Explorations in the Sociology
of Consumption

Explorations in the Sociology of Consumption

Fast Food, Credit Cards and Casinos

GEORGE RITZER

SAGE Publications
London • Thousand Oaks • New Delhi

First published 2001

Apart from any fair dealing for the purposes of research or
private study, or criticism or review, as permitted under the
Copyright, Designs and Patents Act, 1988, this publication
may be reproduced, stored or transmitted in any form, or by
any means, only with the prior permission in writing of
the publishers, or in the case of reprographic reproduction,
in accordance with the terms of licences issued by the
Copyright Licensing Agency. Inquiries concerning
reproduction outside those terms should be sent to the
publishers.

 SAGE Publications Ltd
6 Bonhill Street
London EC2A 4PU

SAGE Publications Inc
2455 Teller Road
Thousand Oaks, California 91320

SAGE Publications India Pvt Ltd
32, M-Block Market
Greater Kailash - I
New Delhi 110 048

British Library Cataloguing in Publication data

A catalogue record for this book is
available from the British Library

ISBN 0-7619-7119-X
     0-7619-7120-3 (pb)

Library of Congress Control Number available

Typeset by SIVA Math Setters, Chennai, India
Printed and bound in Great Britain by Athenaeum Press,
Gateshead

To Casey Maxwell Ritzer:

Love Yet Again

CONTENTS

CONTENTS

PREFACE

This constitutes a preface to both *Explorations in Social Theory: From Metatheorizing to Rationalization* and *Explorations in the Sociology of Consumption: Fast Food, Credit Cards and Casinos*. While each of these books can be read independently of the other, the two volumes taken together offer an overview of my contributions to these two fields. Included are journal articles and excerpts from some well-known books as well as some essays that I hope will get wider visibility as a result of their inclusion in these volumes. Some chapters are taken from material published some time ago, others are derived from more recent publications, and there are several that are being published in these volumes for the first time. Some of the material is derived from books that have been out-of-print for a decade or two. Thus, inclusion of excerpts from these books will bring these works to the attention of a generation or two of sociologists and other social scientists who might otherwise not have access to them.

Virtually all of the material in these two volumes was written with a professional audience in mind. However, as I make clear in Chapter 1 ('Writing to be Read') of *Explorations in the Sociology of Consumption*, I give great importance to writing in such a way that even the most abstract ideas in both social theory and the sociology of consumption are accessible to a wide range of readers. Thus, it is my hope that these volumes will not only be of interest to scholars, but also to many other readers, including both graduate students and undergraduates.

Not only are these two books designed so that they can be read independently of one another, but it is also the case that each of the individual chapters can be read on its own. While I would clearly like readers to proceed from cover to cover, there are many who, given their particular interests, might want to read only a chapter or two from each volume. The desire to have each chapter stand on its own has one drawback for the two volumes. That is, there is a bit more repetition in these books than one might like. Thus, for example, the reader will run into several versions of the basic types of metatheorizing and of the basic dimensions of McDonaldization. I trust that those of you who read the books in their entirety and are irritated by the occasional repetition will bear in mind that such repetition helps make each chapter more meaningful to those who are only reading a selected chapter or two.

The idea for these two volumes came from my dear friend and colleague – Chris Rojek – who also happens to be the sociology editor at Sage Publications in London. I owe him an immense debt for not only coming up with the idea, but allowing me to put together two volumes that I hope will give the reader a good feel for my work in both theory and the sociology of consumption. Other people at Sage have also been of great help including Jackie Griffin and Ian Antcliff.

I also need to thank a number of past and present graduate students at the University of Maryland who co-authored all or part of a number of the essays in these two volumes – Richard Bell, Pamela Gindoff, Doug Goodman, Terri LeMoyne, Elizabeth Malone, James Murphy, Seth Ovadia, Todd Stillman, David Walczak and Wendy Weidenhoft. Also to be thanked are undergraduate research assistants Jan Geesin and Zinnia Cho.

ACKNOWLEDGEMENTS

1-This chapter first appeared in *Contemporary Sociology*, 5, September, 1998: 446–53.

2-This chapter is derived from Chapter 7 of *The McDonaldization of Society*, 2nd edition. Thousand Oaks, CA: Pine Forge Press, 1996: 121–42.

3-This chapter is derived from Chapter 13 of *The McDonaldization Thesis*. London: Sage, 1998: 174–91.

4-This chapter was co-authored by Seth Ovadia and is to be published in Mark Gottdiener, ed. *New Forms of Consumption*. Lanham, MD: Rowman and Littlefield.

5-This chapter is derived from various places in *Expressing America: A Critique of the Global Credit Card Society*. Thousand Oaks, CA: Pine Forge Press, 1995.

6-This chapter is derived from various places in *Enchanting a Disenchanted World: Revolutionizing the Means of Consumption*. Thousand Oaks, CA: Pine Forge Press, 1999; the discussion of the relevance of Walter Benjamin's work to the cathedrals of consumption is published here for the first time.

7-This chapter appears in print for the first time in this volume. It is based on a paper presented at the conference: 'Sociality/Materiality: The Status of the Object in Social Science', Brunel University, Uxbridge, England, September 9–11, 1999.

8-This chapter was published previously in *American Studies*, 41: 2 (Summer), 2000 and was co-authored by Liz Malone

9-This chapter appears in print here for the first time and was co-authored by Todd Stillman

10-This chapter appears here for the first time and was co-authored by James Murphy and Wendy Weidenhoft. It was presented at meetings of the American Sociological Association, Chicago, 1999.

11-This chapter is based on a paper presented at the conference on 'Obscene Powers: Corruption, Coercion and Violence' John Hansard Gallery, University of Southampton, Southampton, England, December 11–12, 1999. It is published here for the first time.

INTRODUCTION

The first volume of this two-volume collection of my work was largely theoretical and metatheoretical (Explorations in Social Theory). This volume focuses on material that involves the application of an array of theoretical ideas to consumption. Thus, these are simultaneously chapters in applied social theory and in the sociology of consumption. However, while they are largely works in applied social theory, they have their metatheoretical elements. For example, Chapter 9 is mainly a metatheoretical analysis of the work related to consumption of a French school of neo-Marxian theory, the situationists, and Chapter 10 does a similar analysis of the path-breaking contributions of Thorstein Veblen to our understanding of consumption. While these two chapters are primarily metatheoretical in character, their main goal is to enhance our understanding of consumption. The chapters in Part Two of the first volume have applied elements, but it is the material in this volume that is more explicitly and directly applied in character. Of course, in a sense virtually everything I do is applied. I either apply theory to the study of theory or to the study of the social world; in many cases both types of applied analysis are found in the same work.

This volume begins with a chapter that excoriates sociology in general, and sociological theory in particular, for not doing more applied substantive work that is accessible, and of interest, to a more general readership. While there is certainly a place for work, like that discussed in Part One of the first volume on metatheory, that is only of interest and accessible to professional sociologists (although I have tried to make even my metatheoretical work accessible), there is a great need for theorists and sociologists more generally to do work that can be read by a more general, literate audience. Sociology should be of interest and relevance to such a readership and should inform public dialogues on a wide range of substantive issues. Unfortunately, very little sociology, especially in the United States, has succeeded in this. This is reflected in the minuscule number of sociologists in the United States with any public visibility, as well as the relatively small number of books written by sociologists that have had appreciable sales. While some books have sold well as monographs aimed at fellow academics and students, almost none has done well in the trade market that caters to the larger public.[1] Sociologists need not write best-sellers, but at least some should be writing books that are read outside the confines of professional sociology and that have an impact on more than a few select members of that field.

American sociologists have largely avoided the sociology of consumption in general, particularly the authoring of books in that area, some of which might well have attracted a broad public audience. One of many reasons for this is that to many mainstream sociologists books on consumption seem 'trivial' in comparison to those on traditional sociological issues (for example, stratification). More generally, works on a wide range of 'important' production-related issues have dominated the field since its inception, but similar contributions in the realm of consumption have been sparse, at best. Thus, a book on a shopping mall, Disney World, or Las Vegas seems far less important to traditional sociologists than one on, say, an automobile factory. Yet, there is no inherent reason why a book on the shopping mall should be any less important than one on the factory. Yet, there have been many books on factories and few on shopping malls. The absence of works on issues related to consumption, issues that would be of interest to many readers who spend far more time in malls than they do in factories, is one of the reasons that sociologists have had so little public impact. This argument sets the stage for several ensuing chapters in this volume which offer excerpts from books of mine that relate to consumption and that were written to be accessible to a general readership. Since this volume (and its companion) is aimed at an academic audience, the excerpts chosen are largely theoretical in nature; much of the substantive detail has been omitted, not only because of the nature of the audience, but also due to space limitations.

Chapter 2 reproduces the chapter in what is, by far, my best-known book, *The McDonaldization of Society* (1996), that deals with the irrationalities of rationality associated with this process. Although the focus of this chapter, and more generally all of my work on McDonaldization, is far broader than simply consumption, virtually all of it is relevant to the sociology of consumption. The paradigm of the process, McDonald's, is of course a site of consumption and, more importantly, it has served as the model for a revolution in sites of consumption and the consumption process more generally. Moreover, many other McDonaldized settings relate to consumption in one way or another.

Many of the specific irrationalities of rationality discussed in Chapter 2 apply very well to many consumption settings, including the fact that McDonaldization often leads to consequences that are the exact opposite of what is intended (for example, the goal of efficiency often leads to a variety of inefficiencies); McDonaldized goods and services are often more expensive than they appear; McDonaldized systems wrap themselves in a variety of illusions; they tend to disenchant the world; they have a wide range of dehumanizing effects on people as workers and consumers as well as on human relationships; and they tend to have an homogenizing effect that often serves to make life far less interesting and exciting.

This idea of the irrationality of rationality is, of course, derived from Max Weber's theory of rationality and may be seen as one of the dimensions of rationalization (and McDonaldization). Those who have taken the lead in McDonaldizing society have certainly not intended to create these irrationalities; they are 'unanticipated consequences' of the process. It is largely in the context of the 'irrationality of rationality' that I am able to offer a critical analysis of McDonaldization. This effort to 'debunk' a variety of the myths associated with McDonaldization is no mere academic exercise; it was – and is – my hope that it will open the eyes of a larger readership to a number of problems associated with the process that are not generally visible to them.

Chapter 3 is derived from my book *The McDonaldization Thesis* (1998), and a number of recent developments in the world of fast-food restaurants are discussed. In that light, the possibility of 'deMcDonaldization' is analysed. There are some storm clouds brewing both for McDonald's and McDonaldization. They include the difficulties McDonald's is encountering in the American market, the growth of McDonald's as a negative symbol around the world, the difficulty of any corporation staying on top forever, the rise of small, non-McDonaldized businesses, the development of 'new regionalism' (as opposed to homogenization) in the United States, and the rise of McDonaldized systems (such as Starbucks) that run counter to at least one of the dimensions (for example, the emphasis on quantity rather than quality) of the process. In spite of such developments, I conclude that while McDonald's will eventually grow less important and may even disappear completely, and the label McDonaldization will become increasingly less important as a result, the underlying process of rationalization will continue apace, and even accelerate. We may need a new name for the concept and even a new paradigm (see Chapter 7 for a discussion of an arena in which we may find new candidates), but the process will be with us, and with a vengeance, for the foreseeable future.

McDonaldization and de-McDonaldization are also examined in the context of the emergence of a postmodern society. In the context of such a society, several scenarios are examined, including rationalized systems surviving on the margins in the predominantly non-rational or irrational postmodern society, the disappearance of rationalized systems in an avalanche of irrationalities, some sort of fusion of rational and irrational elements, and finally the successful resistance by McDonaldized systems and their ultimate triumph over such irrationalities. Given the long-term trend toward rationalization, it is difficult to argue against the latter scenario. It may well be that McDonaldization will outlast postmodernity rather than being drastically changed or eliminated by it.

Chapter 4 deals with the relationship between McDonaldization and consumption more directly and, in the process, offers some clarifications of the concept. First, an effort is made to correct the erroneous impression that McDonaldization is a uniform process that involves a singular 'trajectory'. In fact, the process takes a variety of forms and follows a number of trajectories. Second, not all settings are equally McDonaldized; there is great variation in the degree to which settings are rationalized; even in the fast-food industry, not all settings are highly and equally McDonaldized. Third, not all consumers of McDonaldized goods and services are the same; there are various types of consumers. While McDonaldized systems attempt to mold consumers to behave in a uniform manner, they are never totally successful in their efforts. There are too many different types of consumers, and some types of consumers (for example, the 'rebels') are highly resistant to McDonald's efforts. Finally, there is no uniform relationship between consumers and McDonaldized settings; consumers do not always simply act in accord with the demands of McDonaldized systems. In sum, while McDonaldization is a powerful force that has a variety of overarching effects, it involves a number of variations and complexities. The objective in this chapter is to clarify certain aspects of the McDonaldization thesis in the context of consumption and to offer more of the nuances associated with process.

Chapter 5 is squarely in the realm of the sociology of consumption since it deals with an increasingly important tool in the world of consumption – the credit card. A variety of excerpts from *Expressing America: A Critique of the Global Credit Card Society* (1995) are brought together in this chapter. The argument is made, following Georg Simmel (the major theoretical influence in this work) and his work on money, that the credit card (like money in Simmel's day) can serve as a wonderful window into the nature of society. A variety of Simmel's theoretical ideas are discussed, as are other theoretical ideas (including, again, Weber's theory of rationality, although as is shown Simmel has his own ideas on rationality, some of which are very similar to Weber's) that prove useful in thinking about credit cards. Three theoretical ideas developed by Simmel to analyze money – the 'temptation to imprudence', 'mean machinations', and 'secrecy' – are used to help us analyze credit cards. As we will see, in comparison to money, credit cards lead the consumer to even greater temptations to imprudence, reduce the likelihood of some mean machinations but increase that of others, and create greater 'privacy' than 'secrecy' issues for contemporary society. Next, there is an examination of credit cards from the point of view of the major dimensions of McDonaldization. The argument is made that credit cards can be seen as having McDonaldized credit. Finally, Simmel was concerned with 'Americanization' and we will use this idea to show that the spread of credit cards around the world is more a reflection of Americanization than the more intellectually fashionable notion of globalization (see also, Chapter 8).

Chapter 6 is even more focally concerned with consumption, in particular what I alternately call the 'means of consumption' and 'cathedrals of consumption'; in other words, the sites in which we do our consuming. The chapter consists of a set of excerpts derived from *Enchanting a Disenchanted World: Revolutionizing the Means of Consumption* (Ritzer, 1999). We begin with Marx's theory of the means of consumption. Marx is better known for his ideas on the means of production, but he also developed the idea of the means of consumption that provides the starting point for this analysis. While a debt is acknowledged to Marx, it is clear that his sense of the means of consumption is flawed and inconsistent with his notion of the means of production. An effort is made to redefine the means of consumption so that they better parallel Marx's means of production. A second set of theoretical tools is used to analyze these settings as cathedrals of consumption. Looking at them as cathedrals, and not merely means, leads us to think of these settings in terms of ideas like enchantment, rationalization, disenchantment and re-enchantment. The first three of these lead us back to the theories of Max Weber, while the latter points us toward postmodern social theory and its focal interest in the re-enchantment of the world. Overall, the set of theoretical ideas derived from Marx, Weber and the postmodernists allows us to understand how the sites of consumption cannot only be described as 'means', but also as 'cathedrals'.

A variety of more substantive issues associated with the new means of consumption are then discussed. For example, we will examine how the rationalization of the new means of consumption leads to disenchantment, although we will point out how rationalization can itself be enchanting. Given the trend toward rationalization and disenchantment, we will then deal with the ways in which various postmodern processes – simulation, implosion and manipulations of time and space – can serve to re-enchant the new means of consumption. While it is important that sites be rationalized in order to function effectively, rationalization can be off-putting to consumers. Thus, it is crucial to re-enchant these settings in order to retain old consumers and attract new ones. Finally, there is an effort to reflect on the future and whether we are headed toward a world of disenchanted enchantment.

While Chapter 6 deals with the new means of consumption, Chapter 7 focuses on the very latest electronic means of consumption such as home shopping television and, most importantly, the various sites on the Internet that are revolutionizing consumption of all sorts of things including books, toys, clothing, automobiles, stocks, even pornography. The immaterial nature of e-commerce in general, and e-tail in particular, gives it important advantages over the more material means of consumption that are the focus of Chapter 6. Thus, for example, it is possible to rationalize e-commerce to a far higher degree than shopping malls, superstores, or even fast-food restaurants. This leads to the conclusion that McDonald's may no longer be the paradigm for this process and, as a result, we may need to consider replacing the notion of McDonaldization with a concept that better represents the immaterial nature of consumption on the Internet. Similarly, e-tail has a far greater potential for spectacle and enchantment than the material means of consumption. This means that some of the latter may some-day disappear with the growing success of e-tail. Thus, some bricks-and-mortar shopping malls may eventually fall victim to 'creative destruction' and be replaced by cyber-malls.

The focus in Chapter 8 is on the implications of McDonaldization and the exportation of the new means of consumption (and credit cards) for one of the hottest perspectives in contemporary social theory, globalization theory. While both processes are international in scope, and support many of the basic ideas associated with globalization theory, they are also at odds with that theory at several points. Above all, the concrete examples of McDonaldization and the exportation of the new means of consumption make it clear that globalization theory is characterized by a number of gross generalizations that are in great need of specification. These examples make it clear, for example, that the West in general, and the United States in particular, remain impor-tant players on the global stage. They also demonstrate that the role of the nation-state, especially the United States, cannot be ignored in the rush to focus on global processes that are more or less independent of any nation. Another, partially contradictory, conclusion is that the cor-poration often operates on its own and may now be the most important player on the global stage.

Perhaps the key point in Chapter 8 is that McDonaldization and the exportation of the new means of consumption tend to support the view that in at least some sectors the world is growing more homogeneous than heterogeneous. Globalization theorists tend to focus on the impor-tance of the local and therefore on heterogeneity. However, the issues of concern here tend to be transnational and tend to lead to a high degree of uniformity throughout the world. This is so even though fast-food restaurants and other new means of consumption tend to adapt to local markets in terms of what they sell and how they sell it. Nevertheless, the basic foods and perhaps more importantly the basic procedures tend to remain the same across a wide range of international settings. Of perhaps greater importance are the indigenous versions of fast-food restaurants and other new means of consumption. While they may be native-owned and -run, and may sell local products, they tend to oper-ate on the basis of the same principles as the American entities that created and continue to dominate fast-food restaurants and other new means of consumption. It is these indigenous entities that are of great-est importance in extending McDonaldization and the utilization of the principles that inform the new means of consumption. The forces of homogeneity are far more powerful when they are embedded in indigenous settings than in western imports. The latter can be opposed (as is often the case with McDonald's), but it is more difficult to see, let alone protest against, the basic underlying principles when they inform indigenous settings.

Chapter 9 is, as mentioned above, more metatheoretical in nature. There, the thinking of the French situationists, especially Guy Debord, is analyzed and the relevance of their ideas to the new means of consumption is discussed. The situationists are best known for their critiques of the spectacle and spectacular society. My work on the new means of consumption was influenced by them and it is clear that spectacle lies not only at the core of those means, but also of consumer society more generally. Four key ideas of the situationists – the ceaseless manufacture of pseudo-needs, the marketing of fully equipped blocks of time, the manufacture of mass pseudo-festivals, and the construction of distribution centers – are singled out for discussion and application to the new means of consumption.

What is perhaps most interesting and important about the situationists is their thoughts on resisting the means of consumption and consumption society more generally. Most generally, they see the spectacle as not only oppressive and controlling, but also as offering a utopian image – abundance, festivity, leisure, pleasure – that can inform the revolutionary and serve as a model for an alternative society without the repressive mechanisms of the spectacular society. The situationists also propose a variety of types of actions – *derive* (or drifting), *detourement* (deliberate and subversive misunderstanding), and the construction of real, uncommodified, unmediated situations – that can serve as a base for opposition to the means of consumption and consumer society as a whole.

In Chapter 10 we take a new look at the ideas of Thorstein Veblen, whose stature as a theorist has risen with the growing importance of consumption in the contemporary world. Although Veblen is to be lauded for his work in this area, especially his ideas on conspicuous consumption and leisure, we must not forget that, like the other theorists of his day, he was locked into a productivist bias. This is manifest in his focal concern with the struggle between industry and business. While his ideas on consumption remain relevant today, various changes require that we reconsider many of the details. For example, in this age of hyperconsumption his distinction between conspicuous consumption and conspicuous leisure is no longer so clear-cut since much of consumption today focuses on leisure time activities and pursuits. In spite of these and other problems, Veblen stands out, with Simmel, as a theorist who was not so blinded by the predominance of production that he was not able to see the great and increasing importance of consumption.

Chapter 11 serves, at least in part, as a kind of summary of much of this volume by offering an overview of my critical analyses of consumption, especially of the role played by fast-food restaurants and other McDonaldized systems, credit cards, and the new means of consumption in general. I examine them all though the lens of the notion of the obscene as it is defined by both modernists and postmodernists. From a modern perspective, obscenity can be viewed as part of increasing external (especially corporate) control over our lives, especially as consumers, and as posing threats to social justice, human rights and democratic decision-making. From a postmodern point of view, especially the Baudrillardian view, obscenity relates to the hypervisibility of contemporary phenomena.

Much of the modern obscenity of the phenomena of concern here revolves around the invisibility of much of what transpires in and around them. For example, outside of its obvious manifestations in the fast-food industry, McDonaldization is an invisible process when it infiltrates settings we do not usually associate with it and as it moves into other societies and embeds itself in indigenous enterprises. Hidden from view are such obscenities as homogenization, disenchantment and dehumanization. Then there is the hyperconsumption that is fueled by McDonaldized systems, credit cards and the new means of consumption. Among other things, this involves transforming surprising settings (for example, universities, hospitals) into nothing more than pale imitations of the new means of consumption.

There is a range of specific obscenities associated with all of the phenomena of concern in this volume, but what especially interests me is the hidden mechanisms of control embedded in all of them, especially the new means of consumption. Consumers are led to believe that they are operating freely when, in fact, great effort has been made to control their actions without them being aware of it. They are led to buy and spend more than they intend; they are led into hyperconsumption.

To the postmodernists in general, and Baudrillard in particular, obscenity relates to the lack of a scene, to the lack of concealment throughout our lives. From this perspective, some things must be concealed in order for there to be at least a measure of enchantment in our lives. The fact that everything is made increasingly visible makes for a high degree of disenchantment. Examples of increasing visibility include the obvious spread of the fast-food chains around the nation and the world, the similar spread of credit cards, and the extraordinary visibility associated with spectacles that lie at the base of the efforts of the new means of consumption to become reenchanted.

It is possible to see the modern and postmodern views of obscenity as reconcilable. It could be argued, especially by modernists, that the hypervisibility emphasized by postmodernists serves to conceal the modern obscenities mentioned above. People are distracted by things like spectacles and are therefore less likely to be aware of the ways in which they are being controlled and exploited.

The chapter closes with some thoughts on the obscene consumer from both a postmodern, and especially a modern, perspective. From the latter point of view, the obscene consumer is one who either consumes too little or who consumes what are, from the perspective of consumer society, the 'wrong' things (heroin, guns). (I propose the concept of the 'dangerous consumer' here since it is clear that such consumers can pose a danger to contemporary society.) From a postmodern perspective, the obscene consumer is one who consumes in a highly visible manner. Such a consumer comes very close to Veblen's conspicuous consumer. While an argument can be made that some consumers are obscene from a postmodern point of view, the obscenities associated with McDonaldized systems, credit cards, the new means of consumption and so on are far more important than those associated with the consumer. To focus on the consumer is to 'blame the victim', the focus should be on the crucial sources of the obscenities associated with hyperconsumption.

While this chapter, like much of the rest of my work, is highly critical in nature, it begins with discussion of the many advantages of modern consumer society in general and with things like McDonaldized systems, credit cards and the new means of consumption more specifically. Postmodern theory has alerted us, once again, to the fact that we must not lose sight of these advantages in our rush to delineate the innumerable problems visible from a modern perspective.

Conclusion

Taken together, the material dealt with in the two volumes gives the reader a taste of the metatheoretical, theoretical and applied theoretical work that I have done over the past 25 years (1975–2000). I much prefer to see this as an interim status report than as a final report. That is, I intend to continue working in social theory and hope to make further contributions to it and to the sociology of consumption. While I doubt I will be making another such report in 2025, I feel sure that these two volumes do not represent my last words on this topic. As I write this, I am not certain where the next few years will take me. There is no end of interesting and important metatheoretical, theoretical and applied theoretical issues to explore. Furthermore, changes in both the theoretical and social worlds continually bring new and challenging issues to the fore. The problem is not to find things to think, write, critique and worry about, but how to choose among the plethora of fascinating issues that are continually presenting themselves. There's an intellectual banquet out there for the taking and the offerings are being replenished all the time. I hope to be able to retain a place at the table for a while longer just to be able see and think about what is going to be offered up next. I have no doubt that it will be delicious, but troubling, intellectual fare.

Note

1   Gans's (1997a) research has shown how few books in sociology (leaving aside textbooks) have sold well and even in the case of those books with appreciable sales, the bulk of the buyers have been students and fellow academics. Such sales may indirectly and/or eventually have an impact on the larger public, but only a handful of books in sociology have had any kind of direct effect on public discourse.

WRITING TO BE READ

Why, as Herbert Gans (1997a) has recently demonstrated, do books written by American sociologists sell so poorly, especially to a larger American audience? Why do sociologists have such a meager audience for their work in other disciplines? Why, on the rare occasions when their books do receive general notice, do they review so poorly?

Some Contributing Characteristics of Sociology in the United States

The nature of sociology as it is currently defined in the United States (and, as we will see, it is defined differently in other societies) militates against publishing works of great interest outside of sociology.[1] To begin with, the specialization that increasingly characterizes the field makes it less likely that a sociologist will be able to present a topic with the breadth that will make it attractive to general readers.

Then there are the topics that sociologists choose to study. Most often, specific topics are chosen on the basis of current issues within empirical or theoretical traditions. This means that the subjects flow mainly from concerns within the discipline rather than from the larger society. As a result, much of what sociologists do does not resonate well with larger social issues and concerns. Derived from internal issues, work in sociology tends to be read almost exclusively by those in the discipline with similar interests. The irony is that sociologists routinely deal with general topics – race, stratification, marriage and the family, and so on – that *are* of intrinsic interest to a general audience. However, their specialized, even minute, concerns within those areas tend to prevent sociologists from exploiting this interest. In fact, given the intrinsic interest of the discipline's subject matters, it can only be assumed that sociologists have labored long and hard to avoid attracting broader interest in their work.

Sociologists have also tended to avoid certain topics that might appear to be 'trivial' because of their mundane, everyday character. Thus, in the economy, issues relating to production have – given the discipline's origin in the Industrial Revolution – been deemed important and have always received a great deal of attention. We have well-established specialties such as industrial sociology and the sociology of work. However, the American economy has changed dramatically, and we have arguably moved from a large production to a mainly consumption-oriented society (Bauman, 1992). Yet there has been no parallel shift in the interests of American sociologists; there is, as yet, no specialty in the United States in the sociology of consumption.[2] This is ironic, since the United States is the world's leading consumer society and is actively exporting its consumer tastes (Coke, MTV, *Titanic*, the Big Mac) and means of consuming them (shopping malls, fast-food restaurants, superstores) to the rest of the world. By contrast, there is a well-established field of the sociology of consumption throughout Europe, especially in Great Britain (Corrigan, 1997; Slater, 1997).

An American sociology of consumption is demanded by changes taking place in the society as a whole. Topics in this area could be studied in just as scientific a manner as any other topic in sociology. And it is a field that lends itself to work that would be of interest to a general readership. Why, then, so little work in this area? Part of the reason is that studies of Nike ads, fast-food restaurants, credit cards, and shopping malls seem trivial to many sociologists, who fear that work on them would weaken individual career prospects and the status of the discipline.

Yet another factor is what sociologists consider acceptable data. The data that sociologists generally choose to analyse almost preordain their failure to be relevant to a larger audience. The laborious analysis of mountains of statistical data is unlikely to be very appealing to a general audience (although an emphasis on the conclusions rather than the data and the manipulation of that data would help). Furthermore, large data sets tend to be dated by the time researchers get to them and to date further as scholars analyse (or, worse, reanalyse) them, write them up, and ultimately get the results published. Datedness is not restricted to statistical analyses; long-term observational studies are also likely to seem out of date by the time they make it to the bookstores.

The reward structure in sociology makes it likely that few sociologists (besides a few authors of best-selling textbooks) ever even try to address a large audience. If they are actively publishing, their work – following the accepted academic and scientific model – is aimed mainly at a small number of like-minded peers. It usually takes the form of a journal article or, less likely, a book-length monograph, but rarely a general-interest book. The reward structure (like that in most other scientific disciplines and academic fields) is set up to honor such scientific work with recognition, stature, grant money, and so on. Most actively publishing sociologists are well aware of that reward structure and orient their work to it. This is especially true of aspiring junior faculty members, who are often afraid that their tenure and promotion chances would be adversely affected by any work that does not adhere scrupulously to the scientific norm. The works that are apt to be published in our most prestigious journals and to be most highly rewarded are significant contributions to what Thomas Kuhn (1962/1970) called 'normal science'.[3] Such work, by definition, involves small increments in knowledge and not the bigger paradigm revolutions that are most likely to interest a larger audience. Furthermore, the cutting-edge statistics and the intellectual shorthand (jargon) that allow sociologists to communicate with one another at a high level quickly and easily are not apt to seem good reading to a general reader. And most sociologists have little or no training in writing of any kind, but especially for a larger audience.

Also pointing sociologists toward making incremental contributions to extant paradigms is the fact that there are powerful disincentives for doing more publicly visible work. Affixing the label of 'popularizer' to a sociologist, especially if it is not balanced by other kinds of labels for more 'legitimate' sociology, is likely to lead to much disapprobation.[4] On several occasions, in my role as a consulting editor for book series sponsored by various publishers, I have approached sociologists about doing books on topics with some broad appeal. Several told me flat out that they were afraid to write such books because they felt it would threaten their chances at tenure, promotion, or status in the discipline. And even when tenure or promotion was in hand or status was secure, such works were not forthcoming.

Even if sociologists wanted to do more publicly visible work, in addition to or instead of their more traditional scholarly work, there are powerful and increasing external forces that prevent them from publishing such work. For one thing, the public has become accustomed to *not* reading works in sociology; to put it another way, they have not become acclimated to works emanating from the discipline. Sociology is largely invisible to the general reading public. Few, if any, sociologists have a 'name', and it is clear that in the contemporary book business 'names' sell. For another, the nature of the book-publishing and book-selling businesses creates problems for sociologists aspiring to reach a public audience (Clawson, 1997). There has never been a large number of publishers open to such work, and even the relative few that have been are backing away from sociology. Several years ago I asked the president of a leading publishing house, one that had published some of sociology's best-known works, why the company had deserted sociology. His reply was that his press had not abandoned sociology – sociology had deserted it. This can be interpreted in many ways (for example, sociologists writing fewer high-quality works), but it is clear that one of the implications was that the books being produced by sociologists were mainly of interest to only a handful of fellow sociologists.

Many publishing houses have disappeared, or have folded into others, so there are simply an increasingly small number of publishers available to publish such work. Presses such as Basic Books, Free Press, and Westview, which have been among those more interested in publishing serious, general-interest books by sociologists, have recently been sold, and others have disappeared completely. In addition, the outlets for books by sociologists have increasingly bifurcated into textbook publishers and university presses, and neither of those is well suited to, or necessarily even interested in, publishing general interest books. In the bookstores, the decline of the small shop and its replacement by book superstores (Barnes and Noble, Borders, Crown) has led to the ascendance of the 'blockbuster' book, with correspondingly little room for the books a sociologist, even a best-selling one, might produce. After all, except for a few at the very top, the sales figures of even the best-selling books in the history of sociology would hardly catch the attention of the book superstores. At best, one is likely to find a bookcase or two devoted to sociology in a remote corner of such a superstore, and a surprising number of books on these shelves are likely to be books on social issues written by non-sociologists. Further, sociology has tended to lose some of its already meager shelf space to such fields as media and cultural studies, which have done a far better job of producing books that attract a wide audience.

Another factor that would seem to be associated with the failure of sociologists to attract a large audience is the well-known anti-intellectualism of the American public. While it is undoubtedly a factor, clearly scholars in other fields (as well as European sociologists such as those mentioned below) do reach a wider American audience. One example is the defense of the scientific model by the famous Harvard biologist E.O. Wilson (1998), in a recent issue of *The Atlantic Monthly*. (By the way, Wilson touches on some contemporary topics in sociological theory, such as Foucauldian theory and postmodernism; it is highly unlikely that a sociologist would have a chance at addressing such issues in the pages of the *Atlantic Monthly*.) Our peers in economics, psychology, political science, and history (among others) do a far better job of reaching the general public than we do.[5] Thus, we cannot blame our problems solely on American anti-intellectualism, since more of those in other fields seem better able to overcome it and find a wide audience for their work.

A good portion of the responsibility for sociology's failure to reach a wide audience is traceable to the professional and scientific models that dominate sociology, but it is not my objective to criticize those models. They clearly work, especially for the vast majority of sociologists who see the discipline as a science, or at least a would-be science, and who see their major audience as fellow sociologists. Many, perhaps most, sociologists should be doing such work most, if not all, of the time. In other words, sociologists should pursue the esoteric issues that are at the heart of professional scientific research. One might quibble with this system and argue that maybe sociology should be a little less esoteric, a bit more accessible; but unless practitioners come to the highly unlikely conclusion that sociology's pursuit of the scientific model is fruitless, it is a model they are likely to continue to follow.

There is, however, another model – the public intellectual – and it is one that is not necessarily antithetical to the scientific-scholarly model. Here is the way Joey Sprague, building on the work of Dorothy Smith, describes the goal of at least one kind of work that would be more likely to inform public discourse:[6]

> to help people make sense of the constraints and contradictions in their everyday lives by helping them see how these problems are the outcome of actions taken by powerful parties outside the local context ... In doing so, our agendas might start obliterating the basic/applied dichotomy, because informing discourse on a problem of lived experience would involve putting that problem in a larger social and historical context – including asking such questions as: Who else has this problem? What have they tried to do, and how successful has that attempt been? How does this problem fit into the larger immediate context of social institutions and practices, and how does it shape actual selves in daily interactions? (Sprague, 1998: 26)

As attractive as they might seem, such models of the public intellectual have been rejected, or never even considered, by the vast majority of sociologists. With a few notable exceptions, even our most esteemed colleagues have little in the way of a public following, and their work has had little effect on public policy. Strict adherence to the professional scientific model makes it very difficult (but not impossible) to be a public intellectual. The canons of academic scholarship, the jargon, the elaborate statistics, and so on tend to produce a style of work that is not easily jettisoned when one might wish to reach a wider audience. Furthermore, the style of writing prized by our elite journals and most desirable university presses is decidedly not one that is attractive to a wide, general readership. The latter is an important reason why the work of sociologists tends to do so poorly in the rare instances when it comes to the attention of general book reviewers.

But it is not merely stylistic matters that militate against sociologists writing for a general audience. Such writing tends to be demeaned, or at best merely tolerated, within American sociology; it is certainly not actively supported and rewarded (although it may bring with it other kinds of rewards external to the discipline, such as money, public influence, and an adoring public). We know how to reward the frequent contributor to the *American Sociological Review*, but we have difficulty knowing what to do with scholars, like Richard Sennett or Lillian Rubin, who regularly write books that have a broad international audience (Sennett has four books, one co-authored, and Rubin has three on Gans' original list of 53 books[7] by living sociologists that have sold more than 50,000 copies since the 1940s). Those who have achieved the greatest recognition in sociology are generally those who have been scrupulously faithful to the scientific model and have published almost exclusively scholarly articles and research monographs. Sociology has a number of different kinds of rewards to bestow on its practitioners and they all almost always go to those who have maintained their 'purity' as scholars.

Of course, I am drawing an overly sharp distinction here. There are clearly best-selling sociology books that have also been of significant scholarly influence. From Gans' enumeration these include the only book to top one million in sales, David Riesman's *The Lonely Crowd*, as well as the three books each written by Daniel Bell and Bill Domhoff, and the two each written by Seymour Martin Lipset, Immanuel Wallerstein, and Bill Wilson, as well as, to give just one more example, Glazer and Moynihan's *Beyond the Melting Pot*.

I can also illustrate at least some of this with my own experience with *The McDonaldization of Society* (which did not appear on Gans' list because of its late [1993] publication date and his cutoff date [the end of 1995], but whose total sales would now put it well up on his list). Aimed at being an accessible application and extension of Weber's theory of rationalization to the contemporary world, the book has often been criticized by some (for example, O'Neill, 1999) for being 'pop sociology'. Assuming that that is an appropriate description of the book, the issue is why some of my colleagues think there is no room in the discipline for such a work (especially when economists seem to have little difficulty tolerating the 'pop economics' of someone like Galbraith in, for example, *The Affluent Society*). In any case, if *McDonaldization* is pop sociology, it is simultaneously being taken seriously as a scholarly work, as reflected in the two volumes of essays devoted to it (Alfino, Caputo and Wynyard, *McDonaldization Revisited*, 1998 and Smart, *Resisting McDonaldization*, 1999), a special issue of a Dutch sociology journal (*Sociale Wetenschappen*, 1996) dealing with it, numerous citations in the scholarly literature, and a number of translations.[8] In the case of *McDonaldization*, and many other works, sociologists are too eager to draw a clear line between popular and scholarly works; the two types are not always so easy to distinguish. In addition to drawing such a line, many sociologists want to applaud one type and demean the other. It is possible to produce works that have some popularity, attract an audience outside of sociology, and are of scholarly interest to sociologists!

An interesting case in this context is that of the work of Erving Goffman, whose books were excluded from Gans' list partly because Goffman is no longer alive (although Elliott Liebow was included) and partly because Gans was unable to track down information on the sales of his books. Goffman has been of great scholarly interest to sociologists, but his works have also sold well outside of sociology and, at least to some degree, to the general public. It seems certain that one, and probably several, of his books have sold well in excess of 50,000 copies. A number of them, such as *Presentation of Self in Everyday Life, Interaction Ritual,* and *Stigma,* have had long, successful runs and continue, from all appearances, to sell well. In addition, when he was alive Goffman himself reported that a significant source (perhaps a third) of his total income came from royalties from his books (he claimed that another third came from gambling). In any case, Goffman was, and is, perceived as a successful author with a large and diverse audience, and this perception has contributed to the expression of a number of concerns about his work – the 'triviality' of at least some of his topics, his tendency to cite little and then often to cite more popular than academic sources, his 'jokey' style, and his preference for writing a more 'literary' sociology. As a result, at least in part, of his lack of purity, Goffman has not earned the place in sociology that many feel his work warrants (Fine and Manning, 2000).[9]

A similar point could be made about the work of C. Wright Mills, another deceased sociologist for whose books Gans was unsuccessful in finding sales data. The problem extends beyond the matter of book sales. Norbert Elias faced grave difficulties in gaining acceptance as a social theorist because he dealt with such seemingly trivial issues as spitting, blowing one's nose at the table, and the expelling of wind. Similarly, ethnomethodology is still not accepted in many quarters because of its focus on such mundane topics as turn taking in conversations and how we 'do' walking. As a general rule, issues that are far removed from everyday reality and that can be couched in highly abstract terms are deemed far more acceptable by mainstream sociology. While there is certainly room for the latter within sociology, the field also needs to accord mundane matters a more central place within the discipline. After all, major constituencies of sociology – the larger public, as well as students – live in the everyday world and are naturally most interested in work that relates to it. However, sociologists most often consider colleagues their major constituency and they orient their work largely to peers' interests and expertise.

Actually, the situation confronting the work of American sociologists is worse than it appears at first glance. While few books sell well, the bulk of those that do sell do so because, as Gans notes, they are adopted as supplementary books in classes, especially in sociology. While most of these students are future members of the general public, Gans neglects to make the point that they are buying those books because they are forced to by their instructors. When one deducts sales produced in this way, the situation is much bleaker. Few people buy books written by sociologists of their own free will.

However, one can argue that teaching, and therefore writing books that are aimed at students, does affect public discourse. Sprague (1998) argues that it is primarily through teaching that we can affect public discourse by getting our students to think sociologically. In addition, it is those students who will make up a large portion of the public we will need to address in the future.

The Contrast with Sociology in Other Nations and with Other Disciplines

The difference between American and much of European sociology is quite striking. While many European sociologists share our commitment to scientific purity, many others, a far higher proportion than in the United States, are willing, even eager to play the role of public intellectual. In some cases (for example, Jürgen Habermas), they need not even alter their academic style to write books that approach best-seller status. The same can be said of other important European theorists such as Michel Foucault and Jean Baudrillard. Why can European sociologists, or fellow-travelers, do something that eludes their American peers – write works of interest to a wide readership? In the case of works of Habermas, Foucault, and Baudrillard, their success is not traceable to their works' greater accessibility or freedom from jargon. Their success seems to have much more to do with their intellectual breadth and their ability to write about issues of interest to a wide and diverse readership. It is also deeply indebted to a general reading public in Europe which is much more interested in, and receptive to, works by social thinkers.[10]

Other European sociologists have had to alter their styles to reach a larger audience. Having made his reputation by being one of the most obscure thinkers in sociological theory, a field that values and rewards obscurity, Anthony Giddens has, in the 1990s, turned to writing a series of more accessible books on topics of wide public interest (modernity, the self, intimacy, sexuality). Giddens' work caught the attention of Tony Blair, who reportedly used it to help formulate the agenda that swept him to power (Bryant and Jary, 2000). Giddens has also been rewarded with the directorship of the London School of Economics and with invitations to both 10 Downing Street and the White House.

But it is not merely a question of style; the culture of sociology in many western European countries is entirely different from that in the United States. This is most clearly true in France, the nation most likely to produce scholars who create works of broad public and scholarly interest.

> In the United States, it is not a great exaggeration to say that a good sociologist is unlikely to be taken for an intellectual. In France, however, one criterion of success (even if some sociologists do challenge this) is a person's publicly acknowledged participation in intellectual discussion. The idea of 'vocational' sociology ... has negative connotations in France ... The university

is not the place where the latest sociological publications are analyzed and discussed; a sociologist who publishes a book is usually more concerned with the response of the media than that of the academic journals ... In France, sociologists ... endeavor to influence public opinion and political life through their own debates and discussions. (Wieviorka, 1997: 288–301)

This is not to say that there are not other kinds of problems associated with the kind of direction taken by French sociology. For example, while French sociologists influence public discourse, they have had trouble becoming a significant presence in international debates in professional scientific sociology. In the case of Mexican sociology, at least one observer argues that publicly visible 'intellectual essayism' has gained ascendancy over scholarly work (Brachet-Marquez, 1997). This has operated to the detriment of Mexican sociologists' participation in scholarly debates, especially on research-oriented topics. While American sociology may be in need of more public scholarship, Mexican sociology has no absence of such work, but is lacking in rigorous social research.

In Canada, there is a split between English-speaking sociologists and the French-speaking sociologists of Quebec. The latter have played a major role in formulating public policy, are intellectual leaders, and contribute importantly to the social life of the province and the nation. However, Brym and Saint-Pierre (1997: 546) complain that English-Canadian sociologists 'have largely failed to contribute to public debate on the most pressing issues that face the country'. These sociologists have little or nothing to say on such issues as chronic unemployment, Quebec separatism, and the privatization of the health care system. In fact, Brym and Saint-Pierre argue that English-Canadian sociology compares badly even to that in the United States in terms of the degree to which work emanating from sociologists in the two countries shapes the public debate on policy issues.

Thus, the contrasts among the United States, France, Mexico, and Canada make it clear that there is no one way to do sociology; the four nations differ greatly in the relative importance of professional research and more public work. This has several implications, but the most important is that sociology need not be dominated by those who devote themselves to scientific research. Sociology in the United States could have a different mix of research and publicly relevant work and still be sociology. More generally, there are many different cultures of sociology. The one we now have is not the only alternative; there are other possibilities – our culture could be changed.

There is another important difference between American sociology and the way it is practiced in many other countries. American sociologists who do achieve some general visibility and influence tend to do so in specialized areas. Examples include Bill Wilson and his interest in race and Pepper Schwartz and her concern with sex. In contrast, those who achieve general recognition in other societies, especially in Europe, are more likely to do so on the basis of work that has wide interest and is of much broader influence both within Europe and throughout the world. While specialized influence is not to be denigrated, works of more general influence could also be generated by American sociology.

The contrast between the culture of sociology and those of other fields in the United States is also revealing. Well-respected figures in neighboring disciplines like economics, political science, psychology, and history seemingly have had little trouble writing widely read books and/or influencing public discourse while retaining their reputations as scholars. A good example is John Kenneth Galbraith in economics. Some (for example, the esteemed Paul Samuelson, also in economics) have even 'stooped so low' as to write introductory textbooks without being relegated to the margins of their discipline. In fact, Samuelson was able to win the 1976 Nobel Prize, albeit not for his introductory textbook, but for his work on the monetary system and consumption analysis. Another model in economics is Robert C. Merton (son of sociology's esteemed Robert K. Merton[11]) who (with two others) won the 1997 Nobel Prize for his work on a formula for measuring the value of an option – work that contributed to the massive growth in the derivatives market and to a private enterprise that earned the younger Merton a small fortune.[12]

Conclusion

Sociology is an enormous field. It should be big enough, both in size and professional security, to allow a few of its members to do work that engages a wider audience and to at least not penalize them for doing so. Yet, even if we develop the will to publish such work, and to reward our peers who do so, we face an environment in which it will be more rather than less difficult to get such work published and accepted by the public. Thus, a field that should be among the most relevant of academic fields to the general public is in danger of becoming, if possible, even more irrelevant than it already is. Can a sociology that is largely irrelevant to the general public survive? If so, what kind of sociology will it be? Can we afford to leave the writing about sociological issues to what Gans (1977a: 135) calls 'talented journalists' who 'write on sociological topics with only a limited understanding of society'? More to the point, why should we?

What should sociologists interested in redressing this imbalance do? Among the steps needed are making an effort to write for the general public, learning how to write in an accessible and engaging manner (Sprague, 1998: 26), trying to break down the barriers between specialties and learning to think about issues in more general terms, choosing topics that are of interest and importance to the larger society, widening the sense of what is acceptable data for sociological analysis, altering the culture and the reward structure in the discipline so that contributions to public discourse are not ignored (or at least not demeaned), and realizing that there is no clear line of demarcation between scholarly work and work of general public interest.

Perhaps the most important and most difficult step of all involves striving hard to overcome the insecurity that plagues the discipline. Our own academic insecurity has played an important role in preventing us from writing for a larger audience. In fact, it sometimes appears as if sociology's disciplinary insecurities have led it to be far 'purer' about the work it rewards than are far more secure fields such as economics. Members of more secure disciplines, especially those with some status and seniority, can do this kind of work and still retain their professional status. However, those in a 'weak science' like sociology (Fuchs and Ward, 1994) perceive similar work by their peers as threatening to further weaken the field in the eyes of colleagues in other disciplines, university administrators, granting agencies, and the like. Were we more secure as a science, we would have no problem allowing at least a few of our colleagues to do such work. It is arguable, ironically, that our lack of public visibility further weakens our position in the eyes of grant-giving agencies and university administrators, who routinely deal with other fields that are better able to combine scholarly work with public impact. They must sometimes wonder why a field that deals with the topics that it does has such a meager influence outside of the confines of the discipline. A secure field is able to encourage, not discourage, work of broad public relevance.

Among other things, sociologists need to feel secure enough to write about the seemingly trivial for academic and/or general audiences. The esteemed neo-Marxian theorist Walter Benjamin was able to use the Parisian arcades to cast light on many things, especially the nature of modern commodity capitalism (Buck-Morss, 1989). Adopting a relationistic perspective, Georg Simmel examined many seemingly trivial topics as a way of getting at the essence of society (Levine, 1971). More generally, postmodern social theory points us toward decentering, which, among other things, means focusing not on core phenomena, but rather on the margins (Derrida, 1967/1974: 68). In my view, there are no trivial topics in sociology, only trivial treatments of topics that could be delved into more deeply. There are certainly no trivial topics in the sociology of consumption, yet as we have seen, insecure American sociologists have shunned the topic, even in the face of a society increasingly dominated by consumption.

Of course, there are also factors outside sociology, especially the public attitude toward the field and changes in the structure of the book business, that will affect the success of such efforts. Sociologists cannot alter this situation on their own, but it cannot and will not be changed unless the way in which at least some of us practice our craft is recast.

Notes

This chapter first appeared in *Contemporary Sociology*, 5 (September), 1998: 446–53.

1   While I generally focus on the general reading public, it is worth noting that there are also other relevant audiences, including scholars in other disciplines, elite intellectuals throughout the world, and public-interest scholars, among others. There is some variation from one general audience to another, but as a general rule sociologists do not do well in reaching any of them.

2   One hopeful sign is a new journal, the *Journal of Consumer Culture*, that I am co-editing with Don Slater; another is *Consumption, Markets and Culture*, which has a few American sociologists on its editorial board.

3   In fact, Kuhn's book, with its impact on many fields and even on a general readership, is an example of the kind of book sociologists have such a difficult time writing.

4   Of course, sociology is not the only field in which this is the case. Daniel Yergin, a Cambridge PhD and author of a number of best-selling and oft-translated books such as *The Prize: The Epic Quest for Oil, Money and Power*, recounts the following reactions to him during a period when he was teaching in the government and business schools of Harvard: 'I think they sort of disdained me as a popularizer ... I wrote in short declarative sentences, for example ... They couldn't understand how a faculty member could want to write cover stories for *New York* Magazine on the business implications of some new frozen pizza' (Ringle, 1998: B2).

5   It could be argued that the subject matters of these fields give them a great advantage in reaching such a public. This is especially true of psychology; its micro-orientation (versus the more macro-orientation of most sociology) fits better with the individualist perspective of the general reader. Much the same could be said of the economist's interests in matters related to money, the political scientist's concern with political decisions of great personal import, and the historian's interest in more familiar topics.

6   Although her focus is more on research than it is here.

7   Gans (1977b) later expanded his list to 56 titles.

8   There are currently more than a dozen translations published or in press.

9   A similar argument can be made about the marginality of the work of Georg Simmel in American sociology.

10   Of course, a large and diverse group of Americans buy their books, as well.

11   As important as Merton is as a sociologist, he has had relatively little direct influence on the general public or the political process (Sztompka, 2000).

12   The firm with which Merton was associated eventually experienced a major crisis causing great harm to his reputation. However, that does not negate the essential points being made here.

2

THE IRRATIONALITY
OF RATIONALITY

McDonaldization has swept across much of the social landscape because it offers increased efficiency, predictability, calculability, and control through the substitution of nonhuman for human technology. It also offers many more specific advantages in numerous settings. Despite these assets, there are a number of drawbacks and this chapter presents the great costs of McDonaldization in a systematic manner. Rational systems inevitably spawn a series of irrationalities that limit, eventually compromise, and perhaps even undermine their rationality.

At the most general level, the irrationality of rationality is simply a label for many of the negative aspects and effects of McDonaldization. More specifically, this irrationality can be seen as the opposite of rationality and its several dimensions. That is, McDonaldization can be viewed as leading to inefficiency, unpredictability, incalculability, and loss of control.[1] Irrationality also means that rational systems are disenchanted; they have lost their magic and mystery. Most importantly, rational systems are unreasonable systems that deny the humanity, the human reason, of the people who work within them or are served by them. In other words, rational systems are dehumanizing. (Please note that though the terms rationality and reason are often used interchangeably, in my work they are viewed as antithetical phenomena.)

Inefficiency: Long Lines at the Checkout

Rational systems, contrary to their promise, often end up being quite inefficient. For instance, in fast-food restaurants, long lines of people often form at the counters, or parades of cars snake by the drive-through windows. What is purported to be an efficient way to obtain a meal often turns out to be quite inefficient.

The fast-food restaurant is far from the only aspect of a McDonaldized society that exhibits inefficiency. Interestingly, even the vaunted Japanese industry of the 1980s and early 1990s had its inefficiencies (for more on this, see Ritzer, 2001, Chapter 11). Take the 'just-in-time' system. Because this system often requires that parts be delivered several times a day, the streets and highways are cluttered with trucks. Thus, people are often late for work or for business appointments, resulting in lost productivity. The situation grew even worse because Japanese convenience stores, supermarkets, and department stores also began to use a just-in-time system, bringing even greater numbers of delivery trucks onto the streets. But the irrationalities go beyond traffic jams and missed appointments. All these trucks waste fuel, very expensive in Japan, and contribute greatly to air pollution (Schrage, 1992).

Here is the way columnist Richard Cohen (1990: 5) describes another example of inefficiency in the McDonaldized world:

> Oh Lord, with each advance of the computer age, I was told I would benefit. But with each 'benefit', I wind up doing more work. This is the ATM [automated teller machine] rule of life ... I was told – nay promised – that I could avoid lines at the bank and make deposits or withdrawals any time of the day. Now, there are lines at the ATMs, the bank seems to take a percentage of whatever I withdraw or deposit, and, of course, I'm doing what tellers (remember them?) used to do. Probably, with the new phone, I'll have to climb telephone poles in the suburbs during ice storms.

Cohen underscores at least three different irrationalities – rational systems are not less expensive, they force people to do unpaid work, and, most important here, they are often inefficient. It might be more efficient to deal with a human teller, either in the bank or drive-through window, than to wait in line at an ATM. For many, it would be far more efficient to prepare a meal at home than to pack the family in the car, drive to McDonald's, load up on food, and then drive home again. This may not be true of some meals cooked at home from scratch, but it is certainly true of TV dinners, microwave meals, maybe even full-course meals brought in from the supermarket or Eatzi's. Yet many people persist in the belief, fueled by propaganda from the fast-food restaurants, that it is more efficient to eat there than to eat at home.

Though these and other elements of a rational society may be inefficient for the customer, they are quite efficient for purveyors of goods and services. Banks gain efficiency when people line up at an ATM (unless it breaks down or runs out of money) rather than call on employees for help. McDonald's benefits in a similar way when people use the drive-through window, taking all their wrappings and mess with them.

Supermarkets find it efficient to pack themselves full of foods of all types. A Giant supermarket in Virginia has about 45,000 different products strung out along 23 aisles. In addition, the store includes a 'florist shop, a wine store, a Fanny May candy store, a deli, a soup-and-salad bar, and machines that dispense cold soda and hot coffee, just in case a shopper's strength starts to wane' (Carlson, 1990: 21). While this may be efficient for a consumer looking for a wide range of things, is it efficient for those in search of a loaf of bread and a quart of milk to wend their way through this labyrinth? Of course not, which partly accounts for the popularity of chains such as 7-Eleven.

Although the forces of McDonaldization trumpet their greater efficiency, they never tell us whom the system is more efficient for. Most of the gains in efficiency go to those who push rationalization. People need to ask: Efficient for whom? Is it efficient for consumers to push their own food over the supermarket scanner, swipe their own credit or debit cards, and then bag it themselves? Is it efficient for people to pump their own gasoline? Is it efficient for them to push numerous combinations of telephone numbers before they hear a human voice? Most often, people will find that such systems are *not* efficient for them.

Similarly, rational systems impose a double standard on employees. Those at the top of an organization impose efficiencies on those who work at or near the bottom of the system – the assembly-line worker, the counterperson at McDonald's. The owners, franchisees, top managers, want to control subordinates through the imposition of rational systems. However, they want their own positions to be as free of rational constraints – as inefficient – as possible. They, but not their underlings, need to be free to be creative. Subordinates are to follow blindly the rules, regulations, and other structures of the rational system. Thus, the goal is to impose efficiency on subordinates while those in charge remain as creative (and often as inefficient) as possible.

In general, McDonaldized institutions have also not been notable in the efficient creation of effective new products. There are, for example, Ray Kroc's failures in this realm, notably the Hulaburger. As a general rule, such systems excel at selling familiar products and services in shiny new settings or packages. For instance, the fast-food restaurant wraps that prosaic hamburger in bright packages and sells it in a carnival-like atmosphere. This point extends to many other manifestations of McDonaldization. For example, Jiffy Lube and its imitators sell people nothing more than the same old oil change and lube job, but with well-known logos and bright colors.

High Cost: Better Off at Home

McDonaldization does not ordinarily save people money. For example, in one instance a small soda was shown to cost a franchise owner 11 cents, but it was sold for 85 cents (Perl, 1992: 26). A fast-food meal for a family of four might easily cost 20 or 25 dollars these days. Such a sum would go far further spent on ingredients for a home-cooked meal.

As Cohen demonstrated in the case of ATMs, people must often pay extra to deal with the inhumanity and inefficiency of a rationalized society. The great success and profitability of McDonaldized systems, the rush to extend them to ever new sectors of society, and the fact that so many people want to get into such businesses indicate that these systems generate huge profits.

Bob Garfield noted the expense of McDonaldized activities in his article 'How I Spent (and Spent and Spent) My Disney Vacation' (1991). Garfield took his family of four to Walt Disney World and found that it might be more aptly named 'Expense World'. The five-day vacation cost $1,700; admission to Disney World alone cost $551.30. (And the prices keep going up. In 1998, admission for five days cost a family of four over $800; Horovitz, 1998: B8.) He calculates that in the five days, they had less than seven hours of 'fun, fun, fun. That amounts to $261 c.p.f.h. (cost per fun hour)'. Because most of his time in the Magic Kingdom was spent riding buses, 'queuing up and shlepping from place to place, the 17 attractions we saw thrilled us for a grand total of 44 minutes' (Garfield, 1991: B5). Thus, what is thought to be an inexpensive family vacation turns out be quite costly.

To take one other example, in Chapter 8 we will discuss in vitro fertilization as an example of the McDonaldization of the birth process. A single attempt at in vitro fertilization can cost as much as $10,000 (Oransky and Gottlieb, 1998: 15A).

The Illusion of Fun: 'Ha, Ha, Ha! The Stock Market Just Crashed!'

If it really isn't so efficient, and it really isn't so cheap, then what does McDonaldization, more specifically, the fast-food restaurant, offer people? Why has it been such a worldwide success? One answer – the illusion of efficiency and frugality. As long as people believe it, the actual situation matters little. Perhaps more important, what fast-food restaurants really seem to offer, as Stan Luxenberg (1985) has pointed out, is fun (or Garfield's 'fun, fun, fun'). As another observer notes, 'Restaurants have become a form of entertainment'. Today's diner often looks for theater more than food. Hence the growth of 'eatertainment' chains like Hard Rock Cafe, Planet Hollywood and Rainforest Cafe. This is true even of those who frequent upscale restaurants: 'I would rather eat mediocre food in a fabulous room than sit somewhere dull and boring and eat fabulous food. ... I'm looking for decor, scale, theatrics, a lot going on' (*Time*, 1985: 60). Fast-food restaurants and eatertainment sites are really amusement parks for food, with their bright colors and garish signs and symbols. McDonald's even uses a ubiquitous clown, Ronald McDonald, and an array of cartoon characters to remind people that fun awaits them on their next visit.

Some outlets even offer playgrounds and children's rides and such things are becoming progressively bigger and more 'high tech'. It is not unusual to see a fast-food restaurant dwarfed by its playground. In fact, at one time McDonald's actually went into the playground business. A wholly owned subsidiary, Leaps & Bounds, Inc., eventually opened 49 playgrounds before it was sold to Discovery Zone in September 1994 (Bowman, 1995). The playground equipment at Leaps & Bounds was derived from the sort of equipment found in the playgrounds at many McDonald's restaurants. A McDonald's spokesperson said that the idea grew out of the advertising theme of 'food, folks and fun ... We just turned it around and put the fun first' (Levine, 1991: G4). There are more than a few cynics who would say that McDonald's always put fun before food.

Discovery Zone (DZ) ran into economic trouble and eventually went bankrupt; McDonald's sold its interest in the company (Bloomberg Business News, 1996). However, DZ later emerged from bankruptcy with over 200 outlets in operation (Stanley, 1998). More importantly, Discovery Zone has now been joined by other Children's 'fun centers' such as Jeepers Creepers.

McDonald's in Japan (there were almost 3,000 McDonald's restaurants in Japan at the end of 1998) has joined forces with Toys R Us. A number of Toys R Us outlets will include McDonald's restaurants. In aligning itself more closely with playgrounds and toys, McDonald's is making it increasingly clear that it is in the business of providing 'fun' (Shimbun, 1995).

Furthermore, fast-food restaurants serve the kinds of finger foods bought at the stands in an amusement park. In what may be termed the 'cotton candy principle', people will buy, and even pay comparatively high prices for, a few pennies worth of food as long as it has a strong, pleasant, and familiar flavor. Indeed, as Luxenberg (1985) shows, what fast-food restaurants often sell is 'salty candy'. One of the secrets of the McDonald's french fry is that it is coated with *both* salt and sugar.[2] People taste the salt and the sugar, but rarely if ever the potato slice, little more than an excuse for the rest.

McDonald's offers a kind of 'public theater' (Shelton, unpublished essay). Instead of a private, folded menu, McDonald's offers a marquee that, like the movie options at the local cineplex, presents the diner's alternatives. This notion of public theater is even more descriptive of the eatertainment chains. In this, and many other ways, dining becomes a public rather than a private and personal experience, at times even a public spectacle.

Supermarkets have also increasingly become entertainment centers, selling more and more 'fun foods' such as Count Chocula and Teenage Mutant Ninja Turtles cereals, Snausages in a Blanket (dog food), and Funny Feet fruit snacks. As one observer said,

> When The Shopper was young, Americans used to sing, 'There's no business like show business', but they don't sing it much anymore, probably because just about every business is like show business now. Supermarkets are

certainly no exception. These days, supermarkets are like theme parks. (Carlson, 1990: 20)

The owner of large supermarkets in Connecticut invested a half million dollars in cartoon characters for his stores and has people dressed as Daisy Duck wandering through them. Said the owner, 'This is a people business. Customers are happy here. People come here to shop together with friends because it's fun' (Ryan, 1988: 6).

All this is part of the United States' obsession with amusement. Neil Postman (1985: 3), in his aptly titled book *Amusing Ourselves to Death*, argues that Las Vegas has become the symbol of this obsession because it 'is a city entirely devoted to the idea of entertainment, and as such proclaims the spirit of a culture in which all public discourse increasingly takes the form of entertainment'. If Las Vegas, with its McDonaldized gambling, symbolizes the obsession with entertainment, then McDonald's symbolizes the emphasis on entertainment in the fast-food industry.

Entertainment is also central to the shopping mall. Malls are designed to be fantasy worlds, theatrical settings for what Kowinski (1985) calls 'the Retail Drama'. Both consumers and mall employees play important roles in this drama. After all, many Americans' favorite form of entertainment is shopping. The mall is loaded with props, with a backdrop of ever-present Muzak to soothe the savage shopper. Some of the props remain all year, while others (for example, Christmas decorations) are brought in for special occasions and promotions. Then there are the restaurants, bars, movie theaters, and exercise centers to add to the fun. On weekends, clowns, balloons, magicians, bands, and the like further entertain those on their way from one shop to another. Faced by the threat of shop-at-home alternatives, one marketing expert said, 'You've got to make your centers more fun' (Kowinski, 1985: 371). Thus, people can expect shopping centers to become an even more integral part of show business.

That future has arrived at the Mall of America in Bloomington, Minnesota (Schnedler, 1994). At the center of the Mall of America is a huge amusement park, Knott's Camp Snoopy, including a full-size roller coaster, an arcade, and shooting galleries. A system of acrylic tubes allows visitors to walk through an aquarium. Golf Mountain provides an eighteen-hole miniature-golf course on several levels. The mall also houses an enormous Lego structure. There is a huge sports bar, a Hooters, and a Planet Hollywood. And, of course, there is a movie theater – with 14 screens! Said one critic, 'Mall of America is not a mall, it's a circus' (Swisher, 1991: H1).

Many chains found within shopping malls have come to focus on entertainment and, as a result, have earned the label 'retailtainment'. Examples include Niketown and REI where various structures (for example, one can climb a 65-foot rock at REI in Seattle) and displays (videos on three-storey high screens at Niketown) exist to distract and amuse the customer. Beyond retailtainment and eatertainment, chains of education centers like the Sylvan Learning Center have been called 'edutainment'.

To take one other example from a different realm, journalism has also become more geared to entertainment. For example, *Business Week*, a rationalized magazine, is designed to be not only more efficient to read than the *Wall Street Journal*, but also more enjoyable. An ad for *Business Week* claims, 'We don't just inform you but we entertain you.' Two critics say of this advertisement, 'Is *Business Week* really serious? Are we to expect the following: Ha, Ha, Ha! The stock market just crashed! What a laugh! ... Your company is going down the tubes. What fun!' (Mitroff and Bennis, 1989: 12). Similarly, television news is often described as 'infotainment' because it combines news and show business.

The Illusion of Reality: Even the 'Singers' Aren't Real

Many aspects of a McDonaldized society involve deceptive settings and events – what Daniel Boorstin (1961) calls 'pseudo events', including the package tour, the modern campground, the international villages at amusement parks such as Busch Gardens, Las Vegas casino-hotels like New York, New York, the computer phone call, and false fraternization at Roy Rogers and Nutri/System. All of this may be viewed as part of Ian Mitroff and Warren Bennis' (1989) 'unreality industry'. By this, they mean the fact that whole industries attempt to produce and market unreality. McDonald's, for example, creates the illusion that people are having fun, that they are getting lots of french fries, and that they are getting a bargain when they purchase their meal. In a famous example of such unreality, Milli Vanilli's two 'singers' did not actually sing on their record album (Achenbach, 1990). From the wide range of unrealities, here are a few examples from the supermarket where fewer and fewer things are what they appear to be:

- Sizzlean (fake 'bacon') is made out of beef and turkey, and kosher bacon has no pork.
- Molly McButter and Butter Buds have no butter.
- The turkey flavor in the frozen turkey TV dinner may well be artificial since the natural flavor was removed during processing.
- The lemon smell in the laundry detergent usually does not come from lemons.

Such unreality, along with various pseudo events, has become integral to McDonaldized society.

False Friendliness

Because fast-food restaurants greatly restrict or even eliminate genuine fraternization, what people have left is either no human relationships or 'false fraternization'. Rule Number 17 for Burger King workers is 'Smile at all times' (Reiter, 1991: 95). The Roy Rogers employees who used to say 'Happy trails' to me when I paid for my food really had no interest in what happened 'on the trail'. (In fact, come to think of it, they were really saying, in a polite way, 'Get lost!') This phenomenon has been generalized to the many workers who say 'Have a nice day' as customers depart. In fact, of course, they usually have no real interest in, or concern for, how the rest of a customer's day goes. Again, in a polite and ritualized way, they are really saying, 'Get lost', or move on so someone else can be served.

In addition, people are daily bombarded by a mountain of computer-ized letters, or 'junk mail' (Smolowe, 1990). Great pains are sometimes taken to make a letter seem personal (similarly I now often get calls from telemarketers who start out by saying, 'Hi George'), even though in most cases it is fairly obvious that a computer has generated the let-ter from a database of names. These letters are full of the kind of false fraternization practiced by Roy Rogers' workers. For example, the let-ters often adopt a friendly, personal tone designed to lead people to believe that the head of some business has fretted over the fact that they haven't, for example, shopped in his or her department store or used his or her credit card in the past few months. For example, a friend of mine recently received a letter from a franchise, The Lube Center, a few days after he had his car lubricated (note the use of the first name and the 'deep' personal concern):

> Dear Ken
> We want to THANK YOU for choosing The Lube Center for all of your car's fluid needs ...
> We strongly recommend that you change your oil on a regular basis ... We will send you a little reminder card ... This will help *remind* you when your car is next due to be serviced ...
> We spend the time and energy to make sure that our employees are trained properly to give you the service that you deserve ...
>
> Sandy Grindstaff/Randall S. Simpson
> The Lube Center Management
> [Italics added]

Also, several years ago, I received the following letter from a con-gressman from Long Island even though I live in Maryland. Though I had never met Congressman Downey and knew nothing about him, this didn't prevent him from writing me a 'personal' letter:

> Dear George
> It is hard to believe, but I am running for my NINTH term in Congress! ...
>
> When I think back over the 8,660 votes I've cast ... I realize how many battles *we've shared*.
>
> Please let me know that I can count on *you*.
>
> > Sincerely,
> > *Tom* Downey
> > [Italics added]

A *Washington Post* correspondent offers the following critique of false friendliness in junk mail:

> By dropping in people's names and little tidbits gleaned from databases hither and yon in their direct mail pitches, these marketing organizations are trying to create the illusion of intimacy. In reality, these technologies conspire to *corrupt and degrade intimacy*. They cheat, substituting the insertable fact for the genuine insight. These pitches end up with their own synthetic substitutes for the real thing. (Schrage, 1990: B13)

However false it may be, such junk mail is designed to exert control over customers by getting them to take desired courses of action.

At Nutri/System, counselors receive a list of things to do to keep dieters coming back. Much of this involves scripted interaction. The counselors are urged to 'greet client by name with enthusiasm'. Knowing the client's name creates a false sense of friendliness, as does the 'enthusiastic' greeting. Counselors are also urged to 'converse with client in a sensitive manner'. The counselors are provided with a small, glossy card entitled, 'Personalized Approach at a Glance'. The card rationalizes the personal greeting with pseudo-personalized responses to problematic situations. For example, if clients indicate that they feel they are receiving little support for the diet, the script urges the counselor to say, 'I'm so glad to see you. I was thinking about you. How is the program going for you?' Is the counselor *really* glad to see the client? Really thinking about the client? *Really* concerned about how things are working out for the client? The answers to such questions are clear in a McDonaldized society.

Mention might also be made in this context of greeting cards as well as the cards now available on the Internet. False friendliness would seem to define both.

Disenchantment

One of Max Weber's most general theses is that as a result of rationalization the western world has grown increasingly disenchanted
(Schneider, 1993). Weber derived this notion from Friedrich Schiller. It
relates to the displacement of 'magical elements of thought' (Gerth and
Mills, 1958: 51). As Schneider (1993: ix) puts it, 'Max Weber saw history
as having departed a deeply enchanted past en route to a disenchanted
future – a journey that would gradually strip the natural world both of
its magical properties and of its capacity for meaning'. The process of
rationalization leads, by definition, to the disenchantment of the settings in which it occurs. The term clearly implies the loss of a quality –
enchantment – that was at one time very important to people. While
we undoubtedly have gained much from the rationalization of society
in general, and the means of consumption in particular, we also have
lost something of great, if hard to define, value.

Efficient systems have no room for anything smacking of enchantment and systematically seek to root it out of all aspects of their operation[3]. Anything that is magical, mysterious, fantastic, dreamy and so on
is apt, virtually by definition, to be inefficient. Enchanted systems typically involve highly convoluted means to whatever end is involved.
Furthermore, enchanted worlds may well exist without any obvious
goals at all. Efficient systems, also by definition, do not permit such
meanderings and designers and implementers will do whatever is
necessary to eliminate them. The elimination of meanderings and aimlessness is one of the reasons that rationalized systems were, for Weber,
disenchanted systems.

With regard to calculability, in the main, enchantment has far more
to do with quality than quantity. Magic, fantasies, dreams and the like
relate more to the inherent nature of an experience, and the qualitative aspects of that experience, than, for example, to the number of
such experiences one has or the size of the space in which it occurs.
An emphasis on producing and participating in a large number of
experiences tends to diminish the magical quality of each of them. Put
another way, it is difficult to imagine the mass production of magic,
fantasy, and dreams. Such mass productions may be common in the
movies, but they are more difficult, if not impossible, to produce in
settings designed to deliver large numbers of goods and services
frequently and over great geographic spaces. The mass production
of such things is virtually guaranteed to undermine their enchanted qualities. This is a fundamental dilemma facing McDonaldized
systems (see Chapter 6).

No characteristic of rationalization is more inimical to enchantment than predictability. Magical, fantastic or dream-like experiences
are almost by definition unpredictable. Nothing would destroy an

enchanted experience more easily than having it become predictable, or having it recur in the same way time after time.

Both control and the nonhuman technologies that produce it tend to be inimical to enchantment. As a general rule, fantasy, magic and dreams cannot be subjected to external controls; indeed, autonomy is much of what gives them their enchanted quality. Fantastic experiences can go anywhere; anything can happen. Such unpredictability clearly is not possible in a tightly controlled environment. Now, it is possible that tight and total control can be a fantasy, but for many it would be more a nightmare than a dream. Much the same can be said of nonhuman technologies. Such cold, mechanical systems are usually the antitheses of the dream worlds associated with enchantment. Again, it is true that there are fantasies associated with nonhuman technologies, but they too tend to be more nightmarish than dream-like.

The point of this section has been to argue that McDonaldization is related to, if not inextricably intertwined with, disenchantment. And, the production of a world without magic and mystery is an irrational consequence of increasing rationalization.

Dehumanization: Getting Hosed at 'Trough and Brew'

The main reason to think of McDonaldization as irrational, and ultimately unreasonable, is that it tends to become a dehumanizing system that may become antihuman or even destructive of human beings.

Health and Environmental Hazards

There are a number of ways progressive rationalization has threatened the health, and perhaps the lives, of people. One example is the danger posed by the content of most fast food: a lot of fat, cholesterol, salt, and sugar. Such meals are the last things most Americans need, suffering as many of them do from obesity, high cholesterol levels, high blood pressure, and perhaps diabetes. Fast-food restaurants also help create eating habits in children that contribute to the development of these, and other, health problems later in life. With their appeal to children, fast-food restaurants are creating not only life-long devotees of fast food, but also people who may well grow addicted to diets high in salt, sugar, and fat (Spencer, 1983). In an interesting recent study, it was discovered that the health of immigrant children deteriorates the longer they are in the United States, in large part because their diet comes to more closely resemble the junk-food diet of most American children (Hernandez and Charney, 1998). Said a sociologist whose work was cited in the study, 'The McDonaldization of the world is not necessarily progress when it comes to nutritious diets' (Stearns, 1998: B6).

Attacks against the fast-food industry's harmful effects on health have mounted over the years. As a result, many of the franchises have been forced to respond in various ways. Salads have been one response, although the dressings for them are often loaded with salt and fat. Some fast-food restaurants have ceased cooking french fries in beef tallow and instead use less-cholesterol-laden vegetable oil. Though these restaurants have had to adapt to increasing health concerns, the typical McDonald's meal of a Big Mac, large fries, and shake has more than 1,000 calories, loaded with salt, sugar, and fat. And the recent emphasis on larger and larger portions has only increased the problem. For example, Burger King's Double Whopper with cheese alone has 960 calories (and 63 grams of fat).

McDonaldization poses even more immediate health threats. Regina Schrambling (1991: A19) links various diseases, especially salmonella, to the rationalization of food production:

> Salmonella proliferated in the poultry industry only after beef became a four-letter word and Americans decided they wanted a chicken in every pot every night. But birds aren't like cars: you can't just speed up the factory line to meet demand. Something has got to give – and in this case it's been safety. Birds that are rushed to fryer size, then killed, gutted, and plucked at high speed in vast quantities are not going to be the cleanest food in the supermarket.

Schrambling also links salmonella to the more rational production of eggs, fruit, and vegetables. More generally, she traces a wide range of illnesses to various rationalized production systems. Hudson Foods Inc., a meatpacking company that, among other things, supplied meat to McDonald's and Burger King, was forced out of business not long ago because of an outbreak of *E. coli* that was traced to its frozen hamburgers (*Independent*, 1997).

Then there are the health hazards (and environmental degradation) associated with factory farms and aquaculture. For example, factory farms, especially those involving hogs, produce a huge amount of manure that ultimately finds its way into our waterways and then our drinking water; people have been made ill and women have had mis-carriages as a result of drinking contaminated water (Bell, 1998). The dosing of factory-farmed animals with antibiotics may lead to bacteria that are resistant to antibiotics, thereby putting people at risk who are infected with the bacteria (O'Brien, 1998: 4). Aquaculture creates a similar set of environmental problems and health risks to humans (Woodard, 1998; Wu, 1998).

McDonaldized systems pose a health hazard not only to humans, but also to pets. Pets are affected by many of the things described above, and they are faced with distinctive threats of their own. Chains of supermarket-like pet stores such as Petstuff and Petsmart employed automatic hair dryers to groom dogs. Unfortunately, some dogs were locked in cages and under the dryers for too long. Several died or were injured in the process. Said the founder of a watchdog group, Grooming Accidents, Supervision and Prevention (GASP): 'The whole notion of leaving a dog unsupervised with an electrical heater blowing makes no sense. They are treating animals like cars in an assembly line' (Lipton, 1995: B1).

One Marxist critic, Tim Luke, has attacked the invasion of Russia by McDonald's as well as other aspects of a McDonaldized society. He labels what is being created a 'McGulag Archipelago'. Thus, Luke implies that McDonaldization is a new kind of system to imprison Russian citizens, in other words, a new kind of 'iron cage'. Luke (1990: 42) also attacks McDonald's for a variety of other reasons, such as being 'nutritionally questionable', 'waste-intensive', and 'environmentally-destructive'.

The fast-food industry has run afoul not only of nutritionists, but also of environmentalists. It produces an enormous amount of trash, some of which is nonbiodegradable. The litter from fast-food meals has created a public eyesore across the countryside. It takes hundreds, if not thousands, of square miles of forest to provide the paper needed each year by McDonald's alone (Boas and Chain, 1976). Whole forests are being devoured by the fast-food industry, even though some paper containers have been replaced by styrofoam and other products. In fact, the current trend is back to paper products because even greater criticism has been leveled at the fast-food industry for its widespread use of styrofoam. Virtually indestructible, styrofoam piles up in landfills, creating mountains of waste that simply remain there for years, if not forever.

Many other McDonaldized systems create environmental problems. For example, the factory farms and aquaculture discussed above not only can harm humans, but have a number of negative effects on the environment such as fouled waterways, destroyed forests, and outbreaks of disease in animal and fish populations.

The automobile assembly line has experienced extraordinary success in churning out millions of cars a year. But all those cars, created year after year, have wreaked havoc on the environment, polluted by their emissions. An ever-expanding number of highways and roads has torn up and scarred the countryside. Then there are the thousands of people killed and the far greater number injured each year in traffic accidents.

Dehumanization of Customers and Employees

The fast-food industry offers its employees what I have recently called 'McJobs' (Ritzer, 1998: 59–70). For example, employees labor in dehumanizing work settings. Said Burger King workers, 'A moron could learn this job, it's so easy' and 'Any trained monkey could do this job' (Reiter, 1991: 150, 167). Workers can use only a small portion of their skills and abilities. This is irrational from the organization's viewpoint, because it could obtain much more from its employees for the money (however negligible) it pays them.

The minimal skill demands of the fast-food restaurant are also irrational from the employee's perspective. Besides not using all their skills, employees are not allowed to think and be creative on the job. This leads to a high level of resentment, job dissatisfaction, alienation, absenteeism, and turnover among those who work in fast-food restaurants.[4] In fact, the fast-food industry has the highest turnover rate – approximately 300 per cent a year – of any industry in the United States. That means that the average fast-food worker lasts only about four months; the entire work force of the fast-food industry turns over approximately three times a year.

Although the simple and repetitive nature of the jobs makes it relatively easy to replace workers who leave, such a high turnover rate is still undesirable from the organization's perspective. It would clearly be better to keep employees longer. The costs involved in turnover, such as hiring and training, greatly increase with extraordinarily high turnover rates.

The fast-food restaurant also dehumanizes the consumer. By eating on a sort of assembly line, the diner is reduced to an automaton made to rush through a meal with little gratification derived from the dining experience or from the food itself. The best that can usually be said is that it is efficient and it is over quickly.

Some customers might even feel as if they are being fed like livestock. This point was made on TV a number of years ago in a *Saturday Night Live* skit, 'Trough and Brew', a parody of a small fast-food chain called 'Burger and Brew'. In the skit, some young executives learn that a new fast-food restaurant called Trough and Brew has opened, and they decide to try it for lunch. When they enter the restaurant, bibs are tied around their necks. Then, they discover what resembles a pig trough filled with chili and periodically refilled by a waitress scooping new supplies from a bucket. The customers bend over, stick their heads into the trough, and lap up the chili as they move along the trough presumably making 'high-level business decisions' en route. Every so often they come up for air and lap some beer from the communal 'brew basin'. After they have finished their 'meal', they pay their bills 'by the head'. Since their faces are smeared with chili, they are literally 'hosed off' before they leave the restaurant. The young executives are last seen being herded out of the restaurant, which is being closed for a half-hour so that it can be 'hosed down'. *Saturday Night Live* was clearly ridiculing the fact that fast-food restaurants tend to treat their customers like lower animals.

Customers are also dehumanized by scripted interactions, and other efforts to make interactions uniform. 'Uniformity is incompatible when human interactions are involved. Human interactions that are mass-produced may strike consumers as dehumanizing if the routinization is obvious or manipulative if it is not' (Leidner, 1993: 30). Dehumanization occurs when prefabricated interactions take the place of authentic human relationships.

Garfield's (1991: 5) critique of Walt Disney World provides another example of dehumanized customers:

> I actually believed there was real fun and real imagination in store only to be confronted with an extruded, injection-molded, civil engineered brand of fantasy, which is to say: no fantasy at all.
>
> From the network of chutes and corrals channeling people into attractions, to the chillingly programmed Stepford Wives demeanor of the employees, to the compulsively litter-free grounds, to the generalized North Korean model Socialist Society sense of totalitarian order, to the utterly passive nature of the entertainment itself, Disney turns out to be the very antithesis of fantasy, a remarkable technospectacle ...
>
> Far from liberating the imagination, Disney succeeds mainly in confining it. Like the conveyor 'cars' and 'boats' that pull you along steel tracks through 'Snow White' and 'World of Motion' and the 'Speedway' rides, Disney is a plodding, precise, computer controlled mechanism pulling an estimated 30 million visitors along the same calculated, unvarying, meticulously engineered entertainment experience. It occupies its customers without engaging them. It appeals to everybody while challenging nobody ...
>
> Imagine, for example, a fake submergence in a fake submarine for a fake voyage past fake coral and fake seafood, knowing full well that there are two magnificent aquariums within a 70-minute drive of your house.

Thus, instead of being a creative and imaginative human experience, Disney World turns out to be an uncreative, unimaginative, and ultimately inhuman experience.

The automobile assembly line is well known for the way it dehumanizes life on a day-to-day basis for those who work on it. Henry Ford felt that while he could not do the kind of repetitive work required on the assembly line, most people, with their limited mental abilities and aspirations, could adjust to it quite well. Ford (1922: 105–6) said, 'I have not been able to discover that repetitive labour injures a man in any way ... The most thorough research has not brought out a single case of a man's mind being twisted or deadened by the work.' However, people now know that the dehumanizing character of assembly-line work has profound negative effects on those who work on the line.

Objective evidence on the destructiveness of the assembly line is found in the high rates of absenteeism, tardiness, and turnover among employees. More generally, most people seem to find assembly-line work highly alienating. Here is the way one worker describes it:

I stand in one spot, about a two- or three-feet area, all night. The only time a person stops is when the line stops. We do about thirty-two jobs per car, per unit, forty-eight units an hour, eight hours a day. Thirty-two times forty-eight times eight. Figure it out, that's how many times I push that button. (Terkel, 1974: 159)

Another worker offers a similar view: 'What's there to say? A car comes, I weld it; a car comes, I weld it; a car comes, I weld it. One hundred and one times an hour.' Others do more than describe the work, they get quite sarcastic about it: 'There's a lot of variety in the paint shop ... You clip on the color hose, bleed out the color and squirt. Clip, bleed, squirt; clip, bleed, squirt, yawn; clip, bleed, squirt, scratch your nose' (Garson, 1977: 88). Another assembly-line worker sums up the dehumanization he feels: 'Sometimes I felt just like a robot. You push a button and you go this way. You become a mechanical nut' (Terkel, 1974: 175).

These workers' observations are supported by many scientific studies that show high degrees of alienation among assembly-line workers. This alienation is traceable to the rationality of the line and the fact that it produces the unreasonable consequence of dehumanizing work. Alienation affects not only those who work on the automobile assembly line, but also people in the wide range of settings built, at least in part, on the principles of the assembly line.[5] In our rapidly McDonaldizing society, the assembly line has implications for many of us and for many different settings.

Negative Effect on Human Relationships

Fast-Food Industry: Gone is the 'Greasy Spoon'   Another dehumanizing aspect of fast-food restaurants is that they minimize contact among human beings. For example, the nature of the fast-food restaurant makes the relationships between employees and customers fleeting at best. Because employees typically work part-time and stay only a few months, even regular customers can rarely develop personal relationships with them. All but gone are the days when one got to know well a waitress at a diner or the short order cook at a local 'Greasy Spoon'. There are fewer and fewer places where an employee knows who you are and knows what you are likely to order. Fast being overwhelmed are what Ray Oldenburg (1989) calls 'great good places' such as local cafes and taverns.

Contact between workers and customers at the fast-food restaurant is very short. It takes little time at the counter to order, receive the food, and pay for it. Both employees and customers are likely to feel rushed and to want to move on, customers to their meal and employees to the next order.[6] There is virtually no time for customer and counter person to interact in such a context. This is even truer of the drive-through window, where thanks to the speedy service and the physical barriers, the server is even more distant.

These highly impersonal and anonymous relationships are heightened by the training of employees to interact in a staged, scripted, and limited manner with customers. Thus, the customers may feel that they are dealing with automatons rather than with fellow human beings. For their part, the customers are supposed to be, and often are, in a hurry, so they also have little to say to the McDonald's employee. Indeed, it could be argued that one of the reasons the fast-food restaurants succeed is that they are in tune with our fast-paced and impersonal society. People in the modern world want to get on with their business without unnecessary personal relationships. The fast-food restaurant gives them precisely what they want.

Not only the relationships between employee and customer, but other potential relationships are limited greatly. Because employees remain on the job for only a few months, satisfying personal relationships among employees are unlikely to develop. Again it is useful to contrast this with the Japanese case, where more permanent employment helps foster long-term relationships on the job. Furthermore, Japanese workers are likely to get together with one another after work hours and on weekends. The temporary and part-time character of jobs in fast-food restaurants, and other McDonaldized settings, largely eliminates the possibility of such personal relationships among employees.

Relationships among customers are largely curtailed as well. Although some McDonald's ads would have people believe otherwise, gone for the most part (there are, as we have seen, the occasional 'breakfast clubs') are the days when people met in the diner or cafeteria for coffee or a meal and lingered to socialize. Fast-food restaurants clearly do not encourage such socializing. If nothing else, the chairs by design make people uncomfortable, so that they move on quickly. The drive-through windows completely eliminate the possibility of interaction with other customers.

Family: The Kitchen as Filling Station   Fast-food restaurants also tend to have negative effects on other human relationships. There is, for example, the effect on the family, especially the so-called 'family meal' (Mattox, 1997: A14). The fast-food restaurant is not conducive to a long, leisurely, conversation-filled dinnertime. Furthermore, as the children grow into their teens, the fast-food restaurant can lead to separate meals as the teens go at one time with their friends, and the parents go at another time. Of course, the drive-through window only serves to reduce further the possibility of a family meal. The family that gobbles its food while driving on to its next stop can hardly enjoy 'quality time'. Here is the way one journalist describes what is happening to the family meal:

Do families who eat their suppers at the Colonel's, swinging on plastic seats, or however the restaurant is arranged, say grace before picking up a crispy brown chicken leg? Does dad ask junior what he did today as he remembers he forgot the piccalilli and trots through the crowds over to the counter to get some? Does mom find the atmosphere conducive to asking little Mildred about the problems she was having with third conjugation French verbs, or would it matter since otherwise the family might have been at home chomping down precooked frozen food, warmed in the microwave oven and watching 'Hollywood Squares'? (von Hoffman, 1978: C4)

There is much talk these days about the disintegration of the family, and the fast-food restaurant may well be a crucial contributor to that disintegration. Conversely, the decline of the family creates ready-made customers for fast-food restaurants.

In fact, as implied above, dinners at home may now not be much different from meals at the fast-food restaurant. Families tended to stop having lunch together by the 1940s and breakfast together by the 1950s. Today, the family dinner is following the same route. Even at home, the meal will probably not be what it once was. Following the fast-food model, people have ever more options to 'graze', 'refuel', nibble on this, or snack on that, rather than sit down at a formal meal. Also, because it may seem inefficient to do nothing but just eat, families are likely to watch television or play computer games while they are eating. Furthermore, the din, to say nothing of the lure, of dinnertime TV programs such as *Wheel of Fortune* and of the 'bings' and 'whines' associated with computer games is likely to make it difficult for family members to interact with one another.

A key technology in the destruction of the family meal is the microwave and the vast array of microwavable foods it helped generate (Visser, 1989). The vast majority of American households have a microwave oven. A *Wall Street Journal* poll indicated that Americans consider the microwave their favorite household product. In fact, the microwave in a McDonaldizing society is seen as an advance over the fast-food restaurant. Said one consumer researcher, 'It has made even fast-food restaurants not seem fast because at home you don't have to wait in line.' As a general rule, consumers demand meals that take no more than ten minutes to microwave, whereas in the past people were more often willing to spend a half hour or even an hour cooking dinner. This emphasis on speed has, of course, brought with it lower quality, but people do not seem to mind this loss: 'We're just not as critical of food as we used to be' (*Wall Street Journal*, 1989: B1).

The speed of microwave cooking, as well as the wide variety of microwavable foods, make it possible for family members to eat at different times and places. Even children can 'zap' their own meals with products such as 'Kid's Kitchen', 'Kid Cuisine', 'Fun Feast', and 'My Own Meals' (there are similar products in frozen food). As a result,

'Those qualities of the family meal, the ones that imparted feelings of security and well-being, might be lost forever when food is "zapped" or "nuked" instead of cooked' (Visser, 1989: 40).

The advances in microwave cooking continue. On some foods, plastic strips turn blue when the food is done. The industry has even promised strips that communicate cooking information directly to the microwave oven. 'With cooking reduced to pushing a button, the kitchen may wind up as a sort of filling station. Family members will pull in, push a few buttons, fill up and leave. To clean up, all we need do is throw away plastic plates' (Visser, 1989: 42). What is lost, of course, is the family meal; people need to decide whether they can afford the loss:

> The communal meal is our primary ritual for encouraging the family to gather together every day. If it is lost to us, we shall have to invent new ways to be a family. It is worth considering whether the shared joy that food can provide is worth giving up. (Visser, 1989: 42)

The family meal is not the only aspect of family life threatened by McDonaldization. For example, busy and exhausted parents are being advised that instead of reading to their children at night, they should have them listen to audiotapes (Gisler and Eberts, 1995: 3E). Then there is Viagra which, while it can revive the sex lives of many men and enhance many relationships, can also cause a series of problems between men and their mates. For example, aging males now have access to Viagra, but there is no corresponding medication (at least as yet) for their (female) mates. The result may be tension between an eager man and less than eager mate (Ficklen, 1998; MacGregor, 1998). Newly reinvigorated men may also be motivated to seek out younger, more vigorous partners with the resulting threat to established relationships.

Higher Education: It's Like Processing Meat The modern university has, in various ways, become a highly irrational place. Many students and faculty members are put off by its huge, factory-like atmosphere. They may feel like automatons processed by the bureaucracy and computers, or even cattle run through a meat-processing plant. In other words, education in such settings can be a dehumanizing experience. The masses of students; large, impersonal dorms; and huge lecture classes make getting to know other students difficult. The large lectures, constrained tightly by the clock, make it virtually impossible to know professors personally. At best, students might get to know a graduate assistant teaching a discussion section. Grades may be derived from a series of machine-graded multiple-choice exams and posted impersonally, often by social-security number rather than name. In sum, students may feel like little more than objects into which knowledge is poured as they move along an information-providing and degree-granting educational assembly line.

Of course, technological advances are leading to even greater irrationalities in education. The minimal contact between teacher and student is being further limited by such advances as educational television, closed-circuit television (Honan, 1995), distance learning, computerized instruction, and teaching machines. We may soon see the ultimate step in the dehumanization of education – the elimination of a human teacher and of human interaction between teacher and student.

Health Care: You're Just a Number   For the physician, the process of rationalization carries with it a series of irrationalities. At or near the top of the list is the shift in control away from the physician toward rationalized structures and institutions. In the past, private practitioners had a large degree of control over their work, with the major constraints being peer control as well as the needs and demands of patients. In rationalized medicine, external control increases and shifts to social structures and institutions. Not only is the physician more likely to be controlled by these structures and institutions, but also by managers and bureaucrats who are not themselves physicians. The ability of physicians to control their own work lives is declining. External control as a problem for physicians may manifest itself in increased levels of job dissatisfaction and alienation (perhaps even a turn toward unionization).

From the patient's viewpoint, the rationalization of medicine causes a number of irrationalities. The drive for efficiency can make them feel like products on a medical assembly line. The effort to increase predictability will likely lead patients to lose personal relationships with physicians and other health professionals because rules and regulations lead physicians to treat all patients in essentially the same way. This is also true in hospitals, where instead of seeing the same nurse regularly, a patient may see many different nurses. The result, of course, is that such nurses never come to know their patients as individuals. Then, there is the recent advent (at least in the United States) of the 'hospitalist', doctors who practice exclusively in hospitals. Now instead of seeing one's personal physician (if one still has such a doctor), hospitalized patients are more likely to be seen by physicians who they probably have never seen before and with whom they have no personal relationship (Hundley, 1998).

As a result of the emphasis on calculability, the patient is more likely to feel like a number in the system rather than a person. Minimizing time and maximizing profits may lead to a decline in the quality of health care provided to patients. Like physicians, patients are apt to be increasingly controlled by large-scale structures and institutions, which will probably appear to them as distant, uncaring, and impenetrable. Finally, patients are increasingly likely to interact with technicians and impersonal technologies. In fact, because more and more technologies may be purchased at the drug store, patients can test themselves and thereby cut out human contact with both physicians and technicians. Thus, the rationalization of medicine has increased the dehumanization and depersonalization of medical practice.

The ultimate irrationality of this rationalization would be the unanticipated consequences of a decline in the quality of medical practice and a deterioration in the health of patients. Increasingly rational medical systems, with their focus on lowering costs and increasing profits, may reduce the quality of health care, especially for the poorest members of society. At least some people may become sicker, and perhaps even die, because of the rationalization of medicine. Health in general may even decline. These possibilities can only be assessed in the future as the health-care system continues to rationalize. Since the health-care system will continue to rationalize, health professionals and their patients may need to learn how to control rational structures and institutions to ameliorate their irrational consequences.

Homogenization

Another dehumanizing effect of the fast-food restaurant is that it has increased homogenization in the United States and, increasingly, throughout the world. This decline in diversity is manifest in the extension of the fast-food model to all sorts of ethnic foods. People are hard-pressed to find an authentically different meal in an ethnic fast-food chain. The food has been rationalized and compromised so that it is acceptable to the tastes of virtually all diners. Paradoxically, while fast-food restaurants have permitted far more people to experience ethnic food, the food that they eat has lost many of its distinguishing characteristics.[7] The settings are also all modeled after McDonald's in one way or another.

The expansion of these franchises across the United States means that people find little difference between regions and between cities. Tourists find more familiarity and less diversity as they travel around the nation, and this is increasingly true on a global scale. Exotic settings are increasingly likely sites for American fast-food chains. The McDonald's and Kentucky Fried Chicken in Beijing are but two examples of this. Furthermore, in many nations, restaurant owners are applying the McDonald's model to native cuisine. In Paris, tourists may be shocked by the number of American fast-food restaurants there, but even more shocked by the incredible spread of indigenous forms such as the fast-food croissanterie. One would have thought that the French considered the croissant a sacred object and would have found it obscene to rationalize its manufacture and sale, but that is just what has happened. While the fast-food system has demeaned the quality of the croissant, the spread of such outlets throughout Paris indicates that many Parisians are willing to sacrifice quality for speed and efficiency. (And, you may ask, if the Parisian croissant can be tamed and transformed into a fast-food success, what food is safe?) In any case, the spread of American and indigenous fast food throughout much of the world causes less and less diversity from one setting to another. The human craving for new and diverse experiences is being limited, if not progressively destroyed, by the spread of fast-food restaurants. The craving for diversity is being supplanted by the desire for uniformity and predictability.

Just as the fast-food restaurants are leveling food differences, mail-order catalogues are eliminating seasonal differences. When Ellen Goodman (1991: A19) received her Christmas catalogue just as fall was beginning, she critiqued this particular aspect of rationalization: 'The creation of one national mail-order market has produced catalogues without the slightest respect for any season or region. Their holidays are now harvested, transported and chemically ripened on the way to your home. ... I refuse to fast forward through the fall.' (There is another irrationality here. Those who buy things through catalogues find that their deliveries are often late or they never arrive at all. Said the President of the Better Business Bureau of Metropolitan New York, 'With mail order, the biggest problem is delivery and delay in delivery' (Sloane, 1992: 50).

In sum, contrary to McDonald's propaganda and the widespread belief in it, fast-food restaurants and their rational clones are not reasonable, or even truly rational, systems. They spawn problems for their customers including inefficiency rather than increased efficiency, relatively high costs, illusory fun and reality, false friendliness, disenchantment and dehumanization (threats to health, the environment, and genuine human relationships). None of this denies the advantages of McDonaldization, but these irrationalities clearly indicate the counterbalancing and perhaps even overwhelming problems associated with this process. These problems, these irrationalities, need to be understood because most people have been exposed to little more than an unrelenting set of superlatives created by McDonaldized systems to describe themselves.

Notes

This chapter is derived from Chapter 7 of *The McDonaldization of Society*, 2nd edition. Thousand Oaks, CA: Pine Forge Press, 1996: 121–42.

1   Negative effects other than the ones discussed here, such as racism and sexism, cannot be explained by this process; see Reiter, 1991: 145.

2   Burger King does the same thing to its fries; see Reiter, 1991: 65.

3   I am thinking here of 'authentic' enchantment. In Chapter 6 we will discuss the ways in which the new means of consumption seek to (re-)enchant themselves in various inauthentic (simulated) ways.

4   Leidner (1993: 134) disagrees with this, arguing that McDonald's 'workers expressed relatively little dissatisfaction with the extreme routinization'. One could ask, however, whether this indicates a McDonaldizing society in which people, accustomed to the process, simply accept it as an inevitable part of their work.

5   For a review of the literature on this issue, see Ritzer and Walczak, 1986: 328–72.

6   One exception to the general rule discussed here that diners do not linger is the tendency for retirees to use McDonald's as a social center, especially over breakfast or coffee.

7   In many areas there has been a simultaneous increase in reasonably authentic ethnic restaurants.

3

SOME THOUGHTS ON THE FUTURE OF McDONALDIZATION

The De-McDonaldization of Society?

Perhaps no idea would seem more extreme, at least from the perspective of the McDonaldization thesis, than the notion that we are already beginning to see signs of de-McDonaldization. (An even more heretical argument would, of course, be that the process did not occur in the first place. However, the social world has certainly changed and one of the ways of conceptualizing at least some of those changes is increasing rationalization. Furthermore, such a view would mean a rejection of one of the strongest and most durable social theories; one that has not only endured but grown through the work of such venerable social thinkers as Weber and Mannheim, as well as that of many contemporary social analysts.) If this is, in fact, the case, McDonaldization would seem to be a concept that may have made some sense at a particular time (and place), but that seems to be in the process of being superseded by recent developments. If McDonaldization has already passed its peak, then its worth and utility as a fundamental sociological concept are severely, perhaps fatally, undermined.[1] What evidence can be marshaled in support of the idea that we are seeing signs of de-McDonaldization?

The first is the fact that McDonald's itself, while still the star of the fast-food industry and continuing to grow rapidly, is experiencing some difficulties and does not quite have the luster it once did. If McDonald's is having problems, that may call into question the concept which bears its name and its imprint. The strongest evidence on these difficulties is the increasing challenge to McDonald's in the highly competitive American market. Indeed, the competition has grown so keen that McDonald's focus in terms of profits and future expansion has shifted overseas, where it remains an unparalleled success. Reflective of McDonald's problems in the United States was the recent and much ballyhooed introduction of the Arch Deluxe (Richman, 1996). A great deal of McDonald's past success, especially in the United States, has been based on its appeal to children through its clowns, playgrounds, promotions, and food. However, in recent years McDonald's has become convinced that in order to protect its pre-eminent positioning in the American market it has to become more adult-oriented and to offer more adult foods. Hence the Arch

Deluxe – bigger than a Big Mac, lettuce pieces rather than shreds, tangier Dijon-style mustard, and so on. Whether or not McDonald's succeeds with the Arch Deluxe (and indications are not promising), or any other new product or promotion, the fact is that McDonald's recognizes, and is trying to deal with, problems on its home field. And, if McDonald's continues to lose market share and hegemony within the American market, can trouble in other markets around the world be far behind?

A second worrisome trend to McDonald's, and potential threat to McDonaldization, is the fact that McDonald's is becoming a negative symbol to a number of social movements throughout the world. Those groups that are struggling to deal with ecological hazards, dietary dangers, the evils of capitalism and the dangers posed by Americanization (and, as we will see below, many other problems) often take McDonald's as a symbol of these problems, especially since it can easily be related to all of them. Furthermore, these groups can mount a variety of attacks on the company as a whole (for example, national and international boycotts of McDonald's products), as well as the 20,000 (as of this writing) or so McDonald's outlets around the world. Such outlets make easy, attractive and readily available targets for all sorts of dissident groups.

Much of the hostility towards McDonald's has crystallized in recent years around the so-called 'McLibel' trial in London (Vidal, 1997). McDonald's sued five people associated with London Greenpeace for distributing a pamphlet, 'What's Wrong with McDonald's? Everything They Don't Want You to Know'. Three of the five members apologized rather than face potential ruin, but two others, David Morris and Helen Steel, decided to contest the suit. The case, the longest running libel trial in the history of Great Britain, ended ambiguously in June 1997 with the judge finding for McDonald's on most issues, but substantiating some of the claims against the company.

Among other things, the pamphlet attacked McDonald's (and America) for economic imperialism, misuse of resources by causing the inefficient use of large amounts of grain in the creation of a far smaller quantity of beef, contributing to deforestation, pushing an unhealthy diet on consumers, seducing children into being McDonald's habitués, being responsible for cruelty to animals, providing poorly paid dead-end jobs, and so on. The pamphlet (and the libel case dealing with it) became something of a *cause célèbre*. There is a worldwide web site which keeps interested parties informed about the case and related matters. More importantly, it keeps a wide variety of people and groups around the world informed about actions by, and against, McDonald's and the other fast-food restaurants. In addition, many other related issues (for example, environmental, health) are the subject of communiqués through the web site.

As a result, at least in part, of the McLibel trial, McDonald's has become the symbolic enemy for many groups, including environmentalists, animal rights organizations, anti-capitalists, anti-Americans, supporters of the Third World, those concerned about nutritional issues, those interested in defending children, the labor movement, and many more. If all of these groups can continue to see many of the problems of concern to them combined within McDonald's, then here is a real long-term danger to McDonald's. This problem would be greatly exacerbated if some or all of these groups were to come together and jointly oppose McDonald's. Once, and perhaps still, the model (in a positive sense) corporation in the eyes of many, McDonald's is now in danger of becoming the paradigm for all that is bad in the world in the eyes of many others.

Yet another threat to McDonald's stems from the difficulty any corporation has in staying on top indefinitely. McDonald's may well survive the two threats discussed above, but sooner or later internal problems (for example, declining profits, and/or stock prices), external competition, or some combination of the two, will set McDonald's on a downward course which will end in it becoming a pale imitation of the present powerhouse. While far less likely, it is also possible that these factors will even lead to its complete disappearance.

However, we must not confuse threats to McDonald's with dangers to the process of McDonaldization. McDonald's could disappear tomorrow with few if any serious implications for the continuation of McDonaldization. McDonald's will almost undoubtedly disappear at some point in the future, but by then the McDonaldization process will likely be even more deeply entrenched in American society and throughout much of the world. In the eventuality that McDonald's should some day be down or even out, we may need to find a new paradigm and even a new name for the process, but that process (generically, the rationalization process) will continue, almost certainly at an accelerating rate.

But isn't there a variety of counter-trends that seem to add up to more than a threat to McDonald's, to a threat to the process of McDonaldization itself? Several such trends are worth discussing.

For one thing, there is an apparent rise of small, non-McDonaldized businesses. The major example in my area, the suburbs of Washington, DC, is the opening of many small, high-quality bakeries. There seems to be a reasonably large number of people who are willing to travel some distance and to pay relatively high prices for quality breads made by highly skilled bakers. And there seems to be money to be made by such enterprising bakers. Of course bakeries are not the only example (various health conscious food emporiums would be another); there are many non-McDonaldized small businesses to be found throughout society.

Such enterprises have always existed; indeed they were far more commonplace before the recent explosive growth of McDonaldized systems. Under pressure from McDonaldized competitors, they seemed to have all but disappeared in many sectors, only to reappear, at least in part as a counter-reaction to McDonaldization. While they exist, and may even be growing, it is difficult to see these alternatives as a serious threat to McDonaldization. The likelihood is that they will succeed in the interstices of an otherwise highly McDonaldized society. If any one of them shows signs of being of more than of marginal importance, it will quickly be taken over and efforts will be made to McDonaldize it. It is difficult to envision any other scenario.

Recently, it has been argued that a 'New Regionalism' has developed in the United States and that it constitutes a 'quiet rebellion' against McDonaldization (Myerson, 1996). Identified here is a series of distinctive regional trends, fashions and products that are affecting the nation and ultimately the world. One example offered by Myerson is a salsa originating in San Antonio, Texas and manufactured by Pace Foods. While certainly a non-McDonaldized, regional product, at least at first, the salsa, in fact the company, was purchased by Campbell Soup Company in 1995 for just over $1 billion. Over time, it will just become another McDonaldized product marketed by Campbell Soup. It will probably suffer the fate of Colonel Sanders' original Kentucky Fried Chicken and many other products that at first were highly original and distinctive, but over time were turned into pale, McDonaldized imitations of what they once were.

Another example offered by Myerson is Elk Mountain Red Lager and Red Mountain Amber Ale. These sound like, and reflect the growing importance of, the products of local micro-breweries, but in fact they are produced by the Anheuser-Busch company. Furthermore, they are made from the same hops as Budweiser and Michelob. Anheuser-Busch is, of course, trying to capitalize on the success of local and regional micro-breweries. What they are, in fact, doing is McDonaldizating micro-brewery beer.

Myerson cites the preservation of cities like Savannah, Georgia as yet another example of the new regionalism, but he quickly moves on to the development of 'Disneyesque' simulacra like the Atlanta restaurant Pittypat's Porch, which is named after Scarlet O'Hara's aunt in the book and movie *Gone With the Wind*. He also mentions the 'movie-set' New York that is currently emerging in the resuscitation of Time Square (and in which Disney has a stake). Such examples seem far more supportive of the McDonaldization thesis (as well as of a postmodernist perspective, especially the emphasis on simulacra) than any counter-thesis.

Myerson is correct in arguing that many of America's innovations flow from outlying regions. He takes this as evidence of a trend that runs counter to the ideas of homogenization and McDonaldization. However, he ignores the fact that regional creations that show any sign of success are quickly McDonalized (examples include spicy New Orleans style cooking – Popeye's; southwestern Tacos – Taco Bell). McDonaldized systems do not excel at innovation: they are at their best in implementing and rationalizing ideas stemming from other sources. Thus, innovations are always highly likely to emerge outside of McDonaldized systems. This represents one of the dangers of McDonaldization. As we move closer and closer to the iron cage, where are the innovations of the future to come from?

McDonald's itself has developed a system for coping with its lack of innovativeness. After all, the creations that have generally flowed from the central office (for example, McDonald's Hula Burger – a bun with two slices of cheese surrounding a slice of grilled pineapple) have not been notably successful. It is the ideas that have stemmed from the franchises in the field (the Filet-O-Fish at McDonald's, for example) that have been the most important innovations.

Another counter-trend worthy of noting is the rise of McDonaldized systems that are able to produce high-quality products. The major example is the large and fast-growing chain of Starbucks coffee shops (Witchel, 1994). Until recently, virtually all successful McDonaldized systems have been noted for characteristics like low price and high speed, but not for the high quality of the goods and services that they offer. McDonaldization has heretofore been largely synonymous with mediocrity in these areas. Starbucks has shown that it is possible to create a McDonaldized system that dispenses quality products; on the surface, this poses a profound challenge to McDonaldization and, more generally, to the McDonaldization thesis.

However, Starbucks is, in many ways, an atypical chain. For one thing, it sells variations on what is essentially one simple product – coffee. For another, it is relatively easy, especially with advanced systems and technologies, to consistently produce a good cup of coffee. Third, the patrons of Starbucks are willing to pay a relatively large sum of money for a good cup of coffee. In fact, it may well cost as much to get a cup of 'designer coffee' at Starbucks as to have lunch at McDonald's. Thus, Starbucks indicates that it *is* possible to McDonaldize quality when we are dealing with one (or perhaps a few) simple products, when there are technologies that ensure high and consistent quality, and when enough patrons are willing to pay relatively large amounts of money for the product. Clearly, most chains are *not* able to meet these conditions, with the result they are likely to remain both McDonaldized and mediocre. It is also important to remember that even with the kinds of differences discussed above, especially in quality, Starbucks continues to be McDonaldized in many ways (the different types of cups of coffee are predictable from one time or place to another). However, this is not to say that there are not more chains that will meet conditions enumerated above and follow Starbucks' model. We already see this in the first steps toward the creation of high-quality restaurant chains.

A variety of moderately priced restaurant chains based on the McDonald's model have long since sprung up, including Sizzler, Bonanza, Olive Garden, TGIFriday's, and Red Lobster. In fact, such chains now control 35 per cent of what is called the moderately priced casual market (Bulkeley, 1996). In contrast, chains account for 77 per cent of low-priced restaurant meals. Far behind, with only 1 per cent of the market, are chains (actually, at this level they prefer to be called 'restaurant groups') involved in the high-priced 'linen tablecloth' business where the average patron's bill is in excess of $25. Notable examples include high-end steakhouse chains like Morton's of Chicago (33 restaurants) and Ruth's Chris Steak House (50 restaurants). The challenge in the future is to open high-end chains of restaurants that do not specialize in relatively easy to prepare steaks. Lured by the possibility of large profits, several groups are trying. For example, Wolfgang Puck, noted for his gourmet Spago restaurant in Los Angeles, has opened branch restaurants in San Francisco and Las Vegas (in the highly McDonaldized MGM Grand Hotel) and plans another for Chicago. The problem is that such restaurants depend on a creative chef and it is not immediately clear that one can McDonaldize creativity; indeed the two appear to be antithetical. Said one restaurateur, 'The question is, can ... [one] take a chef-driven concept to a city without a chef?' (Bulkeley, 1996: B1). The editor of *Gourmet Magazine* raises another issue about such chains; one that goes to the heart of McDonaldization and its limitations:

> It's the homogenization of cuisine. Even something as good as Morton's Steakhouse is, nevertheless, still going to be the same meal in Chicago as it would be in Washington. There are some people who value that – the fact that you'll always get a good meal. (Faiola, 1996: 13)

In the context of high-end restaurant chains, it is useful to discuss an analogy between Ford and Fordism and McDonald's and McDonaldization. In the early days of mass production of cars, people had little or no choice; there was virtually no variation in the number and quality of cars. Over the years, of course, and especially today in the era of post-Fordism, people have acquired a great deal of choice as far as their automobiles are concerned. There are many kinds of choice to be made, but one is certainly high quality cars (Mercedes Benz or BMW) versus standard quality (Ford Escort or Plymouth Neon) cars. However, they are all made using standardized parts and assembly line techniques. That is, high-quality cars can be produced using Fordist techniques.

A parallel point can be made about McDonald's and McDonaldization. In its early years, the focus of fast-food restaurants was on the most mundane, standardized products. While various fast-food chains competed for business, they all offered the same relatively low-quality, standardized product. Today, however, people are demanding more choices in foods, including higher quality foods that do not cause them to sacrifice the advantages of McDonaldization. Just as we can produce a Mercedes Benz using Fordist principles, we can offer high-quality quiche using the tenets of McDonaldization. The only thing that stands in the way of a chain of restaurants that offers a range of high-quality quiches is the likelihood that there is insufficient demand for such a product.

As discussed in the case of Starbucks, it is possible to McDonaldize any product, even the highest-quality products, at least to some degree. The secret is to offer one product, or at most a limited number of products. What seems to defy McDonaldization is the essence of a fine restaurant – a range of well-prepared dishes changing from day to day on the basis of availability of high-quality ingredients and/or the whims of the skilled chef. This kind of creativity and variability continues to resist McDonaldization.

The move into high-quality products leads us to question one of the basic tenets of McDonaldization – calculability, or the emphasis on quantity often to the detriment of quality. This is certainly true of virtually all McDonaldized systems that we have known, but it is not necessarily true of Starbucks, or of similar undertakings that we are likely to see in the future. We will see businesses where large amounts of high-quality quiche (to take one possibility) will be purveyed. Don't get me wrong here: I think that most McDonaldized systems continue to forfeit quality in the pursuit of quantity (high speed, low cost, low price). However, McDonaldization, like Fordism, is changing and we will see more systems that are capable of combining quantity and quality.

Does this mean that just as we have moved into a post-Fordist era, we will soon be entering an epoch of post-McDonaldization? To some degree we will, but just as I think that the argument for post-Fordism is overblown, I would not push the post-McDonaldization thesis too far. Just as today's post-Fordist systems are heavily affected by Fordism, tomorrow's post-McDonaldized systems will continue to be powerfully affected by McDonaldization.

Starbucks (and the fledgling high-quality restaurant chains) deviated from other McDonaldized systems largely on one dimension (calculability, or the emphasis on quantity rather than quality), but what of the other dimensions? Can we conceive of successful chains that deviate from the model in other ways? For example, could one build a chain on the basis of inefficiency? (In fact, as I write this, Chili's is running a nationwide television ad campaign claiming that it is *not* an assembly-line operation; that it is a monument to inefficiency.) Or unpredictability? Or on the use of human rather than non-human technology? All of these seem unlikely. But, there might come a time when most systems are so highly McDonaldized that a large market emerges among those who crave a respite. A chain of inefficient, labor-intensive outlets offering unpredictable goods and services might be able to carve out a niche for itself under such circumstances. However, if such a chain was successful, it would quickly come under pressure to McDonaldize. The paradoxical challenge would be to McDonaldize things like inefficiency and unpredictability. Ironically, it could be done – a chain that efficiently manifests inefficiency, one which is predictably unpredictable, uniformly different, and so on. I even have a name for this proposed chain – 'Miss Hap's'. (Miss Hap's would be a burger and fries chain, but there could also be a steakhouse twin – 'Miss Steak's'.)

Imagine, for example, a chain of restaurants that rationalizes inefficiency; in postmodern terms, one that produces a simulated inefficiency. A series of procedures to handle inefficiency would be created; procedures designed to attract customers fed up with efficient systems. These procedures would be broken down into a series of routine steps which would then be codified and made part of the company manual. New employees would be taught the steps needed to perform inefficiently. In the end, we would have a restaurant chain that has rationalized inefficiency. On cue, for example, a counter person at Miss Hap's would effortlessly spill an order of (perhaps fake) fries on the counter. Leaving aside the whimsical example, it is clearly possible to rationalize the seemingly irrational and to produce a system that well might have a ready-made market in a highly McDonaldized society. It would offer more 'fun', more spectacle, than the run-of-the-mill fast-food restaurant. And spectacle is often seen as a key element of the postmodern world (Debord, 1967/1994; Featherstone, 1991). It is certainly in the tune with trends like 'Las Vegasization' and 'McDisneyization'.

Miss Hap's would also offer a range of products that were, or at least seemed, unpredictable. The shape of the hamburgers (Miss Hap's would certainly need to offer hamburgers) would be uniformly different. Instead of being perfectly round (or, in the case of Wendy's, square), the burgers would be irregularly shaped. The shape would *not* be left to chance. A variety of molds would be used to mass-produce several different types of burger with slightly different shapes (this is the 'sneakerization' principle to be discussed below). While the burgers would look different, the differences would not affect the ease with which they could be cooked and served: it would still be possible to produce and sell such burgers within the context of a McDonaldized system. For example, all burgers would fit within the same-shaped bun. While the bun might remain uniformly round, it could be made uniformly irregular in other ways (for example, the hills and crevices on the top of the bun). Similar irregularities could be built into the shakes (which could vary in texture), fries and chicken nuggets (which could vary in length without affecting uniform frying time), and so on.

Another potential threat to McDonaldization lies in the area of customization, or what has been called 'sneakerization' (Goldman et al., 1994). There is considerable evidence that we have entered a post-industrial era in which the movement is away from the kinds of standardized, 'one-size-fits-all' products, that are at the heart of McDonaldized systems. Instead, what we see is much more customization. True customization (for example, made-to-measure suits) is not easily amenable to McDonaldization, but that is not what is usually meant by customization in this context. Rather, it is more niche marketing, of which 'sneakerization' is an excellent example. That is, instead of one or a few styles of sneakers or trainers, we now have hundreds of different styles produced for various niches in the market (runners, walkers, aerobic exercisers, and so on). This, of course, is not true customization; sneakers are not being made to measure for a specific user.

The central point is that sneakerization does *not* reflect a trend toward de-McDonaldization. Large companies like Nike produce hundreds of thousands or even millions of each type of sneaker with the result that each is amenable to a McDonaldized production (as well as marketing, distribution and sales) system. In fact, one future direction for McDonaldization involves its application to products and services that are sold in smaller and smaller quantities. There is undoubtedly some absolute lower limit below which it is not profitable to McDonaldize (at least to a high degree), but it is difficult to specify what that limit might be with any precision. In any case, that limit will become lower and lower with further technological advances. That is, we will be able to apply economies of scale to increasingly small production runs. More and different sneakers, more 'sneakerization', do not represent significant threats to McDonaldization.

A similar argument can be made about what has been termed 'mass customization' (Pine, 1993). Take the case of Custom Foot of Westport, Connecticut (McHugh, 1996). There, a customer puts a foot into an electronic scanner that measures it on a computer screen with the aid of a salesperson. It is during this phase that the customer chooses things like style of shoe, type and grade of leather, color, lining, and so on. Computer software then translates all of this into a set of specifications that are transmitted to subcontractors in several cities in Italy. The shoes are cobbled and sent to the USA within two to three weeks. The cost ranges from $99 to $250, about the same price as ready-to-wear shoes for sale in good New York shoe stores. In contrast, traditional custom-made shoes might cost $1,200 and take several months to arrive. In short, Custom Foot is McDonaldizing the process of making and selling truly customized shoes.

Now clearly this is less McDonaldized than the mass production of thousands, or even millions, of the same shoe. Mass production is more efficient, it permits greater predictability, more of it is amenable to quantification, and it relies more on non-human technologies than the customized production of shoes, even the way Custom Shoe does it. However, the procedures at Custom Shoe are far more McDonaldized than the traditional methods of producing customized shoes. We are talking here, as is usually the case, about degrees of McDonaldization. Custom Shoe has applied the principles of McDonaldization to the production and the sale of custom shoes. The nature of its product, especially in comparison to the mass production of identical shoes, limits the degree to which it can McDonaldize, but it does not affect the fact that it is being McDonaldized.

Thus, two of the directions in the future of McDonaldization are the production and sale of goods and services in increasingly small quantities and of goods that are higher in quality. While these are new directions, they do not represent de-McDonaldization. However, the issue of de-McDonaldization is addressed in another context in the next section.

A Modern Phenomenon in a Postmodern Age

Let us re-examine McDonaldization and de-McDonaldization from the perspective that we are in the midst of the monumental historical change in which a postmodern society is in the process of supplanting modern society. The issue, in this case, is the fate of modern phenomena and a modern process in a postmodern world. Let us assume that we can consider the fast-food restaurant and the McDonaldization process as modern phenomena and that we are currently undergoing a transformation to a postmodern society. Can the fast-food restaurant survive, perhaps prosper, in a postmodern world? What is the fate of McDonaldization in such a world?

If rationality is the *sine qua non* of modern society, then nonrationality and/or irrationality occupies a similar position in postmodern society. Suppose the postmodernists are correct and we are on the verge of the emergence of a nonrational or irrational society. What are the prospects for McDonald's and McDonaldization in such a situation? For one thing, such rational phenomena could continue to exist in a postmodern world and coexist with the presumably dominant irrationalities. In that case, McDonaldized systems would be rational outposts in an otherwise irrational world. People would flock to McDonald's to escape, at least momentarily, the irrationalities that surround them. Visiting a McDonald's would be like frequenting a throwback to an earlier era (much like eating in a diner is today). But surviving in this way, in the interstices of an otherwise nonrational world, would be very different from being the master trend that McDonaldization, at least from a postmodern perspective, once was.

If one possibility is survival at the margins, a second is disappearance in an avalanche of irrationalities. This would be the scenario envisioned by many postmodernists. They would see rational McDonaldized systems as incompatible with the dominant irrational systems and likely, sooner or later, to be swamped by them. The long-term process of McDonaldization would finally come to an end as it grew increasingly unable to rationalize the irrational.

A third, and in many ways highly likely, possibility would be some sort of fusion of the irrational elements of postmodernity with the rational components of McDonaldization: in other words, the creation of a pastiche of modern and postmodern elements. While this appears, on the surface, to be a compromise, in fact such a pastiche is one of the defining characteristics of postmodernism. So this kind of fusion would represent another version of the triumph of postmodernity. Buttressing the case for this alternative is the fact that McDonaldized systems already are well described by many of the concepts favored by postmodernists – consumerism, simulacra, hyperspace, multinational capitalism, implosion, ecstasy, and many others. It could be argued that such systems are *already* pastiches of modernism and postmodernism and therefore already postmodern.

The fourth, and diametrically opposed, possibility, is that McDonaldization will not only resist the irrationalities of postmodernity, but will ultimately triumph over them. Thus, while at the moment we might be seeing some movement toward postmodernism and irrationality, this tendency is likely to be short-lived as it is repulsed by the master trend of increasing rationalization. In this scenario it is postmodernism, not rationalization, that is the short-lived phenomenon. This alternative would obviously be unacceptable to most postmodern thinkers, largely because it means that the advent of a postmodern world would be stillborn. The triumph of McDonaldization means, by definition, the continuation, even acceleration, of modernity.

The logic of the McDonaldization thesis would, needless to say, favor the last of these scenarios. After all, following Weber, the rationalization process has existed and flowered over the course of many centuries. In the process it has encountered a series of monumental barriers and counter-trends. In the end it has not only triumphed over them, but emerged even stronger and more entrenched. Postmodernity *may* prove to be a more formidable opponent; it *may* do what no social change before it has done – alter, halt or even reverse the trend toward increasing rationalization. While such things might occur, it is hard to argue against the continuation, indeed acceleration, of McDonaldization. If history is any guide, McDonaldized systems will survive, even proliferate, long after we have moved beyond postmodern society and scholars have relegated postmodernism to the status of a concept of little more than historical interest.

Notes

This chapter is derived from Chapter 13 of *The McDonaldization Thesis*. London: Sage, 1998: 174–91.

1   The term 'McDonaldization' has found its way into several sociological dictionaries, including Abercrombie et al. (1994) and Jary and Jary (1995).

4

THE PROCESS OF McDONALDIZATION IS NOT UNIFORM: NOR ARE ITS SETTINGS, CONSUMERS OR THE CONSUMPTION OF ITS GOODS AND SERVICES

The objective in this chapter is to deal with four aspects of the McDonaldization thesis that have often been misrepresented. First, we want to make it clear that McDonaldization is *not* a uniform process; it has a variety of 'trajectories'. Second, and relatedly, as a result of varying trajectories, there is great variation in the degree to which settings are McDonaldized; even in the fast-food industry, not all settings are highly and equally McDonaldized. Third, while McDonaldized systems seek to mold consumers so that they behave in a uniform manner, they are never totally successful in doing so; there are various types of consumers. Finally, there is variation in the relationship between consumers and McDonaldized settings; consumers do not always simply act in accord with the demands of McDonaldized systems. Overall, while McDonaldization is a powerful force with quite general effects, it involves a number of variations and complexities. The objective in this chapter is not only to clarify certain aspects of the McDonaldization thesis, but also to offer more of the nuances associated with it.

McDonaldization as Process: Variations in Trajectories

Systems do not undergo the process of McDonaldization in the same manner and to the same degree. Sectors of society are amenable to rationalization in varying degrees and even within the same sector, organizations are transformed in different ways, to different degrees, and in varying time frames. It could be argued that every system has a unique 'trajectory of McDonaldization'; operations become increasingly rationalized over time in a pattern that is a function of the conditions specific to that system. (It is even possible for systems to move in the other direction – to undergo de-McDonaldization; see Chapter 3 of this volume.)

For example, franchised businesses are typically highly McDonaldized operations. Specifically in the fast-food industry, all of the major players have developed advanced systems of efficiency, calculability, predictability, and control, often seeking to keep up with, or even surpass, McDonald's itself. At the same time, McDonald's continues to rationalize further its operations in search of increasing profits and the retention of a competitive edge over other franchises. However, in response to each of McDonald's innovations, other franchises quickly adopt similar practices and strategies. Of course, McDonald's is no longer the sole or even the leading innovator among franchises. Thus, McDonald's must remain sensitive to its competitors and adopt the best and most relevant of their innovations. As a result, not only are fast-food chains, and franchises more generally, all highly rationalized, they also have a tendency to be somewhat indistinguishable from one another. Nonfranchised restaurants are likely to be less McDonaldized than the franchises, but while some remain quite nonrationalized, most experience pressure to rationalize their operations in order to remain competitive.

The health care industry is an example of a sector in which it is more difficult to McDonaldize many operations and, as a result, it has been slower to incorporate the principles of rationalization. While it might appear that medical care is inherently antagonistic toward the process of McDonaldization, the rise of McDoctors, the HMO as the predominant form of health care provision, the increased emphasis on hospitals as businesses, and increased government control over medicine all reflect the fact that McDonaldization has exerted an influence in this area. All elements of the health care process are amenable to rationalization in varying degrees, but some elements of the medical field (McDoctors) are becoming McDonaldized more extremely and more quickly than others (complicated surgical procedures).

A number of factors are influential in determining whether a sector is more or less amenable to McDonaldization. One that appears to play an important role is the degree to which suppliers of goods and services must adapt to the needs of individual customers. There is a strong need and considerable pressure on physicians to adapt their 'service' – medical care – to the specific needs of each patient. While the McDonaldization of medicine has led to doctors being forced to practice a more uniform and structured form of diagnosis and treatment, it is still more resistant to the mechanical 'if–then' mentality that one finds in settings like the fast-food restaurant where there is little need to adapt to the desires of specific customers.

Complexity of tasks is another factor. Simple tasks like the cooking and serving of hamburgers is more amenable to McDonaldization than highly complex tasks like preparing a gourmet meal. Within medicine, simpler tasks (taking vital signs) are more likely to be McDonaldized than complex tasks such as open heart surgery, although even the latter is not without its McDonaldized elements.

We can further distinguish among degrees of McDonaldization in a given sector. In health care, for example, we can see that certain institutional characteristics influence the speed and extent of McDonaldization. For instance, a large hospital in a major city and a general practice doctor's office in a rural area provide similar forms of health care services (in comparison to a drugstore or research laboratory). However, the hospital is likely to be much more McDonaldized, and to become so much more quickly, than the doctor's office.

Another variable that affects the process of McDonaldization is the degree of competition in a sector. The fast-food industry is saturated with intense competitors and customers have many options to any single restaurant or chain. As a result, the pressure to draw upon the benefits of rationalization is great.[1] In contrast, organizations that provide unique products, or enjoy virtual monopolies in their field, are likely to be under less pressure to rationalize their systems. Since customers do not have many options for the product, streamlining production and capturing customers through efficiency and control are not as important.

In terms of specific organizations within a sector, a key factor is organizational size. Since those in charge of large organizations are unable to exercise direct control at all levels, they develop rational systems of accountability and control. These rationalized structures allow administrators to ensure the efficient functioning of the organization without having to be knowledgeable about the activities of all subordinates at all times. For example, most major business firms – IBM, General Motors, etc. – are significantly McDonaldized. The sheer size of these companies, with hundreds of thousands of employees, requires extensive systems of rationalization in order to maximize the likelihood of meeting their institutional goals. The same can be said for large nonbusiness entities, such as the federal and state governments. On the other hand, a small, local print shop is likely to exhibit little in the way of McDonaldization.

Then there is the overall degree of McDonaldization in the environment. As a general rule, restaurants in smaller cities and suburbs will tend to be McDonaldized to a greater degree than those in urban settings. McDonald's began as a smaller city and suburban phenomenon and its strength continues to be in those locales (although in recent years it has made substantial inroads into the city). Competitors to McDonald's in such settings are likely to follow the McDonald's model and become highly rationalized. Seeing the positive effect of McDonaldization on one's institutional neighbors, even in different sectors, will lead owners and administrators to attempt to adapt what makes their neighbors successful to their own organization. However, there is a variety of successful models in a city like New York, many of them with well-established roots and a loyal clientele. Thus, while

McDonaldized fast-food restaurants have established a successful presence, other models are likely to survive and continue to prosper. Thus, the restaurant business, among others, in New York City is less McDonaldized than in Huntsville, Alabama or the suburbs of Washington, DC.

The case of New York City suggests another important factor – the amount of cultural and ethnic diversity in an area. Areas that are fairly homogeneous and dominated by members of the majority group (white, middle-class Americans) are likely to be highly McDonaldized, while those that are highly diverse culturally and ethnically are apt to be less so. A complicating factor is income and wealth. Areas where well-to-do members of the majority group predominate are likely to be able to sustain a variety of less McDonaldized settings. Areas where ethnic minorities predominate are likely to support many non-McDonaldized settings even though income may be low. We would hypothesize that areas dominated by poor and middle-class members of the majority group are most likely to be highly McDonaldized.

Specific relationships and hypotheses aside, the key point is that there is great variety in the degree of McDonaldization in various economic and social settings. While there is a general trend toward the McDonaldization of such settings, it is not manifest uniformly across various domains or even within a specific domain. McDonaldization is *not* a monolithic process.

The Variety of Settings for Consumption

As a result of the varying trajectories, there is great differentiation in consumption settings. We can use Pierre Bourdieu's concept of 'field' to help us think about these diverse settings. The field is a network of relations among the objective positions within it (Bourdieu and Wacquant, 1992: 97). Positions may be occupied by either agents or institutions and they are constrained by the structure of the field. There are many semi-autonomous fields within the social world. Each has an objective structure that can be mapped.

We could talk of a field at the macro-social level, but also at a number of sub-levels. Thus, for example, we could conceive of each of the following as fields – retail establishments; restaurants; traditional, non-McDonaldized restaurants; fast-food restaurants; the McDonald's chain, and so on. In deciding where to dine, the consumers' practice is determined, in part, by the overall structure of these fields, as well as the more specific field that they are led, or forced, to choose. Of course, that choice is also affected by characteristics of the consumer, especially in Bourdieu's terms the consumer's habitus and capital (see below).

Thus, we can discuss a wide range of fields under the heading of McDonaldization. If we define American restaurants as the field, then there is a wide variety of positions ranging from highly McDonaldized chains to almost totally non-McDonaldized gourmet restaurants. If we take American health care as the field, then the range might be from McDoctors to surgical theaters. We could refine both of these further and think, for example, of McDonaldized chains of restaurants as the field and then identify different positions in the field – McDonald's, Burger King, Olive Garden, Morton's, and so on. The important point here is that there is a wide range of fields and subfields and this serves to underscore the point that there is great variety in consumption settings, and many other settings, as well.

The Variety of Consumers

Throughout the development of the sociology of consumption, there has been very little consensus on consumers and their characteristics. Some of the earliest authors on consumption, such as Veblen (1899/ 1994) and Simmel (1904/1971), tended to view consumers as conscious, empowered agents who use the symbolic system of consumption as a way of establishing class differences and distinct personal identities. Later theorists of consumption have been divided between the visions of consumers as empowered or as victims. However, between these two extremes lies a broad range of types of consumers, some of which overlap and others of which differ substantially from one another.

In *The Unmanageable Consumer* (1995), Yiannis Gabriel and Tim Lang attempt to organize these conceptualizations into a typology of the modern consumer. They argue that 'different traditions or discourses have invented different representations of the consumer each with its own specificity and coherence, but willfully oblivious to those of others' (Gabriel and Lang, 1995: 2). Their catalog of consumer types is not a comprehensive list, but it does illustrate the range of consumers. They are the consumer as chooser, communicator, explorer, identity-seeker, hedonist or artist, victim, rebel, activist, and citizen. By themselves, none of these is sufficient to describe fully any single consumer (in this sense, Gabriel and Lang are outlining types of acts of consumption of which all consumers are capable at one time or another). Most consumers can be seen as fitting into different types at different times, and often, multiple types within a single act of consumption. Certain combinations of these consumer roles overlap quite often, as in the case of the communicator and identity-seeker roles. Other combinations are somewhat exclusive of one another, such as the victim and the rebel.

Gabriel and Lang argue that the emergence of these multiple consumer types is a characteristic of later capitalism and an indication that the idea of the consumer as a singular figure is losing its coherence. 'Precariousness, unevenness, and fragmentation are likely to become more pronounced for ever-increasing sections of Western populations', and as the consumer becomes more of a mercurial character, attempts by marketers, producers, and social scientists to define the consumer will become untenable (Gabriel and Lang, 1995: 190). They foresee a future in which consumption is an opportunistic act, and the providers of market goods are increasingly unable to target their products to consumers in rational and systematic ways.

This conclusion is opposed to the view of the consumer implicit in both the McDonaldization thesis and Weberian theory in general. McDonaldized organizations seek to control the consumer, irrespective of the consumer's desires or needs. For example, fast-food restaurants and many other highly rationalized systems have strict codes and practices that constrain the options of the consumer. Even less McDonaldized systems seek to limit the options available to consumers. In either case, the interpretation of the consumer as 'unmanageable' does not fit with the idea of increasing McDonaldization. Rationalized organizations are too dependent on control to meet their own needs for efficiency and profit to allow consumers to escape from the boxes in which the system places them.

However, Gabriel and Lang are correct in recognizing that in spite of increasing McDonaldization and the best efforts of McDonaldized systems, the consumer is not likely to be reduced to a singular, highly predictable figure. Consumers will continue to be agents and the various roles that individuals can take on must be considered part of developing a full understanding of the relationship between McDonaldized systems and the consumers of their goods and services.

In order to illustrate the diversity of consumers, let us look at the way in which each of Gabriel and Lang's types of consumers might relate to highly McDonaldized settings in the fast-food industry. This is obviously a highly simplified analysis, not only because we rely on ideal-typical rather than fully complex human consumers, but also because we focus on only one type of setting. Yet, this allows us to begin to think in a more fully adequate way about consumers in a McDonaldized society.

Choosers are likely to be led by rational factors into opting to eat in McDonaldized fast-food restaurants. For example, low price, convenience, and the lack of available alternatives (an increasing likelihood in an increasingly McDonaldized society) would lead such a consumer to a franchised restaurant. The fast-food restaurant is a 'rational choice' in a society where speed and efficiency are valued, consumers want to be sure that they are getting what they expect, and cost is an important consideration. Other choosers are likely, for other equally rational reasons, to opt out of eating in such restaurants, at least to the degree that they can find viable alternatives. Such reasons might be the adverse effect of the nature of the food served on consumers' health, the dehumanizing character of 'dining' in fast-food restaurants, and the negative impact such restaurants have on the environment.

Communicators would be led in the direction of a wide variety of restaurants depending on what it is they want to communicate. In eating in a chain of fast-food restaurants, they might be communicating that they are frugal, sensible, and that they belong to that group of people that frequents such restaurants in general and the specific chain in particular. In terms of the latter, those who frequent Burger King may be communicating that they are somehow different from McDonald's consumers. Those who prefer higher-priced McDonaldized chains, such as the Olive Garden, may be seeking to communicate the fact that they are different from those who choose lower-end chains. Those who eat in chains of any type may be seeking to communicate the fact that they are more 'down to earth' than the 'swells' who dine at expensive, chic restaurants.

Explorers would be drawn to the chains as one of many different types of restaurants that they wish to experience.[2] Similarly, they may be drawn to a wide variety of them because of their desire to experience the full range of restaurant chains rather than committing to one or another. One would also expect explorers to sample any new chain as soon as it opens. Of course, the explorer, assuming there are no major economic limitations, will not be restricted to franchises and will seek to experience a wide range of restaurants, including expensive, less McDonaldized settings.

Identity seekers may, paradoxically, establish their identity based on one of the highly McDonaldized chains. They may revel in thinking of themselves as 'Burger King kind of people', or as members of an informal 'breakfast club' that meets at the chain every morning. The paradox involves finding an distinctive identity in a system that offers uniformity, the same identity to all. This is identified by Miles (1998) as the problem of trying to purchase an identity 'off the peg'. In other words, it is the question of whether purchasing an identity created and mass-produced by McDonaldized systems constitutes a 'true' identity.

Hedonists go to McDonaldized chains because they derive pleasure from being there and consuming the food and perhaps even the 'ambience' of such a place. The hedonist would also be drawn by the emphasis on large portions and the idea that there is going to be plenty of food to devour. The artists, a type that Gabriel and Lang closely link to hedonists, would be drawn to the franchises by the desire to be creative and the need to express themselves. This again gives rise to a paradox, as one wonders how artists can express themselves in a creative fashion in such a structured environment? Possibilities include making special requests ('hold the catsup'), mixing several different types of drinks at the self-service counters, or making creative salads or other innovative concoctions at the salad bar. Of course, both hedonists and artists, assuming cost was not an insurmountable barrier, would probably be drawn more to the high-end, non-McDonaldized restaurants where there are far more possibilities for creative ordering of dishes and the dishes are more likely to please the eyes of the artist and the taste buds of the hedonist. In fact, the recent emphasis on elegant designs for the presentation of food on the plate is designed with the artist in mind. However, it is worth noting that in at least one sense the artist has more leeway for creativity in the chains than in the elite restaurants. The self-service available in fast-food restaurants offers the artist more opportunities for self expression than in the elite restaurants where everything is done for the diner.

Consumers can be seen as victims in all types of restaurants, although the nature of the victimology differs from one type to another. In the fast-food restaurant, consumers are victimized by the structure (the limited menu, the drive-through window, the uncomfortable seats) and by being forced to do things that they might prefer not to do. They are also victimized by the food which, given the large number of calories and the high fat, cholesterol, salt and sugar content of much of it, is likely to have an adverse effect on their health in the long run. Consumers can also be seen as being victimized by the efforts of the fast-food restaurants to lure their children into being lifelong devotees of fast food (and its poor nutritional value). However, these forms of victimization are not exclusive to the fast-food end of the spectrum. Consumers at expensive restaurants can also be seen as victims of often unhealthy food (say a large slab of prime rib or an entree with very rich sauce) and, distinctively, of extraordinarily high prices.

It is possible to be a rebel in a fast-food restaurant, but its rigid structure makes it difficult to be one. Rebels could demand such things as table service at a fast-food restaurant, but the nature of the setting makes it virtually impossible that they will get it. More extremely, consumers could cover the walls with graffiti as an expression of rebellion against the system. Interestingly, fast-food restaurants in general, and especially McDonald's, are often the site of violence. In the past decade, there have been a number of well-publicized murders at fast-food restaurants. Overseas, people unhappy with the United States in general, or with the invasion of fast-food restaurants in particular, often take out their anger by attacking McDonald's outlets or those of other chains based in the United States. For example, during the 1999 NATO bombing of Yugoslavia, one response of the Serbians was the smashing of windows at two McDonald's restaurants in Belgrade (Dinmore, 1999). Similarly, an American decision to add a 100 per cent tariff on Roquefort cheese led to protests in that same year that included the dumping of rotten vegetables and piles of manure at, and the trashing of, local McDonald's restaurants in France (Cohen, 1999; Swardson, 1999). One is far less likely to see acts of rebellion of this, or any other type, mounted against elite non-McDonaldized restaurants. They simply do not have the same semiotic significance as McDonald's or other well-known American chains.

Also as a result of their powerful symbolic importance, there is likely to be much more activism mounted against McDonaldized chains than against an elite restaurant. This is well reflected in the worldwide community discussed in Chapter 3 that has emerged as a result of the so-called McLibel trial in Great Britain (Vidal, 1997).

The consumer as citizen is, to a large degree in our society, contrasted to the consumer being depicted in most of this discussion. Except for the rebels and the activists, the types of consumers are virtually all self-interested in one way or another. In contrast, the consumer as citizen is interested in the good of the collectivity. In our society, which emphasizes self-interested consumption, it is very difficult to be a citizen in the world of consumption. Buying 'green' products might be an example of good citizenship in the realm of consumption, but perhaps the best thing that the citizen can do is to abstain from consumption as much as possible. The difficulty of being a citizen has been exacerbated in recent years by the government policies, epitomized by the war cry 'no new taxes', that have tended to de-emphasize the collective good and have focused instead on individual self-maximization. As a general rule, the consumer as citizen would have problems with both McDonaldized and non-McDonaldized restaurants, but the nature of the problem might be different. A citizen might object to the elite character and high cost of 'elite' restaurants, but the opposition to McDonald's would deal more with things like health concerns and environmental damage.

Thus, there are many different types of consumers and each would relate differently to McDonaldized restaurants, to say nothing of the full range of restaurants. In addition, we should think of this overview as relating to acts of consumption and not just consumers. All of us may engage in each of these types of consumer behavior at one time or another. The key point is that means of consumption are confronted with a wide array of consumers and acts of consumption. They may seek to impose great uniformity on consumers and consumption, and while they are often largely successful, those actions are always going to be limited by the great diversity among consumers and in acts of consumption.

Consumers and McDonaldization

We can see, therefore, that a McDonaldizing society is characterized by neither singular consumers nor singular settings; there is considerable variation in both. One type of consumer will relate differently to highly McDonaldized settings than another type. Furthermore, from one act of consumption to another, the same individual is capable of taking on a variety of different roles and role combinations. Similarly, the settings of consumption vary in their degree of McDonaldization (and many other things, as well). The issue, then, is: What can we say about this complex relationship between a wide range of types of consumers (and acts of consumption) and a similarly wide range of settings in terms of their degree of McDonaldization?

Such a specific issue brings us into the realm of social theory associated in the United States with micro–macro relationships and in Europe with the agency-structure linkage. We can think of individual consumers as a micro-level phenomenon and the settings in which they consume, varying in terms of degree of McDonaldization, as macro-level phenomena. Alternatively, most consumers have agency, at least some of the time. And the settings in which they consume can be seen as structures. There is a dialectical relationship between the agency of the consumer and the nature of the structures. The form and outcome of that relationship depends upon the characteristics of both within a particular setting. Agency-structure theories tend to be richer than micro–macro theories and one that suggests itself, especially since we have already deployed the concept of field, is Pierre Bourdieu's theory of practice. We will not delve deeply into that theory, nor will we employ it slavishly, but it does offer a useful general orientation to the relationship between various consumers and the range of McDonaldized settings for consumption.

In *Distinction* (1984: 101), Bourdieu offers a formula for social action that takes into account both the agency of individuals and the structures in which they are situated: [(habitus) (capital)] + field = practice. While the 'mathematics' of the formula are not expounded upon, and the nature of the details are not of significance to us here, the important point is that Bourdieu is arguing that individual practice is the result of individual agency, the product of an individual's habitus[3] and the capital (cultural, social, etc.) of that individual, and the structure, as expressed by the field in which the agents find themselves. Differences in agency and/or field will lead to different practices. Further, there is recognition here that there are important variations in both agency and field.

Consumer behavior is generated, in part, by the habitus of the individual consumer. A person's habitus is 'a structured and structuring structure', from which, among other things, practice, classificatory schemes and taste arise. The individual's habitus facilitates the performance of certain consumer roles and discourages the adoption of others. In addition, the relevant stocks of capital that the individual possesses play a role in determining consumer practices. Capital, in its various forms (social, educational, economic), interact with the habitus of the consumer to create 'stances' *vis à vis* the field of consumer settings. For example, consumers who lack economic capital are unlikely to be very discriminating (to be 'choosers') when it comes to the settings of consumption; they will use what they can afford. The consumer as citizen requires social capital in order to be an effective presence in the face of the power of McDonaldized systems. Capital, like habitus, leads to specific practices, and tends to discourage others, in certain circumstances. As we have seen, Bourdieu uses the concept of the field to designate the array of settings and it is there that people engage in practices that express their habitus and employ their various stocks of capital. The practice of the individual is the result of the interaction of the habitus and capital(s) and the nature and structure of the field. The structure of the field affects the range of practices that are available to the individual; the individual chooses among the practices available within the field. The result is the practice which, in this discussion, is an act of consumption.

Bourdieu's concepts of habitus, capital and field suggest a way that we can think of the relationship between the consumer and the means of consumption (one of which is the fast-food restaurant; Ritzer, 1999) so that both influence the form and outcome of the interaction. By understanding the act of consumption (practice) as the product of the consumer as agent (habitus and capital) and the specific means of consumption (field), we have a dynamic rather than a static vision of consumption. The consumer and the means of consumption interact in a dialectical relationship, as each influences the form of the other, and the overall interaction is one that is dynamic in both the specific interaction and over time.

Using Bourdieu as our inspiration, we can now begin to think about ways in which the consumer and the means of consumption encounter one another and the range of possible results that emerge from that interaction.[4] In a highly McDonaldized society, especially one that has been so for quite some time, we can expect the habitus of most people to be endowed with a strong propensity to prefer McDonaldized settings. This is especially likely to be so for young people, with older people less inclined to McDonaldized settings if, for no other reason, than the fact that it is likely that they were born into a less McDonaldized society. As time passes and the older generations die off, we can expect a more uniform propensity toward McDonaldized settings across generations.

In terms of social class, we would expect a propensity toward McDonaldization across all social classes, but there would be differences among classes. The lower and middle classes would be most strongly inclined in that direction while the upper class would have a propensity that would lead to somewhat less of a draw toward McDonaldized settings.

The social class differences, to the extent that they exist, are related to capital. The possession of economic capital by the families of upper-class children would permit them to expose their children to non-McDonaldized settings from a young age. Similarly, their cultural capital (for example, appreciation of fine cuisine) would lead them to want to take their children to fine restaurants and, in the process, develop their cultural capital in this realm (and many others). At the other extreme, the lower classes, lacking in economic and cultural capital, would be led not only to expose their children to McDonaldized settings, but also extol the virtues of those settings. The middle class would have the economic capital to expose their children to McDonaldized settings much more frequently than the lower class. However, they would, on occasion, have the resources to expose them to non-McDonaldized settings. Similarly, the moderate cultural capital of the middle classes would lead them to stress the virtues of McDonaldized settings, although there would also be an appreciation of non-McDonaldized settings. Thus, there is greater likelihood for ambivalence in the middle classes than at the two poles of the class system.

When one turns to the field in a highly McDonaldized society, one obviously finds it dominated by McDonaldized settings. The greater the predominance of such settings, the less the likelihood that anyone has any choice, whatever the relationship between their habitus and capital. In a fully McDonaldized field, there would be no choice. This, in Bourdieu's terms, is what Weber meant by the 'iron cage'. Of course, no field will ever be totally McDonaldized, but it is likely that many will achieve a high degree of McDonaldization. In such a field, even those whose combination of habitus and capital inclines them to seek out non-McDonaldized settings will have a hard time finding them. In many cases, they will be forced into a McDonaldized setting even though they are inclined to, for example, eat in some other kind of setting.

The preceding is but a brief illustration of the direction Bourdieu's theory can take one in thinking about the relationship between agency and structure in a McDonaldized society. As with our discussion in the previous sections on process, settings, and consumers, the critical point is that there is no simple conclusion to be drawn about, and there is great complexity in, that relationship.

Conclusion

This effort to add nuance and specificity to the McDonaldization thesis has only scratched the surface of a complex set of issues. There is much more to be said about trajectories of McDonaldization, differentiation within McDonaldized settings and between those that are highly

McDonaldized and those that are less so, diversity among types of consumers and acts of consumption, and most importantly about the relationships between consumers and the range of McDonaldized settings. A fuller analysis of acts of consumption needs to allow the levels of McDonaldization to range across the full spectrum. The types of consumers require further specification; Gabriel and Lang's nine types are a useful starting point, but there may be other types of consumers that have been overlooked. Much more needs to be done with translating Gabriel and Lang's types of consumers into types of consumer practices. In addition, far more can be done with the analysis of the consumer within the range of McDonaldized settings based on nature of habitus, amount and types of capital, and so on.

Most importantly, perhaps, much more can be said about the dialectical relationship between the consumer and the means of consumption. One way in which the dialectical process might be analyzed is in a study of the patterns of association between specific consumer types or types of consumer practices and settings at various points on the trajectory of McDonaldization. Studying the reasons why people consume where they do, and how the settings attract certain types of customers rather than others, begins to get at the dialectical association between consumers and means of consumption. Another way to explore this process is through a study of the 'negotiations' that take place once a consumer begins interacting with a specific setting. How the consumer and means of consumption mutually determine the role that the consumer will play in the act of consumption is a dialectical process that often goes unnoticed by consumers, organizations, and those who study both. Consumption, like McDonaldization, is devilishly complex.

Notes

This chapter was co-authored by Seth Ovadia and is to be published in Mark Gottdiener (ed.), *Consumers and Culture*. Lanham, MD: Rowman and Littlefield, 2001.

1   Of course, this does not explain why the fast-food industry (although it had precursors) pioneered McDonaldization. Ray Kroc was not faced with a saturated market for such restaurants.

2   One 'explorer', Peter Holden, has set about to visit as many McDonald's restaurants as he can. As of mid-1999 he had been to 10,893 of them, about 80 per cent of McDonald's North American outlets (see Connors, 1999).

3   While we will not go into it here, there are problems involved in thinking about agency from the point of view of such a structuralist notion as habitus. Given his structuralist bias, Bourdieu does not have as strong a theory of agency as, say, Anthony Giddens.

4   However, a consideration of the system of consumption in its full complexity is well beyond the scope of this chapter.

5

EXPRESSING AMERICA: A CRITIQUE OF THE GLOBAL CREDIT CARD SOCIETY

A Window on Society

The credit card, as well as the industry that stands behind it and aggressively pushes its growth and expansion, is not only important in itself, but also as a window on modern society. The idea of analyzing the credit card in order to understand society is derived from the theories of ... Georg Simmel. Among his innumerable insights was the view that 'any item of culture can be the starting point for sociological research into the nature of the totality' (Turner, 1986). Simmel was a 'relationist', meaning that he saw each aspect of society as related to every other aspect (Ritzer and Gindoff, 1992; Ritzer, 2001, Chapter 6). In his view, the study of any element of society will, if carried far enough, lead us to every other societal component and ultimately to a better sense of the social world in its entirety.

Simmel chose the study of money as a way of gaining insight into society. I am replacing money with the more contemporary credit card, but my goal is the same as Simmel's: to explore some fundamental characteristics of the social world. Why, if everything is related to everything else, should we use money and the credit card to study society? The advantage of both is that they are so centrally important in modern consumer society that they take us very quickly to the core of that world. Choosing something else would eventually accomplish the goal, but by a lengthier and more laborious route.

What will be discovered about the social world through this analysis of credit cards is a set of social problems that goes far beyond credit cards, including rampant consumerism, escalating indebtedness, pervasive fraud and crime, invasions of privacy, dehumanization of our daily lives, and increasing homogenization of the world's cultures. These are problems of concern to all of us, but we get a new and different sense of those problems by approaching them from a unique direction and by viewing them in an atypical way.

Credit cards also illustrate other important social problems. For example, the credit card industry tends to favor men over women. Thus, full-time homemakers may have difficulty obtaining credit cards because they lack outside income. In addition, the credit card business operates to the advantage of the relatively well-to-do and to the disadvantage of those who are not so well off economically. Those who are well off may be able to get lower interest rates or have their annual fees waived. More importantly, they are better able to pay their credit card bills in full each month, thereby avoiding usurious interest rates. The degree to which our culture values materialism is well reflected in the widespread popularity of the credit card. The individualism at the core of our cultural system is manifest, among other places, in the tendency to blame individual consumers, not our consumer society, for their problems with excessive debt.

Beyond this litany of specific problems is one that many sociologists consider to be the essential problem in the modern world: the oppressive and deforming impact of large-scale social structures on individuals. In the words of a popular analyst of the credit card business, Terry Galanoy (1980: 33), that industry and its products have 'invaded, saturated, and altered our lives forever'. Galanoy (1980: 15) asks,

> Which is the real plastic – your Visa or MasterCard or you?
> Like those cards, you are being formed, shaped, plied, impressed. You are also being deformed continuously and permanently to go in the direction the pressure of the moneymen wants you to go.

Thus, the credit card industry and the larger consumer society are just as oppressive and distorting as the other large-scale social structures (for example, capitalism and bureaucracies) that have long come under the scrutiny of sociologists.

A Sociology of Credit Cards

Sociology in general, and sociological theory in particular, offers a number of ways of dealing with the credit card industry and the individuals affected by it. Throughout much of the twentieth century, sociological theory has been divided between macro theories (such as structural functionalism and conflict theory) that would be most useful in analyzing the credit card industry itself and micro theories (such as symbolic interactionism and phenomenological sociology) that would be most helpful in analyzing individuals within our consumer society. However, sociological theory has generally been plagued by an inability to deal in a fully adequate manner with micro–macro relationships such as the linkages between the credit card industry and individuals. Sociologists have grown increasingly dissatisfied with having to choose between large-scale, macroscopic theories and small-scale, microscopic theories. Thus, there has been a growing interest in theories that integrate micro and macro concerns. In Europe, expanding interest in what is known there as agency–structure integration parallels the increasing American preoccupation with micro–macro integration (Ritzer, 1991a, 1991b).

Mills' Personal Troubles, Public Issues

These theoretical approaches have important implications for the study of sociological issues in general – and in particular for the kinds of social problems discussed in this chapter.[1] Micro–macro and agency–structure integration leads the sociological study of social problems back to one of its roots in the work of the American social critic and theorist C. Wright Mills (1916–62).

Mills is important to us here for two reasons. First, in 1953 Mills co-authored, with Hans Gerth, a now almost-forgotten theory of micro–macro integration: *Character and Social Structure*. As the title suggests, the authors were interested in the relationship between micro-level character and macro-level social structure. According to Gerth and Mills (1953: xvi), one of their goals was 'to link the private and the public, the innermost acts of the individual with the widest kinds of socio-historical phenomena'. Thus, their thinking is in line with the most recent developments in sociological theory.[2]

Of more direct importance here is the now-famous distinction made by Mills (1959) in *The Sociological Imagination*, between micro-level personal troubles and macro-level public issues. Personal troubles tend to be problems that affect individuals and those immediately around them. For example, a father who commits incest with his daughter is creating personal troubles for the daughter, other members of the family, and perhaps himself. However, that single father's actions are not going to create a public issue; that is, they are not likely to lead to a public outcry that society ought to abandon the family as a social institution. Public issues, in comparison, tend to be problems that affect large numbers of people and perhaps society as a whole. The disintegration of the nuclear family would be such a public issue.

What, then, is the relationship between these two sets of distinctions – personal troubles/public issues and character/social structure – derived from the work of C. Wright Mills? The character of an individual can certainly cause personal troubles. For example, a psychotic individual can cause problems for himself and those immediately around him. When many individuals have the same character disorder (psychosis, for example), they can cause problems for the larger social structure (overtax the mental health system), thereby creating a public issue. The structure of society can also cause personal troubles for the individual. An example might be a person's depression resulting from the disjunction between the culturally instilled desire for economic success and the scarcity of well-paying jobs. And the structure of society can create public issues, as exemplified by the tendency of the capitalist economy to generate periodic recessions and depressions. All these connections and, more generally, a wide array of macro–micro relationships are possible. However, the focus here is the credit card industry as an element of social structure and the way it generates both personal troubles and public issues.

A useful parallel can be drawn between the credit card and cigarette industries. The practices of the cigarette industry create a variety of personal troubles, especially illness and early death. Furthermore, those practices have created a number of public issues (the cost to society of death and illness traceable to cigarette smoke), and thus many people have come to see cigarette industry practices themselves as public issues. Examples of industry practices that have become public issues are the aggressive marketing of cigarettes overseas, where restrictions on such marketing are limited or nonexistent, as well as the marketing of cigarettes to young people in this country (for example, through advertisements that featured the controversial 'Joe Camel'). Similarly, the practices of the credit card industry help to create personal problems (such as indebtedness) and public issues (such as the relatively low national savings rate). Furthermore, some industry practices – such as the aggressive marketing of credit cards to teenagers – have themselves become public issues.

One of the premises here is that we need to begin adopting the same kind of critical outlook toward the credit card industry that we use in scrutinizing the cigarette industry. Interestingly, Galanoy (1980: 110) has suggested a warning label for credit cards, like the ones found on cigarette packs:

> Caution: Financial experts have determined that continued bank card use can lead to debt, loss of property, bankruptcy, plus unhealthful effects on long-lived standards and virtues.

Mills' ideas give us remarkably contemporary theoretical tools for undertaking a critical analysis of the credit card industry and the problems it generates. His conception of the relationship between personal troubles and public issues is the major (although not the only) theory undergirding this analysis.

Micro–Macro Relationships

The various theoretical resources underpinning this analysis are all brought to bear on a central issue in the sociological study of a particular social problem: personal troubles, public issues, and the burgeoning credit card industry. Although the focus is on the way the macro-level credit card industry creates a variety of public issues and personal troubles, it is important to realize that people, at the micro level, create and re-create that industry by their actions. Not only did people create the industry historically, but they help to re-create it daily by acting in accord with its demands and expectations. However, people also have the capacity to refuse to conform to the demands of the credit card industry. If they were to do so on a reasonably large scale, the industry would be forced to alter the way it operates. People can also be more proactive in their efforts to change the credit card industry.

However, there are limits to what individuals, even when acting in concert, can do about macro-level problems. In many cases, macro-level problems require macro-level solutions. Thus, it is important that the credit card industry, as well as the government, take actions to deal with the public issues and personal troubles discussed throughout this chapter. The theoretical approach underlying this analysis allows us to understand both the adverse effects of the credit card industry and the steps that people and larger social structures can take to ameliorate or eliminate them.

Marx: Capitalist Exploitation

In addition to adopting Mills' general approach, I will draw on several other important theoretical sources to deal with more specific aspects of the relationship between people and the credit card industry. One is the work of Karl Marx, especially his ideas on the exploitation that he saw as endemic to capitalist society. To Marx, this exploitation takes place in the labor market and the workplace, where capitalistic firms exploit their workers by paying them far less in wages than the value of what they produce. In Mills' terms, Marx believed that capitalistic firms create personal troubles for workers by exploiting them so greatly, and the impoverished state of the workers eventually becomes such an important public issue that the workers are likely to rise up and over-throw the capitalist system and replace it with a communist system.

Mills was in fact one of the first major American sociologists to be drawn in the direction of Marxian theory. However, time has not been kind to Marxian theory, and many of Marx's predictions have not come to pass. There have been many changes in the capitalist system, and a variety of issues have come to the fore that did not exist in Marx's day. As a result, a number of neo-Marxian theories have arisen to deal with these new capitalist realities. One that concerns us here is the increasing importance to capitalists of the market for goods and services (Baran and Sweezy, 1966). According to neo-Marxians, exploitation of the worker continues in the labor market, but capitalists also devote increasing attention to getting consumers to buy more goods and services. Higher profits can come from both cutting costs and selling more products.

The credit card industry plays a role by encouraging consumers to spend more money, in many cases far beyond their available cash, on the capitalists' goods and services. In a sense, the credit card companies have helped the capitalists to exploit consumers. Indeed, one could argue that modern capitalism has come to depend on a high level of consumer indebtedness. Capitalism could have progressed only so far by extracting cash from the consumers. It had to find a way to go further.

Capitalists' reliance on widespread consumer credit parallels early capitalists' exploitation of the labor market. In an effort to increase profits, the latter sought to progressively lengthen the workday in order to exploit more of the laborer's time and effort. When they had pushed the workday to unconscionable lengths, the government was forced to intervene by restricting work hours. The capitalists then sought new ways to exploit workers, and they eventually did so with technological advances that allowed workers to produce more in less time. When the capitalists reached a point of diminishing returns in their efforts to squeeze more out of workers for less, they turned their attention to consumers. With the aid of the credit card industry, as well as the advertising and marketing industries, they eventually discovered new ways of acquiring more of the consumer's economic resources, even resources the consumers did not yet have.

Simmel: The Money Economy

Writing more than 40 years before the invention of the credit card, Georg Simmel (1907/1978) focused (as mentioned earlier) on money, but much of what he had to say about the money economy and the personal troubles it creates is of help to us in understanding the modern world of credit cards.[3] Simmel pointed to many problems associated with a money economy, but three are of special concern to this analysis of credit cards.

1　Credit Card Debt: Beware the Plastic Loan Shark[4]　We generally have a very intimate relationship with money in the form of currency or even the sum at the bottom of our monthly bank statements. However, as Georg Simmel recognized, the advent of credit tended to distance us from money. Money that exists in the form of a line of credit (to take an example from Simmel's day) seems more distant from us than cash in our wallets or in our bank accounts. Because it is far more removed from us and far less tangible, credit, in Simmel's view, leads to a strong 'temptation to imprudence' (Simmel, 1907/1978: 479). In other words, when we have credit available to us, we are far more likely to spend to excess and to plunge into debt, sometimes deeply, than we are when we are restricted to cash on hand and in the bank.

However, it is not only the distance associated with credit that leads to imprudence. Credit also leads to a more rapid circulation of money than in a currency-based economy, for two main reasons. First, credit expands the amount of money available beyond cash on hand, thereby increasing the number of possible transactions. Second, with currency, transactions are usually limited to face-to-face dealings with others, but with credit they can more easily involve people and organizations that we do not interact with directly. Thus, credit serves not only to increase the amount of money available but also the size of the population with which we deal.

Each additional transaction made possible by credit leads to still other deals, with the result that both the number and the speed of economic transactions in general increase dramatically. With the increasing number and rapidity of transactions, any single deal and each dollar spent in that deal become progressively less important. As a result, it grows increasingly easy for us to part with money – and so we part with more of it, more often. In Simmel's (1907/1978: 194) words, the 'rapid circulation of money induces habits of spending and acquisition; it makes a specific quantity of money psychologically less significant and valuable'.

2 *Credit Card Fraud: Screw You, Mac – I Got Mine*[5] The point of departure for this brief discussion of credit card fraud is Georg Simmel's (1907/1978: 432) argument that the money economy is a 'fully compliant instrument for the meanest machinations'. In its currency form money makes all sorts of unethical and criminal acts easier and more likely than they were with earlier forms of value exchange. Simmel (1991: 29) noted, 'Persons who are otherwise honest may participate in deceitful "promotions", and many people are likely to behave more unconscientiously and with more dubious ethics in money matters than elsewhere.' For example, bribes are easier and more secret in a cash form than they are in the form of, say, a herd of cattle. Slipping an assassin an envelope stuffed with cash is simpler and easier to hide than shipping a load of timber as payment for the dastardly deed. Cash payments leave no physical traces, but payments with cattle or timber are likely to be visible to many people and to leave physical signs that can be easily traced.

One issue implied in Simmel's position is that there is a historical progression in mean machinations corresponding to developments in the form of money. But are even meaner machinations more likely with credit cards than they are with currency? The answer is no. Because the use of credit cards leaves an electronic and paper trail, many of the meanest machinations are less likely to occur (Coleman, 1992: 835).

Drug deals, contract murders, and assassinations are more likely to be done on a cash basis than they are to be charged to Visa or MasterCard. In his study *Reducing Crime by Eliminating Cash*, David Warwick (1993: 8, 10) puts the issue this way:

> The lack of any type of recording and the unrestricted negotiability of cash makes it the most detection free medium of exchange criminals can use. It makes cash their most desired commodity, their prime target, and the epi-center of most crime. One only needs to read the familiar sign affixed to many delivery trucks, 'Driver carries no cash', to realize the worst feature of cash: Simply possessing it puts one at risk of being robbed, of being assaulted, or worse.
>
> The most frequent crimes committed in America consist of thefts of cash itself or of property to sell for cash ...
>
> Theft of cash often involves more than mere loss of property. Every minute, coast to coast, Americans are assaulted and/or murdered for the cash they possess, no matter how small the sum ...
>
> There is the *indirect* relationship of cash to crime to consider as well. Murder-for-hire, arson, kidnaping and bribery are all commonly committed for payment in cash. Billions of dollars worth of stolen goods are fenced for cash each year. We also know ... that the estimated $300 billion-a-year nar-cotics trade in the United States is conducted in cash.

As a result, Warwick suggests credit cards (as well as the various forms of electronic money) as a *solution* to cash-based crime.

3   Secrecy, Privacy, and Credit Cards: Who Isn't in their Files?   One of Georg Simmel's (1907/1978: 385) most provocative theses is that 'money, more than any other form of value, makes possible secrecy, invisibility and silence of exchange'. Simmel is quite right about secrecy in a cash economy, but the ability to keep transactions secret is generally less possible with credit cards than it is with currency. A prominent member of the community would be foolish to use a credit card to pay a prostitute, for example. One's name is associated with a credit card transaction, whereas a cash transaction may well remain anonymous. Furthermore, there are no records of a secret cash transaction, but paper and elec-tronic evidence exist of a credit card deal. Potentially, many people can have access to the records of a credit card transaction.

A specific example of the lack of secrecy and the resulting personal troubles associated with credit card transactions is the case of Craig Spence, a one-time Washington lobbyist. In February 1989 the Secret Service raided a Washington house that was allegedly the site of a homosexual prostitution ring and confiscated hundreds of credit card vouchers. A few months later, it was reported that Spence had been a major client of the ring. Spence's career was ruined, and a series of events was set in motion that helped lead to Spence's suicide in November 1989 (*Washington Times*, 1989).

Access to credit card records represents a problem not just for the criminal or one who deviates from society's norms, but for everyone. Credit records, in combination with records associated with other types of documents (for example, Social Security cards, driver's licenses, and bank statements), make up huge centralized banks of information on many millions of people (Rule et al., 1980). The fact that a variety of people and organizations have access to this information is a profound threat to individual privacy and has caused personal troubles for many individuals. Furthermore, that private threat poses the danger of the public issue of totalitarianism and even greater incursions into, and control over, people's personal lives. As Galanoy (1980: 18) put it,

> Ultimately, the danger here is not merely a loss of privacy, but of a *1984* scenario where 'Big Banker' replaces 'Big Brother' in becoming all-seeing, all-knowing, all-controlling, capable of destroying any resistance.

Thus, the advent of credit cards (and related phenomena such as ATMs and debit cards) has turned Simmel's theory of the relationship between money and secrecy on its head. Although money in the form of currency affords more secrecy than its predecessors, credit cards generally greatly reduce the possibility of secrecy. But it is not just that credit cards make secrecy more difficult. They also heighten enormously others' ability to invade our privacy. According to the general counsel of Citicorp's bank card program, 'There's no question privacy is quickly evolving into one of the most important issues of the 1990s' (Kleege, 1994: 15).

Exacerbating the threat posed by this invasion of privacy is the fact that inaccuracies often creep into the records of credit card (and other) transactions (Stewart, 1991). It is not unusual for people to get poor credit ratings because of erroneous information in their files. Invasions of privacy are an enormous danger in themselves, but the dangers are heightened when they are based on misinformation. Many individuals have encountered personal difficulties as a result of the existence of misinformation on their credit card records.

The invasion of privacy, either as a private trouble or a public issue, is not a matter that seems to trouble the credit card organizations very much. They are likely only to become mobilized when there is a public outcry over it or the government threatens to become involved because of pressure from the public. There is, however, a comparatively minor issue that does seem to trouble the credit card industry: merchants writing on charge slips the telephone numbers, or sometimes even the addresses, of those using credit cards. It is not the fact that merchants are invading the privacy of customers or the potential for further invasion that troubles the industry but ... the fact that such inquiries undermine the legitimacy of credit cards. In the view of the industry, credit cards should be accepted on their own, without any additional information. A request for additional information is seen as casting doubt on the credit card as a legitimate instrument in its own right. As usual, the industry focuses on its self-interest and only becomes concerned with customers' well-being when its own interests are imperiled.

Weber: Rationalization

The next issue of concern has to do with the 'rationalization' of society and its relationship to credit cards. Although Simmel wrote on rationalization, the premier theorist on the rationalization process was, as we have seen, Max Weber. The credit card industry has been an integral part of the rationalization process. By rationalizing the process by which consumer loans are made, the credit card industry has contributed to our society's dehumanization.

Interestingly, one school of neo-Marxian theory, critical theory, has brought together ideas from both Marx and Weber that are relevant to this analysis of the credit card industry (Wiggershaus, 1994). While building on Marx's concern with the economy, the critical school focuses on culture. Mass culture is seen as pacifying and stupefying. It could be argued that the consumer culture that credit cards help foster has such effects on people by helping to keep them immersed in the endless and mindless pursuit of goods and services. The critical school also disparages the rationalization process – especially the tendency to engage in technocratic thinking, in which the focus is merely the discovery of the optimum means to ends that are defined by those in control of the larger society. The credit card can be seen as a product of such thinking. Because it works so well as a means, people are discouraged from reflecting on the value of the ends (the goods and services of a consumer society), critically analyzing those ends, and finding alternatives to them.

McDonaldization

The credit card, like the fast-food restaurant, is not only a part of the process of McDonaldization but is also a significant force in its development and spread. Just as McDonald's rationalized the delivery of prepared food, the credit card McDonalidized the consumer loan business. Prior to credit cards, the process of obtaining loans was slow, cumbersome, and nonrationalized. But obtaining a modern credit card (which can be thought of as a noncollateralized consumer loan) is now a very efficient process, often requiring little more than filling out a short questionnaire. With credit bureaus and computerization, credit records can be checked and applications approved (or disapproved) very rapidly. Furthermore, the unpredictability of loan approval has been greatly reduced and, in the case of preapproved credit cards, completely eliminated. The decision to offer a preapproved card, or to approve an application for a card, is increasingly left to a nonhuman technology – the computer. Computerized scoring systems exert control over credit card company employees by, for example, preventing them from approving an application if the score falls below the agreed-on standard. And these scoring systems are, by definition, calculable, relying on quantitative measures rather than qualitative judgments about things like the applicant's 'character'. Thus, credit card loans, like fast-food hamburgers, are now being served up in a highly rationalized, assembly-line fashion. As a result, a variety of irrationalities of rationality, especially dehumanization, have come to be associated with both.

It is worth noting that the McDonaldization of credit card loans has played a central role in fostering the rationalization of other types of loans, such as automobile and home equity loans. Automobile loan approvals used to take days, but now a loan can be approved, and one can drive off in a new car, in a matter of hours, if not minutes. Similarly, home equity loans can now be obtained much more quickly and easily than was the case in the past. Such loans rely on many of the same technologies and procedures, such as scoring systems, that are used in decision making involving credit cards (Varney, 1994). Thus, just as the process of rationalization in society as a whole has been spearheaded by the fast-food industry, it is reverberating across the banking and loan business led by the credit card industry. We can anticipate that over time other types of loans, involving larger and larger sums of money (mortgages and business loans, for example), will be increasingly rationalized. Virtually every facet of banking and finance will be moving in that direction.

We can get a glimpse of the rationalized future of banking at one branch of Huntington Bancshares of Columbus, Ohio. The branch in question is the busiest of the bank's 350 outlets, processing as many home equity loans as 100 typical branches and handling as many new credit cards as 220 of those branches. It is distinguished by the fact that none of its business is done in person – it is all done by telephone. Of the fear of alienating customers because of the dehumanization associated with this type of banking, the chairman of Huntington Bancshares says, 'I don't mind offending customers and losing them if it benefits the bank in the long run ... I'd rather have fewer customers and make an awful lot of money on them than have a lot of customers and lose our shirt' (Hansell, 1994: D1, D13).

Whatever its impact on customers, the branch is certainly efficient. For example, it is able to approve a loan in 10 minutes, even if the request is made by telephone in the middle of the night. Here is the way the system works:

> As soon as a 'telephone banker' types the first few identifying details of an application into the computer, the machine automatically finds the records of the customer's previous activity with Huntington and simultaneously orders an electronic version of the applicant's credit bureau file. The phone banker then contacts by pager one of two seasoned loan officers who roam the maze of office cubicles in the telephone center.
>
> With printouts of the banking records, credit file and computer-analyzed loan application in hand, a loan officer can generally make a decision in less than a minute. The bank says its credit problems are no greater than for loans from its branches. (Hansell, 1994: D13)

Huntington Bancshares' so-called 'telephone banker' appears to be the counterpart to the McDonald's counterperson or the worker at the drive-through window. Telephone bankers are clearly far less skilled than their predecessors. They are reduced to glorified computer operators, with the truly important and difficult work (analyses of credit records and loan decisions) being done by the computer and the loan officers. Thus, 'McDonaldized' banking brings with it deskilling and the further rationalization of bank work. It is forecast that about 40 per cent of the 100,000 bank branches in the United States are likely to be closed over the next decade. Some of these closures will be due to mergers, but many will be due to the replacement of the less efficient, conventional branches and traditional bankers with new, more efficient branches and telephone bankers.

The Internet has made even Huntington Bancshares seem primitive. It is now possible to get virtually instantaneous approval for a credit card over the Internet by providing the credit card company with a few bits of information.

Credit cards (and related phenomena like debit cards, ATMs, electronic funds transfers), like the fast-food restaurant, can be seen as part of the McDonaldization process. The growth of the credit card industry (like the fast-food industry) is a reflection of the increasing McDonaldization of society, and the industry is in turn furthering the rationalization process. This is an extremely important point. That is, credit cards are not merely key elements of a McDonaldizing society. They are also crucial to the efficient operation and the continued expansion of the rationalized business world. Debit cards additionally help the banking industry to grow more efficient, and other types of electronic funds transfers (EFTs) hold out the promise of a far more rationalized and efficient system of, among many others, health and medicine. Thus, credit cards and related phenomena are deeply implicated in the further rationalization of many aspects of society. It is in this sense that credit cards are central not only to the future McDonaldization of society but also to the emergence of the problems and irrationalities that are such worrisome aspects of a rationalizing society.

Calculability: The All-Important Credit Report The credit card industry emphasizes things that are quantified, although this more conservative industry generally shies away from the clever names employed in the fast-food industry. (However, one is led to wonder just how long it will be before we see something like the 'Whopper Card'.) Among the most visible of the quantified aspects of credit cards are their credit limits, interest rates, and annual fees (or lack thereof). Credit cards permit people to maximize the number of things they can buy and optimize the amount of money they can spend. By offering instant credit up to a predefined but expandable limit, credit cards allow people not only to spend all their available money but also to go into debt for, in many cases, thousands of dollars. Furthermore, in an effort to increase their level of debt, people often seek to maximize the credit limit on each of their cards and to accumulate as many cards as possible, each with as high a credit limit as possible. In fact, increasingly important status symbols in our society are the number of credit cards one has in one's wallet and the collective credit limit available on those cards. The modern status symbol is thus debt rather than savings. In sum, credit cards emphasize a whole series of things that can be quantified – number of cards, credit limits, amount of debt, number of goods and services that can be purchased, and so on.

Calculability involves not only an emphasis on quantity but also a comparative lack of interest in quality ... The emphasis on the quantity of credit card debt allowed tends to lessen people's interest in the quality of the things that they can acquire while running up that debt. With a finite amount of cash on hand or in the bank, consumers tend to be more careful, buying a relatively small number of high-quality goods that promise to have a long and useful life. But consumers who buy things on seemingly ever-expandable credit often have less interest in quality. The accent is on buying large numbers of things, with comparatively little concern that those things might deteriorate swiftly. After all, if things wear out quickly, they can be replaced – perhaps when one's credit card has an even higher credit limit.

Relatedly, the ready availability of virtually anything and everything on credit leads to a leveling in the value of products. This leveling of everything to a common denominator leads to the cynical attitude discussed by Simmel: that everything has its price, that anything can be bought or sold on the market. Because anything can be bought at any time, people develop a blasé attitude toward things. Simmel (1907/1978: 256) describes this as a view of 'all things being of an equally dull and grey hue, as not worth getting excited about'. In slightly different terms, the credit card (and before that, money) is the absolute enemy of esthetics, reducing everything to formlessness, to a purely quantitative phenomenon ... [6]

A particularly revealing example of quantification in the credit card industry is the use of 'credit scoring' in determining whether an applicant should be issued a credit card (or receive other kinds of credit). Of course, in the end the majority of applicants are approved by one credit card firm or another, because the profits from the credit card business are extraordinarily high. Credit card firms can afford to have a small proportion of cardholders who are delinquent in paying their bills or even who default on them. Nonetheless, it is obviously in the interest of the card companies to weed out those who will not be able to pay their bills.

Credit scoring is usually a two-step process (Updegrave, 1987). First, the application itself is scored by the credit card company. For example, a homeowner might get more points than a person who rents. If an application scores a sufficient number of points, the lender then buys a credit report on the applicant from a credit bureau. The score on the credit report is key to the decision to issue a card. Said a vice president of a company in the business of designing scoring models for lenders: 'You can have an application that's good as gold, but if you've got a lousy credit report, you'll get turned down every time' (Updegrave, 1987: 146). In other words, it is the numbers, not qualitative factors, that are ultimately decisive.

Scoring models vary from one locale to another and are updated to reflect changing conditions. Despite great variation from report to report, the following items usually receive the most weight:

- *Possession of a number of credit and charge cards* (30 per cent or more of the points). Having too many cards may cost points, but having no cards at all may be an even more serious liability.
- *Record of paying off accumulated charges* (25 per cent or more of the points). Being delinquent on a Visa or MasterCard is likely to cost more points than being late on a payment to a department store. The credit card companies have found that when people are having economic difficulties, they try to stay current on their credit card payment but might let their department store bill slide. Thus being delinquent on credit card bills is a sign of serious financial difficulties. Delinquencies of 30 days might not cost an applicant many points, but delinquencies of 60 days or more might well scuttle one's chances of getting a card.
- *Suits, judgments, and bankruptcies involving the applicant.* Bankruptcies are likely to be particularly costly. The president of a credit scoring firm said, 'Lenders aren't very forgiving about bankruptcy ... They figure a bankrupt ripped off a creditor and got away with it legally' (Updegrave, 1987: 147).

- *Measures of stability*. These include applicants' tenure on the job and in their place of residence. Someone who has lived in the same place for three or more years might get twice as many points as someone who has recently moved.
- *Income*. The higher the income of the applicant, the greater the number of points on this dimension.
- *Occupation and employer*. The highest-rated occupations, executives and professionals, are likely to earn an applicant a large number of points. Similarly, being in the employ of a stable and profitable firm is likely to garner the applicant many points, whereas employment in a firm on the edge of bankruptcy is likely to be very costly.
- *Age*. Generally, the older the applicant, the greater the number of points.
- *Possession of savings and checking accounts*. Checking accounts, because they tend to require more ability to manage finances, generally get twice as many points as savings accounts.
- *Homeownership* (often 15 per cent of the total points). An applicant who owns a home is more stable than one who rents, has a sizable asset to protect, and is responsible for regular payments.

Scoring systems clearly quantify the decision making process. In doing so, they reduce human qualities to abstract quantities. That is, they reduce the individual quality of creditworthiness to a simple, single number that 'decides' whether or not an applicant is, in fact, worthy of credit. The more human judgment of an official of a credit card firm is then considered unnecessary. One banking consultant claims that 'the character of an individual is much more important than [a credit score]. You can't decide who to lend to by using a computer' (Shiver, 1988: 145). However, with a crush of applicants brought in large part by active recruiting efforts, credit card firms are increasingly relying on computerized scoring systems and paying more attention to quantifiable scores.

Scoring systems are not used just to weed out applicants but are also increasingly employed to evaluate existing credit card customers. Said the president of a company with 2 million credit card accounts:

> The software goes in and looks at attributes of a customer's account and how that account is being handled [by the customer]. And through a statistical methodology ... [i]t looks at payment patterns, usage patterns ... We look at every account automatically and assign a behavior score. That score is, if you will, an odds quote, 100 to 1 or 1,000 to 1.
> It can't predict a specific account ... It can look at a lot of accounts and predict that out of that pool of, say 10,000 accounts that one of them will go delinquent. So we can look at that pool and get a sense of risk from the profile. (Crenshaw, 1991: H4)

A scoring system is used on existing credit card users with a number of different purposes in mind. First, the scoring system helps the credit card firm decide whether to increase a current cardholder's credit limit. The computer evaluates whether an increase in the limit is likely to lead the cardholder into delinquencies. Second, the scoring system helps with decisions on authorizing transactions over a credit card's limit. The computer can make such an authorization on its own, or it can pass the decision to a human evaluator. Third, a credit card company might develop scores based on its own records or on those of the credit bureaus that it can use to determine whether cardholders are likely to pay their bills, Fourth, a scoring system helps decide whether cardholders who have just become delinquent will eventually return to 'current' status (that is, no longer be delinquent) or become more seriously delinquent. The firm can then decide whether action is needed and, if so, what type of action (for example, wait to see what happens, begin a collection effort, or cut off the account completely). Fifth, scoring is sometimes used to determine which cardholders are likely to become bankrupt. Finally, accounts are scored to assess which ones are likely to be most profitable. Those that offer little in the way of profits (especially the accounts of convenience users) are likely to be dropped or not renewed (Detweiler, 1993).

Efficiency: The Faster the Better   The credit card is a highly efficient method for obtaining, granting, and expending loans. Applicants need do little more than fill out a brief application (or provide a few bits of information over the Internet), and in the case of preapproved credit cards, even that requirement may be waived. In most cases, the customer is granted a line of credit, which is accessed and expended quickly and easily each time the card is used. Assuming a good credit record, as the credit limit is approached it will be increased automatically, thereby effortlessly increasing the potential total loan amount.

Furthermore, the credit card tends to greatly enhance the efficiency of virtually all kinds of shopping. Instead of carrying unwieldy amounts of cash, all one needs is a thin piece of plastic. There is no need to plan for purchases by going to the bank to obtain cash, no need to carry burdensome checkbooks and the identification needed to get checks approved. With their credit cards, consumers are no longer even required to know how to count out the needed amount of currency or to make sure the change is correct.

Credit (and debit) cards are also more efficient from the merchant's point of view. The average cash transaction at, for example, a supermarket is still fastest (16 to 30 seconds), but it is closely followed by card payment (20 to 30 seconds); a check transaction lags far behind (45 to 90 seconds). Although it might be a tad slower than cash at the checkout counter, a card transaction is ultimately far more efficient than a cash deal because it requires little from the merchant except the initial electronic transmission of the charge. Handling cash is, as one supermarket electronic banking services executive points out, 'labor intensive. From the time it leaves the customer's hands to the time it hits the bank, cash may get handled six to eight different times, both at the store and at the bank level' (*Chain Store Executive*, 1992). All these steps are eliminated in a charge (or debit) transaction.

Credit cards and debit cards are unquestionably more efficient than checks as far as the merchant is concerned. Debit cards, which can be thought of as 'electronic checks', are more efficient because the amount of the bill is immediately deducted from the customer's account. Eliminated with both credit and debit cards are bounced checks and all the inefficiencies and costs associated with trying to collect on such checks. Furthermore, it is quicker to get a card transaction approved than it is for the customer to write a check and have it approved. Like other businesses, 'grocery stores like the cards because they speed up the checkout line' (Quint, 1990: 43). Other electronic funds transfers, such as paying bills by computer or telephone, promise even greater efficiencies because the customers do not interact on a face-to-face basis with the merchant's staff.

Predictability: Avoiding Those Painful Lulls The credit card has made the process of obtaining a loan quite predictable. Consumers have grown accustomed to routine steps (filling out the questionnaire, for example) that lead to the appearance of a new card in the mail. After all, many people have gone through these same steps many times. In the case of preapproved credit cards, the few remaining unpredictablities have been eliminated, because offer and acceptance arrive in the very same letter.

Whenever human beings are involved in a transaction, unpredictability increases. Thus both fast-food restaurants and credit card companies seek to minimize interaction between their staff and customers. However, there is far less such human contact in the credit card industry than in the fast-food business. (And there is painfully little genuinely human contact in fast-food restaurants.) The limited contact that does exist in the credit card business is likely to take place over the telephone (or increasingly, via the Internet). It might take the form of unsolicited calls made in an effort to recruit new card users. More likely it involves calls by cardholders to the company to inquire about bills or by employees of the company to cardholders to find out why payments are late. However one comes into contact with employees of the credit card firms, much of the interaction is likely to be scripted. The telephone solicitors are clearly reciting scripts mindlessly. Even those responding to customer inquiries or complaints have been trained to select the appropriate scripts and subscripts depending on the nature of the inquiry or complaint and the direction taken by the conversation.

The credit card also serves to make consumption in general more predictable. Before credit cards, people had to spend more slowly, or even stop consuming altogether, when cash on hand or in the bank dipped too low. This unpredictability at the individual level was mirrored at the societal level by general slowdowns in consumption during recessionary periods. But the credit card frees consumers, at least to some degree, from the unpredictabilities associated with cash flow and the absence of cash on hand. It even frees them, at least for a time, from the limitations of depleted checking and savings accounts. Overall, the credit card has a smoothing effect on consumption. We are now better able to avoid 'painful' lulls when we are unable to participate in the economy because of a lack of ready cash. Most generally, the credit card even allows people to consume, at least to some degree, during recessionary periods. For the purveyors of goods and services, the availability of credit cards makes the world more predictable by helping to ensure a steadier stream of customers during bad times as well as good ones.

Nonhuman for Human Technology: No Visitors, No Staff   A variety of nonhuman technologies are found in the fast-food restaurant: soft-drink machines that shut themselves off when the cups are full, french fry machines that buzz when the fries are done and automatically lift the baskets out of the oil – and soon robots rather than real human beings to serve customers. These technologies control employees, deskill jobs by transferring skills from people to machines, and ultimately replace people.

The credit card is itself a kind of nonhuman technology. More important, it has given birth to technologies that intervene between buyer and seller and serve to constrain both. Most notable is the vast computerized system that 'decides' whether to authorize a new credit card and whether to authorize a given purchase. Shopkeeper and customer may both want to consummate a deal, but if the computer system says no (because, for example, the consumer's card is over its credit limit), then there is likely to be no sale. Similarly, an employee of a credit card firm may want to approve a sale but be loath, and perhaps forbidden, to do so if the computer indicates that the sale should be disapproved. The general trend within rationalized societies is to take decision making power away from people (customers, shopkeepers, and credit card company employees alike) and give it to nonhuman technologies.

With the advent of smart cards, the card itself will 'decide' whether a sale is to be consummated. Embedded in the card's computer chip will be such information as spending limits, so the card itself will be able to reject a purchase that is over the limit.

Not only do some aspects of our credit card society take decision making away from human beings, but other of its elements eliminate people altogether. Thus, widespread distribution of the smart card may eliminate many of the people who now operate the credit card companies' extensive computer systems. Today, ATMs have been increasingly replacing bank tellers. A bank vice president is quite explicit about the substitution of ATMs for human beings: 'This might sound funny, but if we can keep people out of our branches, we don't have to hire staff to handle peak-time booms and the like. That drives down costs' (*American Banker*, 1991: 22A). A similar point can be made about debit cards, which involve far less human labor than do the checks they are designed to replace. The growth of debit cards has undoubtedly led to the loss of many bank positions involved in clearing checks. Similarly, because credit cards are designed to be used in place of cash, the increasing use of such cards has led to the loss of positions involved in a cash economy (for example, bank tellers needed to dole out cash).

The most recent steps in this historical process involve the further development of Internet banking. Increasingly, people will not need to leave their homes in order to conduct financial transactions. They will be able to use their ATM, debit, and credit cards to transfer funds through their telephones, home computers and television screens (Piskora and Kutler, 1993: 1A). The result will be even more nonhuman technology and even less contact with other human beings.

Various pressures have forced the credit card industry to pursue ever higher levels of McDonaldization through new nonhuman technologies. For example, both consumers and shopkeepers want quick authorizations of credit card sales, so more sophisticated computers and computer programs have been developed. The credit card companies also have a strong interest in seeing charges entered speedily into customer accounts so that the bills will be paid sooner or, better yet, so interest charges can begin accruing sooner on unpaid balances. The search for speedier billing has led to further technological advancement.

Consider Visa's computer system, Visanet, which serves as the intermediary among the merchant, the merchant's bank, and the card-issuing bank. Visanet is a huge network encompassing '9 million miles of fiber-optic cable ... 20,000 banks and other financial institutions, and 10 million merchants in 247 countries and territories worldwide' (*Los Angeles Times*, 1993). This system handles an average of 11,000 transactions per minute. Most of them go through two 'super centers' in Virginia and England, as well as 1,400 smaller Visa computers. From swiping the card through the point-of-sale terminal to approving the transaction, the entire process ordinarily takes between 6 and 20 seconds. In this process, the system determines whether the card is stolen, whether the transaction exceeds the card's credit limit, and whether it is an unusual purchase that might not have been authorized by the cardholder.

On-line systems like Visa's Internet and MasterCard's Maestro also permit the instantaneous transfer of funds when a debit card is used.

Transfers of funds using far less sophisticated off-line systems take a few days to complete.

Another pressure toward further technological advancement and greater control is the need to quickly and correctly approve credit applications. As mentioned earlier, more of these decisions are being made by computerized credit scoring systems these days. The computer may even generate the acceptance or rejection letter, in which case the application might be handled without any human involvement whatsoever.

Perhaps the most visible example in the credit card business of taking control from humans and building it into the technology is the movement away from 'country-club' billing to 'descriptive billing'. In country-club billing, customers receive with their monthly bills copies (or facsimiles) of the actual charge slips used for each purchase. As of this writing, American Express continues to provide this service but it is an expensive undertaking. In the main, credit card companies have adopted descriptive billing, in which cardholders merely get a list of the charges, dates, and amounts. The problem with descriptive billing is the loss of control by consumers. With copies of receipts, which include authorizing signatures, cardholders can clearly see whether or not they actually made the purchase. With only lists included in the bill, cardholders must rely on memory or on their own record keeping to verify purchases. People often get frustrated with the bother and assume the list of charges is correct, thereby surrendering control to credit card companies and their computers.

By the way, the consumer's need to keep credit card records and to verify long lists of bills is indicative of another characteristic of a McDonaldizing society: making consumers do more of the work without being paid. In the fast-food restaurant, customers collect their own food and dispose of the remnants when they are done eating, thereby serving as their own servers and buspersons. In the credit card business, since most companies no longer provide us with copies of receipts, customers are required to keep the copies and check them against the list provided with their monthly bills. Consumers have also become responsible for detecting and correcting errors in their credit bureau records. As Gerri Detweiler (1993: 10, 39; italics added) puts it, '*The system is not user-friendly: you have to do all the work.*'

Irrationality of Rationality: Caught in the Heavy Machinery   The irrationality of rationality takes several forms. At one level, irrationality simply means that what is rational in planning does not work out that way in practice. Take, for example, the Discover Card's program to allow its cardholders to access Sprint's long-distance service. To make a long-distance call with the card, 'all you need to do is dial Sprint's 11-digit access number. Then 0. Then a 10-digit phone number. The 16-digit account number from your Discovery Card. Then a four-digit "Personal Access Code"'

(*Consumer Reports*, 1992). A highly inefficient string of 42 digits must be entered just to make one long-distance telephone call. To take another example, the credit card companies are supposed to function highly predictably. Thus, for example, our bills should be error free. However, billing errors do find their way into monthly statements. For example, there are many charges that we did not make or the amount entered may be incorrect.

The credit card world is also highly dehumanized because people generally interact with nonhuman technologies, with such products as bills or overdue notices, or with people whose actions or decisions are constrained if not determined by nonhuman technologies. Horror stories abound of people caught in the 'heavy machinery' of the credit card companies. Pity the poor consumers who get charged for things they did not buy or who are sent a series of computer-generated letters with escalating threats because the computer erroneously considers them to be delinquent in their payments. Then there are the many complaints of people who get turned down for credit because erroneous information has crept into their credit reports. Trying to get satisfaction from the technologies, or from their often robotlike representatives, is perhaps the ultimate in the dehumanization associated with a rationalizing society ...

Various irrationalities are associated with rationalization of the process of granting credit card loans. Besides the dehumanization associated with the process, computerized credit approval is associated with a greater likelihood of delinquency and default (Huntington Bancshares is an exception) than when financial institutions employ more traditional methods. Credit card companies have been willing to accept these risks (at least until recently) because of the relatively small amounts involved in credit card loans and the fact that credit cards in general are so profitable. Such losses are hardly noticeable.

The largest set of problems is associated with actions taken by credit card companies to increase revenues and profits. For example, credit card companies have been known to alter their accounting methods so that customers end up paying more in interest than they expect to or should pay. Initially, General Motors' co-branded card featured a potentially costly 'two-cycle billing method', which worked in the following way:

> A $500 purchase made Jan. 1 does not have to be paid off until late February under typical grace periods. If only a minimum payment is made, most cards calculate interest for the March billing period on the unpaid charges from the February bill. Under the two-cycle method, a card issuer will go back two cycles and calculate the interest from the time the purchase was made.
>
> This extra charge will be levied only once for people who carry balances from month to month. But for those who constantly switch from paying off to carrying a balance, this two-cycle method can be costly. (Bryant, 1992: 35)

It is interesting to note that GM was forced to drop its two-cycle billing method because of negative publicity and cardholder complaints.[7]

In spite of this successful effort, few customers are knowledgeable enough to understand the implications of such rational accounting procedures or even that they have been implemented. The problem, however, is more general: 'A number of banks took advantage of consumer complaisance by changing annual fees, rates, grace periods, late charges, and other card restrictions without attracting a great deal of consumer attention' (Mandell, 1990: 79). Few consumers have the will or the ability to carefully oversee the activities of the credit card companies.

Perhaps the most persistent and reprehensible activities of the credit card companies ... are their efforts to keep their interest rates high even when interest rates in general are low or declining. Of course, many other irrationalities of the rationalized credit card industry have been discussed above – the tendency of credit card companies to engage in practices that lead people to spend recklessly, the secrecy of many aspects of the credit card business, the invasion of the privacy of card-holders, and the fraudulent activities engaged in by various players in the credit card world.

Personal Troubles, Public Issues, and McDonaldization   Let us look now more explicitly at the process of McDonaldization as it applies to credit cards from the perspective of the twin themes of personal troubles and public issues. McDonaldization can be seen as a large-scale social process that manifests itself in the credit card industry (among many others) and is, in the process, creating personal troubles for individuals as well as public issues that are of concern to society as a whole.

Although my focus here is the problems that McDonaldization creates, it certainly carries with it a wide array of benefits. In fact, most of the major components of rationalization may be seen as advantageous. Most of us regard the emphasis on things that can be counted (rather than qualitative judgments), efficient operations, predictable procedures and results, and the advances offered by nonhuman technologies as highly positive characteristics of a rational society.

Still, rationalization creates many personal troubles:

- *Calculability*. Consumerism's emphasis on buying large numbers of easily replaced things leaves us surrounded by poor-quality goods that do not function well and that fall apart quickly. More important, when we can easily acquire, and reacquire, many of the things that we desire, we are left with a cynical and blasé attitude toward the world. In addition, the scoring systems relied on by credit card firms reduce all of us to a single number. Our fundamental character means little, and so society becomes a little more flat, dull, and characterless. Decision making is taken away from human officials and handed to the computers that calculate and assess credit-worthiness. Consumers are left feeling that they are controlled by cold, inhuman systems. A perfect example of this control is the fact that, once the credit bureaus have a file on a person, it is impossible for that person to opt out of the system.

- *Efficiency*. The greater efficiency of making purchases with credit cards in comparison to the alternatives, especially cash and checks, exacerbates our society's emphasis on speed. Lost in the process is a concern for the quality of the experience and the quality of the goods and services obtained. Overall, something important but indefinable is lost in a world that sometimes seems to value speed and efficiency above all else.
- *Predictability*. A similar point can be made about the personal troubles associated with predictability. Something very important is lost when all the things that we consume and all the experiences that we have are highly predictable. Life becomes routine, dull, boring. The excitement associated with at least some unpredictability – a surprising discovery or an unexpected experience – is lost. When people had to rely on cash they were likely to experience self-denial at times. But when the cash supply was replenished, there was excitement in finally being able to afford some object or participate in some experience. The tendency to reduce or eliminate periods of self-denial eliminates, in the process, the excitement of obtaining something for which someone has had to wait.
- *Substitution of nonhuman for human technology*. A considerable amount of humanity is lost when people are in the thrall of large-scale computerized systems like those in the credit card industry. Instead of being in control, people are controlled by these systems. This phenomenon is well illustrated by the switch from country-club to descriptive billing in most of the credit card industry. Similarly, the technologies associated with credit cards tend to reduce or eliminate human interaction; tend to eliminate jobs, leaving people without work and the income and meaning that work accords; and tend to bring with them greater speed and efficiency and thus other kinds of problems.
- *Irrationality of rationality*. Each of the major components of the rationalization of the credit card industry can be seen as causing personal troubles for individuals. Many of those troubles relate to the irrationality of those rational systems, especially their tendency toward dehumanization. In many ways our lives are less human because of the advances in the credit card industry and the rationalization process of which they are part.

What is the public issue associated with McDonaldization and credit cards? At one level, the aggregation of all these personal troubles can be seen as a public issue. At another level, the policies of the credit card industry that cause these problems can also be viewed as a public issue. However, the broadest public issue is the threat of totalitarianism posed by the credit card industry in concert with the other major elements of the rationalizing society. In *Charge It*, Terry Galanoy (1980; see also, Nocera, 1994: 307) called such a totalitarian system Lifebank, the logical derivative of the credit card society. In the Lifebank system, he speculated, all of a person's assets will be combined into one account, which will be controlled by one or more banks or financial institutions and their computers. All of a person's credit cards will be replaced by a single Lifebank card. Virtually all consumption will be on credit. As the bills come due, they will be automatically deducted from each person's Lifebank account. However, each person will be granted an allowance for day-to-day expenses. There will, as a result, be little cash and little need for it. Checking accounts as we know them will have largely disappeared. Lifebank's computers will make virtually all economic decisions for individuals. Credit ratings will be continually updated. The Lifebank card will be the key to virtually everything, and those without such a card will not only not have any credit in a society that depends on credit but will literally have ceased to exist as far as Lifebank's computers are concerned. In sum,

> We will have lost control. Even the banks will have lost control. The Lifebank-type system will have its own reasoning, its own standards, its own momentum, its own energy, its own life; and operating without conscience, without soul, without social logic, it will also be out of control by all standards we should still live by today. (Galanoy, 1980: 215)

Although such a system has yet to come into existence, many developments and technological advancements in the credit card industry have made something like Lifebank more possible today, and continued technological advances make it an even greater possibility in the future.

Lifebank does resemble the 'iron cage of rationality' that underlay Weber's concern with the rationalization process. Weber feared that the world was moving toward a seamless web of rational systems that would control more and more aspects of our lives. Furthermore, we would be less and less able to escape from the rational society. Eventually, all the escape routes would be closed off (or rationalized). We would be left with little more than the ability to choose among rational systems.

It is clear that the credit card industry has become highly rationalized and taken its place as a key element of our rational society. What is particularly disturbing about the role of the credit card is that it has become one of the preferred means to an increasingly wide array of rationalized ends and thus contributes to the further rationalization of all the ends to which it provides access. It should be pointed out that the credit card can also provide access to nonrationalized ends. In that sense, it can help to liberate people from rationalization, at least until the bills come due. However, credit cards (and related phenomena) are playing a distinctive and unusually powerful role in the emergence and solidification of the iron cage of rationalization. That is the central public issue as far as credit cards are concerned, and it subsumes the wide range of more specific issues discussed in this section that should also be of great public concern.

Globalization and Americanization

A sociology of credit cards requires a look at the relationship among the credit card industry, personal troubles, and public issues on a global scale. It is not just the United States, but also much of the rest of the world, that is being affected by the credit card industry and the social problems it helps create. To some degree, this development is a result of globalization, a process that is at least partially autonomous of any single nation and that involves the reciprocal impact of many economies (Featherstone, 1990; Robertson, 1992). In the main, however, American credit card companies dominate the global market. Thus, I will deal with the spread of the credit card industry around the world under the heading of Americanization rather than globalization. For this issue, instead of drawing on the ideas of long-dead thinkers like Mills, Marx, Simmel, and Weber, I will rely on more contemporary work (Kuisel, 1993).

The central point is that, in many countries around the world, Americanization is a public issue that is causing personal troubles for their citizens. I address the role played by the credit card industry in this process of Americanization and in the homogenization of life around the world, with the attendant loss of cultural and individual differences.

As we will see in greater detail in Chapter 8 of this volume, unlike those who concentrate on Americanization, globalization theorists generally refuse to focus on any single nation, or even to use the nation as the unit of analysis. Rather, globalization implies a focus on worldwide processes that are, at least to some degree, independent of nations. Furthermore, there is a refusal to think of culture as flowing largely in one direction; rather, there is a focus on the resistance of other cultures and of their independent significance in shaping world culture. Although there is much merit in the concept of globalization, at this point in history the idea of Americanization is more helpful in understanding the worldwide impact of credit cards.[8] After all, the credit card is an American innovation. Credit cards emanating from the United States are encountering little serious resistance from foreign competitors, and the credit cards stemming from other parts of the world are having little impact on the American market. At some time in the future, the credit card world might be better described by the term globalization, but at the moment Americanization is a far more accurate description.

An idea derived from globalization theory that does seem to have some relevance to the credit card world at the moment is 'third cultures', or partially autonomous cultures that transcend national boundaries and exist on a global basis (Featherstone, 1990: 1). Exchanges of information, knowledge, goods, and people take place within these third cultures. For example, the global 'finanscape' is a third culture dealing with the 'movement of megamonies through national turn-stiles at blinding speed' (Appadurai, 1990: 298). Clearly, the credit card industry – and even more, the things like electronic funds transfers – are crucial components of this finanscape. The credit card society can also be seen as part of the 'ethnoscape', especially in terms of the movement of people through tourism, and the 'technoscape', in that it employs technologies that girdle the world. To some degree, then, the credit card world is already part of these third cultures, and it is likely to grow progressively detached from its American roots and increasingly autonomous of any single nation. Yet at the moment it is dominated by the United States, and this is likely to be the case for the foreseeable future.

The concept of Americanization has a long intellectual tradition, most of the important work having been done by nonsociologists (for example, Duhamel, 1931; Duignan and Gann, 1992; Servan-Schreiber, 1968; Williams, 1962). However, Georg Simmel was concerned with the growing 'Americanism' of his day. To him, Americanism stood for the 'enormous desire for happiness of modern man' and, more negatively, for 'modern "covetousness"' (Simmel, 1991: 27). It is interesting to note that Simmel not only anticipated all the other major themes discussed here in relationship to credit cards but the motif of Americanization as well.

Americanization has been characterized in various terms, few of them flattering. For instance, Georges Duhamel (1931: 215) of France described America as 'the devouring civilization':

> American civilization ... is already mistress of the world ... There are on our continent ... large regions that the spirit of old Europe has deserted. The American spirit colonizes [or taints] little by little such a province, such a city, such a house and such a soul.

In the most famous work in this tradition, J.-J. Servan-Schreiber (1968: 3), also French, saw Americanization primarily in economic terms: 'Fifteen years from now it is quite possible that the world's third greatest industrial power, just after the United States and Russia, will not be Europe, *but American Industry in Europe'*. However, time has not borne out Servan-Schreiber's prediction ...

Francis Williams (1962: npi) came closer to the mark from the vantage point of Great Britain:

> The American invasion is going on all over the world: American ideas, American methods, American customs, American habits of eating, drinking and dressing, American amusements, American social patterns, American capital.

Although Williams (1962: npi) regarded America's investment of capital in Europe as important, he considered the 'impact of American ideas, ... American social attitudes and ways of life ... even more profound and all-pervasive'.

In *Seducing the French: The Dilemma of Americanization*, Richard Kuisel (1993: 4) argues that 'there is a kind of global imperative that goes by the name of Americanization'. He seems to have several different ideas in mind when he refers to Americanization, ideas that are all useful in helping us think about credit cards:

- By Americanization Kuisel means that the French, and more generally other nations, accept a wide range of American exports. That is, they 'accept American economic aid and guidance; borrow American technology and economic practice; buy American products; imitate American social policy; even dress, speak and (perhaps worst of all) eat like Americans' (Kuisel, 1993: 3).
- Kuisel (1993: 10) associates Americanization and rationalization (and implicitly McDonaldization): '*Americanisme*, defined as the quest for abundance through standardized mass production and consumption, evoked Henry Ford's assembly line, ubiquitous billboards, rows of simple wood houses, packaged foods, and tractors plying vast farms.' In the 1930s, the French referred to this process as becoming 'Fordized' (Kuisel, 1993: 11). Indeed, Fordism – especially its emphasis on mass, standardized production using assembly-line technology – can be seen as an excellent example of rationalization and as one of the precursors of a McDonaldized society.
- Kuisel often seems to equate Americanization with modernity and modernization. For example, he describes his book as being concerned with how France 'became modern or "Americanized" and yet remained French'; later, he describes the 'process of modernization that has swept across postwar France' (Kuisel, 1993: x, 4).
- Kuisel (1993: 4) disengages Americanization from America and sees it as the process by which more and more societies can be described as 'consumer societies'. As he puts it, 'Although the phenomenon is still described as Americanization, it has become increasingly

disconnected from America.[9] Perhaps it would be better described as the coming of the consumer society.'

The expansion of credit cards into France, Europe, and the rest of the world can be seen to varying degrees, as an example of Americanization in the several senses of the term discussed by Kuisel. In the main, we can say that the credit card is an American export that is bringing with it other American goods and services, rationalization, modernism, and consumerism.

Acceptance of American Exports How does Kuisel's first meaning of Americanization relate to credit cards? First, because credit cards were invented in America, they are in a sense exports. Interestingly, France is the leader in Europe in the use of credit cards, and its use of credit cards has increased substantially.

Credit cards can also be used to purchase, among other things, a wide range of American products. However, as Kuisel (1993: 36) notes, American exports to France were not always the finest expressions of American industry and culture. Chewing gum, Hollywood films, and comics did not convey the noblest images of the United States. Nevertheless, France and much of the rest of the world have eagerly become Americanized through the use of credit cards, at least in the sense that they have used the cards to buy an array of American products.

Rationalization   Not only does Kuisel see a general association between Americanization and rationalization (McDonaldization) in France, but he also sees linkages with more specific elements of rationalization. For example, there was concern in France over the American emphasis on calculability – the focus on quantity rather than quality. Kuisel (1993: 11) singles out American films on this dimension: 'American film making as an "industry" that produced meters of banal celluloid escapism for profit [and] subordinated quality to box office receipts.' More generally, American society was viewed as being 'mechanized' (that is, dominated by nonhuman rather than human technologies) and 'monotonous' (that is, predictable). Above all, Americanization was seen as producing the irrationality of rationality:

> Machines and factories degraded work and worker. The economy should be in the service of human beings, not the other way round ... *dehumanized* ... America [exhibits] the 'new barbarism' reducing human beings to animalistic needs, enslaving them to an economic monster, and defining them by their functions. (Kuisel, 1993: 13)

The 'functional anthill' of the United States was seen as threatening the nonrationalized, premodern world of traditional France, which was dominated by 'the small pleasures of mischief, exuberance, uniqueness, and spontaneity as well as the sterner values of frugality, camaraderie, and heroism' (Kuisel, 1993: 13).

More generally, as discussed above, credit cards are both a part of and a contributor to the process of rationalization. Although that process might not have had its origins in the United States, it has come to be closely associated with it.

At this point, it might be well to look at the related issue of Fordism, because the French closely linked Fordism with rationalization and Americanization (Clarke, 1990). Credit cards are Fordist in several senses. For one thing, credit cards are mass-produced. Second, they are products of inflexible technologies, are themselves a kind of inflexible technology, and rely on inflexible computerized systems for the approval and processing of credit card transactions. Third, they are based on economies of scale in the sense that credit card companies are driven to maximize the number of credit cards in the hands of consumers; the greater the number of cards in use, the greater the profits. Finally, credit cards can be used to purchase mass-produced, homogeneous products. They also help to foster a national, even an international market for those products.

Yet at the same time, credit cards help in various ways to foster a post-Fordist society. With credit cards, consumers can purchase more of both mass-produced and customized products. Greater sales of customized and specialized products help to foster the development of smaller and more productive manufacturing systems. More is required from the workers in those systems, who thus need higher and more diverse levels of skill in order to handle the more sophisticated technologies. These more differentiated workers, in turn, lead more differentiated lifestyles than their predecessors working on the assembly line and in other Fordist production systems. People who live more differentiated lifestyles require, in turn, more diverse products and services.

Thus credit cards contribute to the maintenance of elements of a Fordist society as well as to the development of at least some aspects of a post-Fordist society. This analysis of credit cards leads to the conclusion that the real world is far more complex than simple models and theories would have us believe.

This analysis also casts some doubt on the association between credit cards and the rationalization process in general. If credit cards can be linked to post-Fordist societies, then why can they not be associated with a 'postrational' society as well? In some ways they can be, especially in terms of many of the irrationalities of rationality. Fundamentally, however, at this juncture credit cards have far more in common with rationalization and Fordism than they do with the theoretical alternatives. But someday, just as it might be more appropriate to think about credit cards in terms of globalization rather than Americanization, it might also be more appropriate to think of them in postrational or post-Fordist terms.

Modernism   Credit cards could also qualify as a modern phenomenon and thus, to the degree that we equate modernity with Americanization, as an example of Americanization in this sense of the term as well. The equation of modernity and Americanization is characteristic of what is called modernization theory, in which it is considered 'self-evident that contemporary American society, its institutional structures, and its normative matrix [is] the society most advanced in modernity' (Tiryakian, 1992: 79). However, modernization theory has fallen into disrepute for a variety of reasons, not the least of which is its assumption that the United States is the model to be emulated by the rest of the world. But in associating modernity, the United States, and credit cards, I am not saying that any or all of them are unequivocally positive. Indeed, much of this discussion has dealt with problems associated with credit cards and therefore implicitly with problems with American society and modernity. The point here is that both the United States and credit cards have a variety of modern characteristics and that credit cards have played a key role in bringing Americanization and modernity, for good and ill, to much of the rest of the world.

A related issue is the relationship between modernity and post-modernity. The credit card was certainly a product of the modern era; its creation and development predated the emergence of postmodern society. Nevertheless, some would argue that the credit card might be better thought of as a postmodern phenomenon. Are credit cards better thought of as being modern or postmodern? Let us consider one difference between these two types of society – rigidity (and rationality) versus flexibility (and nonrationality). Credit cards are associated more with the rigidity of a modern society than with the flexibility of a post-modern society. Among those rigidities are the fact that computerized systems handle all credit card transactions in the same way, most credit cards have fixed limits, and they lead everyone to consume in much the same way.

The paradox, however, is that the rigid, seemingly modern credit card permits all sorts of flexible, postmodern behaviors and realities. For example, instead of doing our shopping only during a store's business hours, we can order products any time of the day or night through catalogs, the Internet, or television shopping networks and charge our purchases to our credit cards. The cards can also be used to buy the most unusual and unique products; they need not be used to buy only standardized merchandise. The result is the development of all sorts of small market niches and a wider range of options for everyone (Hage and Powers, 1992). Indeed, segmentation is one of the growing trends in the credit card industry. Furthermore, we are better able to go anywhere we want any time we like with credit cards. We do not need to engage in lengthy planning and preparations; we can simply get up and go. Thus, credit cards are simultaneously inflexible instruments and ones that provide great flexibility; in other words, they have characteristics of both modern and postmodern society.

There are a number of other ways in which credit cards are part of both the modern and the postmodern worlds. Time and space compression are characteristic of both modern and postmodern societies (Harvey, 1989), and the credit card is a particularly good example of both types of compression. The credit card permits us to obtain things immediately rather than wait until we have accumulated enough cash, and in many cases, it eliminates the need to travel to distant locales to obtain unusual products. We can simply order them over the Internet or by telephone, pay for them with a credit card, and wait at our doorstep for our purchases to arrive from all corners of the globe. Given their capacity to compress time and space, credit cards would seem to be associated with both modern and postmodern society.

Both types of society are also characterized by simulations. In terms of the means of exchange, both currency (associated with modern society) and credit cards (associated here with postmodern society, although the association is not clear-cut) can be seen as simulations: at one time currency simulated gold, and today credit cards simulate currency. (Note that credit cards are thus a simulation of a simulation.) Furthermore, both currency and credit cards can be used to purchase either authentic or simulated experiences. Thus, we can use cash or a credit card to pay for a simulated Amazon River trip at an amusement park or for the real thing.

In sum, although credit cards are certainly a product of modern society, they are also consistent in many ways with postmodern society. Thus they help put the lie to the idea of a radical disjunction between modern and postmodern society. Yet, in the end, one must conclude that there is a stronger association between credit cards and modernity. Although it has postmodern elements, the United States remains primarily a modern society (it is, for example, still better described as rational and inflexible) and the credit card is best viewed as an agent and an aspect of modernity.

Consumerism The final meaning of Americanization suggested by Kuisel is perhaps most unambiguously associated with credit cards. With America's heavy industries in decline, the consumer culture and its products, and the means of consuming them, have become the nation's major export:

> It should come as no surprise that the global consumer culture – particularly in the realm of movies, music and food – has remained almost an American

monopoly in a time when America's hegemony in other industries, ranging from automobiles to consumer electronics, has been shattered irrevocably. (Rieff, 1994: C1, C4)

America, the source and center of the consumer society, is equally the source and center of the credit card society.

More important, the credit card has given the consumer society an enormous boost. We can safely say that the consumer society has expanded greatly as a result of the advent and growth of the credit card. Consumption that otherwise would not take place now occurs because the credit card is available. People are able to spend all that they have, and then to go well beyond that level, with their credit cards. More generally, related phenomena – debit cards, ATMs, and electronic funds transfers – also help to feed consumption-oriented society.

Anti-Americanism and the Credit Card

Although some would equate Americanization and anti-Americanism, the two are in fact different.[10] Whereas Americanization incorporates a range of attitudes, anti-Americanism is a negative state of mind – as Kuisel (1993: 8) defines it, 'sets of attitudes that are predominantly, if not systematically or permanently ... critical' of America. He makes it clear that a single critical comment does not qualify as anti Americanism; it must be part of a larger complex. He also argues that 'petty complaints' should not be considered as reflective of anti-Americanism: 'Distaste for chewing gum or Hollywood does not qualify. Contempt for Americans or American foreign policy or consumer society as "the American way of life" does' (Kuisel, 1993: 8–9).

We cannot examine the Americanization of the credit card world without asking whether credit cards have inspired anti-Americanism. The first point to be made about the relationship between credit cards and anti-Americanism is that, except for American Express, nothing overt about the general-purpose cards indicates that they are associated with America. In fact, the names of the general-purpose cards – Visa, MasterCard, Discover, Optima, Diners Club, and Carte Blanche – are generic expressly to avoid simple identification with any nation. In addition, other nations are issuing at least some of these cards and producing their own cards, such as Japan's JCB, Great Britain's BarclayCard, even the fledgling Great Wall card of China.

However, the most important point about credit cards and anti-Americanism is that, unlike most other American products, credit cards are means rather than ends. As a result, they can be used to purchase the goods and services of any nation and thus support any nation's economy. For this reason, credit cards are far less likely to spawn anti-Americanism than are other American products, which are likely to compete with and displace indigenous products. Of course, American credit cards do compete with and displace the cards of other nations. But far more commonly, Big Macs get eaten instead of Britain's fish and chips, people drive Fords instead of Sweden's Volvos, and people drink Coca-Cola in place of French wine. However, credit cards can just as easily be used to purchase fish and chips, Volvo parts (if not Volvos themselves), and French wine as they can be used to buy American substitutes.

This is a good place to take issue with Kuisel's point that 'petty complaints' do not qualify as anti-Americanism. It seems to me that chewing gum, hamburgers, or even credit cards can easily be objects of anti-Americanism. Just because they are 'petty products', part of 'low culture' rather than 'high culture', why shouldn't hostility to credit cards qualify as anti-Americanism?[11] (As we have seen, McDonald's has come to be the object of protests against the United States in various parts of the world.) In fact, that hostility can be a surrogate for broader hostility to 'the American way of life'. Indeed, hostility to the American Express card, or McDonald's, is in some ways a better indicator of anti-Americanism than opposition to American foreign policy. Comparatively few people have direct contact with American foreign policy, but virtually everyone comes into contact with America's seemingly 'petty products'. Furthermore, many of these seemingly minor objects are likely to be part of the American cultural express and, as such, are likely to evoke powerful reactions, both pro and con.

In many ways, it is possible to see the credit card as the most dangerous of America's exports to the world. Because it is a means, not an end like most other American exports, it seems either benign or a great boon to the consumers of every nation. Concealed beneath this surface appearance are the malignant effects of credit cards.

From the point of view of other societies, the most important malignant effect of credit cards and the most likely cause of anti-Americanism is the threat of homogenization. Homogenization can be both a cause of private troubles and a public issue. As the use of credit cards spreads, individuals are threatened with the destruction of long-cherished cultural practices and the elimination of the things that have made their lives meaningful. Similarly, societies are under threat because their distinctive features appear to be eroding, to be replaced by American culture. Even though credit cards can be used to support indigenous economies and cultures, they have also very effectively brought American products, processes, and values to most of the nations of the world. One journalist described 'the general tidal pull toward homogenization at play everywhere in the world ... The general direction in the world is toward greater similarity, at least on the levels of material ambitions, architecture, food and ambient noise – a.k.a. music' (Rieff, 1994: C4).

Here is what Francis Williams (1962: 11–12) had to say about the homogenization and Americanization of English culture:

> The impact of American ideas, and still more of American ways of life, is now so large, the drive of America to Americanize so great, that to ask how much of what is specifically English in our civilization will remain in a decade or two if the trend continues is by no means absurd ... An All-American world would be the last sad surrender to conformity. [What is endangered is] much that gives to English life its colour and zest and character.

The fear of homogenization appeared in France in a flap over another American product, Coca-Cola in the 1940s. There was fierce opposition to Coke, especially from the political left, and to the 'coca-colonization' of France:

> The day when opposite Notre Dame there is a poster of 'The Pause That Refreshes' and on restaurant tables one sees as many Coke bottles as carafes of red wine, it will be not only the French, but also Americans, who will feel poorer. (Kuisel, 1993: 63)

Such fear continues in France to this day. For example, a French official was quoted in 1994 as saying that, if the American cultural invasion is not resisted 'there will soon develop a standardized world culture created according to American norms' (Rieff, 1994: C4).

By helping to make all societies similarly modern, credit cards thereby help to destroy many societies' characteristics. In fact, Kuisel (1993: 13) describes French opposition to Americanization in the 1930s as 'distinctly premodern'. Credit cards certainly play a key role in the consumer society that the French associated with the United States and feared so much. Credit cards can also help to make all societies similarly rationalized, thereby destroying their nonrational and irrational elements.

The French probably resist Americanization more than the people of most other nations. Perhaps they are so resistant because France shares with the United States an exalted view of itself and its role in the world. As Kuisel (1993: 127) puts it, 'France and the United States clash because they are the only two Western nations that harbor universal pretensions.' Nevertheless, many other far less pretentious nations have had their share of anti-Americanism.

Despite anti-Americanism in many places in the world, there have been few, if any, overt signs of national opposition to credit cards. Sometimes an American Express office is the object of protest or attack, but that company's obvious association with the United States, and not the credit card per se, is the likely irritant. Again, the credit card's

status as a pure means, rather than an end, makes it a less likely target
for anti-Americanism. Ironically, in many ways the credit card should
be a prime target of anti-Americanism, because as a means it fosters
many of the types of Americanization that elicit hostility in so many
nations.

It is instructive in this regard to compare the French reactions to
credit cards and to the Euro Disney theme park. As an end Euro Disney
became a lightning rod for hostility, as Coca-Cola had been earlier, but
as a means the credit card has largely escaped criticism.

At a cost of $5 billion, Euro Disney opened with great fanfare in a
suburb of Paris in April 1992. It ran into problems even before it opened.
Labor unions were upset about the demand that male employees have
short hair, be clean shaven (including no mustache), and wear only
one ring per hand. Female employees were forbidden to wear showy
jewelry, eye shadow, or false eyelashes and were instructed to wear
'appropriate undergarments' (*Chicago Tribune*, 1992: 2).

After it opened, Euro Disney came under attack from all sides. One
American journalist claimed that it reeks of 'a kind of sterile Americana'
(Robins, 1992: L1). But the reaction of French journalists and intellectuals was far worse. Among many other things, Euro Disney was called
'a terrifying giant step toward world homogenization', 'a cultural Cher-
nobyl', and a 'conservatory of nothingness' (Kuisel, 1993: 228).

As a result of such criticisms – as well as a number of other factors,
such as poor weather, the high price of admission (higher than Disney's
American parks), high hotel room rates ($345 per night at the premier
park hotel) and food prices, and most important, a recession in Europe –
Euro Disney was, at least at first, a dismal failure financially (Gumbel
and Turner, 1994). It lost $920 million in its first full year of operation
and was in danger of being shut down unless its finances were restruc-
tured (Cohen, 1993). In fact, in 1994 the parent Disney Company did
agree to spend about $750 million to bail out Euro Disney, and a Saudi
Arabian prince agreed to chip in up to $439 million (Coleman and
King, 1994). In spite of these financial woes, 18 million people visited
Euro Disney between its opening and early 1994, 'making it the single
largest tourist attraction in France, far surpassing even the Eiffel Tower
and the Louvre' (Kraft, 1994).

Although the world has been Americanized to a great degree, the
case of Euro Disney (at least from a financial point of view and in its
early years) demonstrates that Americanization has its limits. Francis
Williams (1962: 146) argued that it 'is probably true that the complete
Americanization of any country other than America itself is impossible'. A French culture will survive, even if (as now seems assured) Euro
Disney does ultimately succeed. For reassurance, one has only to look
to Japan, where Tokyo Disneyland has been a huge success but has
elicited little hostility and has done little or nothing to change Japanese

culture. (Of course, the orderly park does fit well with Japan's highly ordered society; Sterngold, 1994.) As sociologist Todd Gitlin (cited in Kuisel, 1993: 230) noted, American culture is likely to become 'everyone's second culture'.

The credit card will increasingly become a part of and one of the preferred means in this second culture; the credit card will allow those in other cultures to use an Americanized means to attain a variety of Americanized ends. In this sense, it does pose a more profound threat than Euro Disney. Yet at the same time the credit card is unlikely to be more than a significant part of the second culture. Furthermore, as we have seen, the credit card can be used to purchase indigenous ends. The net result, paradoxically, is that the credit card represents both a threat to other cultures and a means by which those other cultures can be nurtured and sustained. Thus, although credit cards pose the danger of homogeneity, they can also foster heterogeneity (Appadurai, 1990). It is perhaps for this reason, in addition to its comparative invisibility, that the credit card has escaped criticisms like those aimed at Euro Disney and other manifestations of the American Express.

In sum, the credit card is important not just in and of itself but also in its ability to shed light on other issues. Examining credit cards helps us understand the essence of the modern world, as well as some of the most pressing personal troubles and most fundamental public issues of our time.

Notes

This chapter is derived from various places in *Expressing America: A Critique of the Global Credit Card Society*. Thousand Oaks, CA: Pine Forge Press, 1995.

1 For an application of a micro–macro approach to the sociological analysis of money, see Baker and Jimerson, 1992.
2 For a discussion of Gerth and Mills' *Character and Social Structure* in light of the recent movement toward more integrative theoretical perspectives, see Ritzer, 1981: 193–8.
3 In fact, Simmel did have a few things to say about credit: see Simmel, 1907/1978: 479–81.
4 See Tobias, 1994.
5 See Galanoy, 1980: 193.
6 For a dissenting view on this issue, at least as far as money is concerned, see Zelizer, 1994.
7 Personal communication from Gerri Detweiler, former executive director of Bankcard Holders of America.
8 Similarly, in describing the worldwide dominance of American lawyers and legal services, Dezalay (1990: 281) says, 'This globalization is for the most part an Americanization.'

9   If, indeed, the consumer society has become disconnected from the United States, then it might be better thought of in terms of globalization.

10   One author who equates the two defines Americanization as anti-Americanism: 'a catchall for anything of which the speaker morally and emotionally disapproves'. See MacCreary, 1964: 1.

11   In any case, the distinction between high and low culture has come to be viewed as increasingly valueless. See, for example, Pierre Bourdieu, 1984.

6

ENCHANTING A DISENCHANTED WORLD: REVOLUTIONIZING THE MEANS OF CONSUMPTION

This chapter deals with the almost dizzying proliferation of settings[1] that allow, encourage and even compel us to consume so many goods and services. The settings of interest to us here will be termed either the 'new means of consumption' or the 'new cathedrals of consumption'. Whatever we call them, they are, in the main, settings that have come into existence or taken new forms since the close of the Second World War and which, building upon but going beyond earlier settings, have dramatically transformed the nature of consumption. Because of important continuities, it is not always easy to distinguish clearly between new and older means of consumption (Nasaw, 1993; Oldenburg, 1989), but it is the more contemporary versions, singly and collectively, that concern us here.

The following are the major new means of consumption with notable examples and the year in which they began operations:

- Franchises (McDonald's, 1955)
- Shopping malls (the first indoor mall, Edina, Minnesota, 1956)
- Mega-malls (West Edmonton Mall, 1981; Mall of America, 1992)
- Superstores (Toys R Us, 1957)
- Discounters (Target, 1962)
- Home shopping television (Home Shopping Network, 1985)
- Cybermalls (Wal*Mart, 1996)
- Theme parks (Disneyland, 1955)
- Cruise ships (Sunward, 1966)
- Casino-hotels (Flamingo, 1946)
- Eatertainment (Hard Rock Cafe, 1971)

Social Theory and the New Means of Consumption

Three basic and interrelated theoretical perspectives inform this analysis. The first is the approach of Karl Marx and neo-Marxian theory (including the early work of Jean Baudrillard). Marxian and neo-Marxian theory are the origins of the concept 'means of consumption'. In addition, that theory highlights the fact that the success of modern capitalism and the cathedrals of consumption is highly dependent on the control and exploitation of the consumer. The second perspective is Max Weber's work on rationalization, enchantment, and disenchantment. Rationalization helps to transform the cathedrals of consumption into highly efficient selling machines, thereby enhancing their ability to control and exploit consumers. However, rationalization tends to lead to disenchantment and, therefore, to cold, inhuman settings that are increasingly less likely to attract consumers. Weber saw little possibility of enchantment in the modern world, but the neo-Weberian, Colin Campbell, extended Weber's ideas to include the possibility of such enchantment. The work of Rosalind Williams and Michael Miller demonstrates that the early French department stores were *both* highly rationalized and enchanted 'fantasy worlds'. The theory of the relationship among rationalization, enchantment and disenchantment highlights the difficulties faced by the cathedrals of consumption in attracting and keeping large numbers of consumers. This is related to Marxian theory in the sense that in order to be controlled and exploited, consumers must be attracted, and continually return, to the cathedrals. Enchantment and rationalization help to bring large numbers of consumers to these settings, but their attractiveness to consumers is continually threatened by the prospects of disenchantment.

Marxian and Weberian theory are modern perspectives; the third theoretical orientation is postmodern social theory, especially ideas drawn from the later theories of Baudrillard. These ideas of the postmodern theorists are especially helpful in explaining how the new means of consumption overcome the problems associated with disenchantment and attain the reenchantment needed to continue to lure, control, and exploit ever-increasing numbers of consumers. Paradoxically, at least one of the postmodern processes leading to reenchantment ('implosion' into the home) is posing a profound threat to the nature, if not the existence, of most of the new means of consumption. Consistent with the contradictory character of postmodern society, the new means of consumption are both bolstered *and* threatened by postmodern developments.

Marxian Theory and the Means of Consumption

Like most other modern theorists, Marx focused mainly on production – that is, he had a productivist bias. Given the realities that he was dealing with (the early days of the Industrial Revolution and capitalism) a focus on production in general, and the means of production in particular, was sensible. However, in recent years, to the degree that production and consumption can be clearly separated,[2] production has grown increasingly less important (for example, fewer workers are involved in goods production), especially in the United States, whereas consumption has grown in importance. In such a society, it makes sense to shift our focus from the means of production to the means of consumption.

Marx had a great deal to say about consumption, especially in his well-known work on commodities. Much less well known and visible is the fact that Marx (following Adam Smith (1789/1994), as he often did) employed the concept 'means of consumption'.

Marx (1884/1981: 471) defined the *means of production* as 'commodities that possess a form in which they ... enter productive consumption'. The *means of consumption* he defined as 'commodities that possess a form in which they enter individual consumption of the capitalist and working class' (Marx, 1884/1981: 471). Under this heading, Marx differentiates between subsistence and luxury consumption (Smith made a similar distinction). On the one hand are the 'necessary means of consumption', or those 'that enter the consumption of the working class' (Marx, 1884/1981: 479). On the other are the 'luxury means of consumption, which enter the consumption only of the capitalist class, i.e., can be exchanged only for the expenditure of surplus-value, which does not accrue to the workers' (Marx, 1884/1981: 471). Basic foodstuffs would be subsistence means of consumption whereas elegant automobiles would be luxury means of consumption.

There is a logical problem in the way Marx uses the concept of the means of consumption, especially in comparison to the paired notion of means of production. The means of production occupy an intermediate position between workers and products; they are the means that make possible both the production of commodities and the control and exploitation of the workers. In contrast, the way Marx uses the idea, the means of consumption are not means but rather the end products in his model of consumption; they are those things (either subsistence or luxury) that are consumed. In other words, there is *no* distinction in Marx's work between consumer goods and what I term the means of consumption.[3] To put it another way, in his work there is no parallel in the realm of consumption to the mediating and expediting role played by the means of production.

I distinguish the means of consumption from that which is consumed. Fast-food restaurants are different from the hamburgers we eat in them.[4] The means of consumption will be seen as playing the same mediating role in consumption that the means of production play in Marx's theory of production. That is, just as the means of production are those entities that make it possible for the proletariat to produce commodities and to be controlled and exploited as workers, the means of consumption are defined as those things that make it possible for people to acquire goods and services and for the same people to be controlled and exploited as consumers.[5]

The concept of the means of consumption appears, at least in passing, in various other places (Simmel, 1907/1978; Williams, 1982; Zukin, 1991), but most notably in one of Baudrillard's (1970/1998) early works, *The Consumer Society*. At this point in his career Baudrillard was still heavily influenced by Marxian theory, although he was to break with that approach in a few years en route to becoming today's preeminent post-modern social theorist. Baudrillard does not define the concept, but the way he uses it makes it clear that (unlike Marx) he is not conflating the means of consumption with the commodities to be consumed but is following the definition I am using. Baudrillard's paradigm of the means of consumption is the Parisian 'drugstore':

> Any resemblance to an American pharmacy is tucked into one small corner. The rest of this amazing establishment is more like a mini-department store with everything from books to cameras, toys, French and foreign news-papers and magazines, clothing, and a booming takeout business in carved-on-the-spot sandwiches, salads, and soft drinks as well as caviar, pâté de foie gras, and elaborate picnic hampers. Le Drugstore's outdoor café offers what it claims is an 'authentic' American menu. (Rothenberg and Rothenberg, 1993: 38)

The Parisian 'drugstore' is clearly a means of consumption in that it is a social and economic structure that enables consumers to acquire an array of commodities. Baudrillard goes on to talk about an entire community as the 'drugstore writ large'. In this context he describes a community, Parly 2, with its shopping center, swimming pool, clubhouse, and housing developments. The shopping center and at least a version of the kind of community described by Baudrillard (the elite gated community) are examples of the new means of consumption. Other examples discussed by Baudrillard are holiday resorts and airport terminals.[6]

Baudrillard was prescient in writing about the significance of these new means of consumption in the late 1960s. However, he did little with the idea and related phenomena. Furthermore, he erred in focusing on the Parisian drugstore because of its limited impact on the rest of the world. In fact, today that drugstore has been swamped by the importation of the kinds of means of consumption that occupy our attention: fast-food restaurants, chains of all sorts, Euro Disney and so on. Nonetheless, Baudrillard's sense of the means of consumption is the closest in the literature to the way the concept is employed here.

Exploiting and Controlling the Consumer Marx's theory, especially as it relates to the means of production, focuses on the control and exploitation of workers (the proletariat), as discussed previously. In twentieth-century capitalism, the focus shifted increasingly from production to consumption, resulting in a parallel shift from control and exploitation of workers to that of consumers. Consumers could no longer be allowed to decide on their own whether to consume, how much or what to consume, and how much to spend on consumption. Capitalists felt that they had to devote more time, energy, and money in an attempt to influence, if not control, those decisions. This idea is explicit in Baudrillard's early work. He views consumption as 'social labor' and compares its control and exploitation to that of productive labor in the workplace. Capitalism has created a controllable and exploitable 'consuming mass' to complement the control and exploitation of the 'producing mass' (Gane, 1991: 65).

The Marxian theory of the exploitation of workers was clear-cut because all value came from the workers. If they got anything less than everything, they were being exploited (when in fact they received barely enough to subsist).

In what sense can the consumer be said to be exploited? There are many ways to respond to this question. For example, advertisements are designed to lure people into buying things they might not otherwise consume. And it is the consumers who must ultimately pay for the cost of the advertisements as part of the purchase price of goods or services. In fact, as neo-Marxists Paul Baran and Paul Sweezy (1966) showed long ago, capitalists prefer competition on the basis of advertising campaigns (and other sorts of sales competition) to price competition because it enables them to keep prices high and to pass the costs of advertising campaigns on to consumers. However, our focus is not on the way advertisements are used to exploit consumers, but on how the new means of consumption perform a very similar function.

At one level, the new means of consumption are set up to lead people to consume more than they intend and perhaps more than they can afford (Schor, 1998). At another level, the sometimes astronomical cost of constructing and maintaining the cathedrals of consumption leads to high prices that are driven even higher by the desire of those involved in the cathedrals to reap large profits. Credit cards (see Chapter 5) aid the ability of the new means of consumption to exploit consumers by leading them to buy more. Furthermore, credit cards are exploitative in themselves in the sense that people are lured into debt that many find it difficult to extricate themselves from and into paying usurious interest rates on balances that serve to stretch indebtedness out for years, if not decades. Consumers can be said to be exploited by the new means of consumption by being led to buy more than they need, to pay higher prices than need be, and to spend more than they should (Schor, 1998).

It is true that it is far harder to argue that the consumer is exploited than it was for Marx to contend that the proletariat was exploited. The proletariat had no choice. If they wanted to work, they had to sell their labor time to the capitalist in exchange for access to the means of production and ultimately a subsistence wage. In contrast, the consumer appears to have the option of avoiding the new means of consumption and obtaining goods and services in other ways (for example, making commodities themselves or using older means of consumption). However, the fact is that the proliferation of the new means of consumption is making it more difficult and less attractive for consumers to obtain goods and services in other ways. It is increasingly the case that if consumers want to consume, they *must* use ('labor' in) one of the new means of consumption. In a sense, consumers must give the capitalists their 'consumption time' in exchange for access to the means of consumption. Consumers are then able to get goods and services only by placing themselves in a context in which they are likely to buy more, to pay higher prices, and to spend more money than they intend.

In a similar way, consumers are not *forced* to use credit cards. They could pay in cash and avoid many of the problems associated with credit cards. However, in the case of an increasing number of transactions through, for example, cybermalls or home shopping television networks, it is almost impossible to consume without credit cards. Even in the many cases that consumption can be accomplished in other ways, the credit card proves to be an irresistible lure.

So although the analogy between workers and consumers is far from perfect, there is a sense in which both have become 'exploitable masses'. With the proliferation of the new means of consumption, the choices open to consumers are declining. Although they may not be subject to much, if any, overt coercion, consumers are the objects of a variety of softer, more seductive controlling techniques. And such techniques are one of the defining characteristics of a postmodern society. Consumers can still choose venues other than the new means of consumption; they can opt not to pay exorbitant prices and not to buy things that are not absolutely needed; but at the same time we must not forget that enormous sums of money are spent on advertising and on the new means of consumption (among other sales mechanisms) to get people to buy and pay more. On balance, the evidence seems clear that this money is well spent and people often do what is expected of them.

Take the case of the lottery, a new means of consuming gambling that is traceable to Colonial America but which boomed in the 1970s and 1980s as a result of state government efforts to raise money (Chinoy and Babington, 1998a, 1998b). Jackpots have reached astronomical levels and a wide array of new games have proliferated. Outlets that sell lottery tickets tend to be concentrated in poor areas and to target those with lower incomes and education. Heavy players may gamble as much as 10 per cent or more of their annual income on the lottery. A great deal of money is spent in advertising lotteries and luring people into playing for the first time or to continue being regular players. Advertisements are clever and target specific groups such as low-income players who tend to prefer specific types of games such as Keno, the superstitious with the Lucky Numbers game, and the more affluent players with games based on themes, such as 'Star Trek'. Players are often ill-informed about payout percentages and the slim chances of winning. For all of these reasons, and more, it could be argued that the lottery is an exploitative means of consuming gambling.

Nevertheless, the analogy between the exploitation of workers and consumers is far from ideal. However, various neo-Marxists have offered us a different way of looking at the analogy between the capitalist's treatment of workers and consumers. They contend that the real focus in contemporary capitalism is no longer the *exploitation* of workers, but rather their *control* (Braverman, 1974; Edwards, 1979). If control is the central concern as far as contemporary workers are concerned, then that must certainly be the case for consumers. We are on far firmer footing simply arguing that the new means of consumption concentrate on the control of consumers in order to get them to spend as much as possible. This allows us to skirt the bothersome issue of exploitation without losing any of the focus and power of our argument. And we can retain at least a partial theoretical footing in (neo-) Marxian theory.

Weberian Theory and Enchantment, Rationalization, and Disenchantment

Although Max Weber shared Marx's interest in capitalism, he came to see it as just one of a number of developments that were unique to the Occident. Just as Marx believed that capitalism created a number of social advances, Weber noted the positive contributions of the western institutions of interest to him. And like Marx, Weber was deeply concerned with the problems created by these changes. However, whereas Marx was a radical hoping for a revolution that would overturn capitalist society, Weber was much more pessimistic about doing anything about the problems associated with the distinctive set of Occidental institutions.

The key factors in Weber's theorizing are enchantment, rationalization, and disenchantment. His argument is that the modern process of rationalization in the Occident, as exemplified in capitalism and in the bureaucracy, has served to undermine what was once an enchanted (that is, magical, mysterious, mystical) world. Rational systems in general, and the bureaucracy in particular, have no room for enchantment. It is systematically rooted out by rational systems, leaving them largely devoid of magic or mystery ...

Disenchantment Weber derived the notion that as a result of rationalization the western world has grown increasingly disenchanted from Friedrich Schiller (Schneider, 1993: ix). It relates to the displacement of 'magical elements of thought' (Gerth and Mills, 1958: 51). As Schneider (1993: ix) puts it, 'Max Weber saw history as having departed a deeply enchanted past en route to a disenchanted future – a journey that would gradually strip the natural world both of its magical properties and of its capacity for meaning'. Or,

> In the face of the seemingly relentless advance of science and bureaucratic social organization, he believed, enchantment would be hounded further and further from the institutional centers of our culture. Carried to an extreme, this process would turn life into a tale which, whether told by an idiot or not, would certainly signify nothing, having been evacuated of meaning. (Schneider, 1993: xiii)

The theme of disenchantment recurs in many places in Weber's work, but especially in his sociology of that most enchanted of domains: religion.[7] For example, he saw a historical process of rationally and professionally trained (and, therefore, disenchanted) priests gaining ascendancy over magicians who acquired their positions through irrational means and who clearly have a more enchanted view of, and relationship to, the world than priests. Weber (1958: 139) argued that in the modern world, 'One need no longer have recourse to magical means in order to master or implore the spirits, as did the savage, for whom such mysterious powers existed.'

Prophets, who as a group are more enchanted than the priests, receive a personal calling and engage in emotional preaching. They are either the founders, or the renewers, of religion. Weber differentiated between ethical (for example, Muhammed and Christ) and exemplary (for example, Buddha) prophets. Ethical prophets believe that they have received a commission directly from God and they demand obedience from followers as an ethical duty. Exemplary prophets demonstrate the way to salvation to others by way of example. Both types are useful in creating a group of followers, but once they have succeeded in creating such a group, they tend to be replaced by the disenchanted priests who are far better than either type of prophet at the pastoral, day-to-day affairs of managing such a group. In the process, religion begins to lose its enchanted character and comes under the sway of the rationalized church that houses the priests. The priests derive their authority from their position within the church, whereas prophets derive theirs from their service to a sacred (and enchanted) tradition.

Weber also argued that the Protestants, especially the Calvinists, developed an idea system, 'The Protestant Ethic', that helped give birth to the spirit of capitalism. Weber is here working at the level of ideas rather than material structures. Weber depicted a world that is, at least initially, enchanted. The Protestant Ethic sprang from the Calvinist belief in predestination. Believing that whether or not they were saved was preordained, the Calvinists looked for particular signs as a way of telling whether or not they were among the saved. The most important of those signs became economic success. The Calvinists came to work hard, and to reinvest profits in their businesses, to help ensure that they would, in fact, see the signs of their salvation. This was clearly an enchanted world. That is, the Calvinist was making decisions on the basis of mystical ideas ('signs', 'salvation') rather than rational, matter-of-fact principles and procedures.

The capitalist economic system eventually lost all vestiges of enchantment and came to be a highly disenchanted world without room for ideas such as predestination and salvation. In fact, it became inhospitable to the Calvinists, indeed to all religions, because of the tie between religion and enchantment. There was little patience in the rationalized and disenchanted world of capitalism for such enchanted worlds as religion.

Enchantment   Weber's thinking on magicians, prophets, the Protestant Ethic, and charismatic and traditional leaders had a great deal to do with enchantment. However, his thinking on more recent developments, especially in the West, had much more to do with rationalization and disenchantment, enchantment having been largely driven out by the machine-like bureaucracy and rational-legal authority. A formally rational world is a disenchanted world. In a modern context it is not unusual to associate Weber with the imagery of disenchanted and rationalized iron cages, but it is unusual to link him to the idea of enchantment. However, such a connection has been made by Colin Campbell (1989) who has extended Weberian theory, at least as it relates to the Protestant Ethic thesis, in such a way that it is able to encompass the ideas of enchantment, dreams, and fantasies.

In *The Romantic Ethic and the Spirit of Modern Consumerism*, Campbell does not contest Weber's basic argument about the central role of early Calvinism in the rise of capitalism, but merely contends that Weber did not take his analysis far enough. That is, Weber analyzed the Protestant Ethic up to approximately 1700, but it continued to evolve after that point and began to move in a very different direction. Although Campbell pointed out that there was more emotion[8] in early Calvinism than Weber recognized, he argued that later Calvinism became even more accepting of emotion. In other words, there were elements of enchantment in later Calvinism.

Although the early Calvinists required signs of success in order to help them to determine whether they were to be saved, later Calvinists sought evidence of their good taste. Good taste was linked to beauty and beauty to goodness. The Calvinist who demonstrated good taste simultaneously displayed goodness. In other words, pleasure-seeking came to be linked with the ideals of character. An easy mechanism for demonstrating that one had good taste was to show that one was in fashion. The later Calvinists grew 'eager to "follow fashion" and hence to consume "luxury" goods with avidity' (Campbell, 1989: 153).

The later Protestant Ethic led, albeit unintentionally, to the spirit of modern *consumerism*. Defining this spirit was what Campbell called 'autonomous, self-illusory hedonism'. This hedonistic spirit stood in stark contrast to the asceticism of the early Protestants as well as of the spirit of modern capitalism. It also was individualistic and involved illusions, day dreams, and fantasies; in other words, it was a world of enchantment. The key is individual fantasies because, as Campbell pointed out, fantasies can be far more important and rewarding than reality. In fact, he argued that disappointment inevitably occurs when people are able to fulfill their fantasies, especially with a variety of consumer goods and services. Each time they venture forth into the marketplace, people delude themselves into believing that this time it is going to be different; the material reality is going to live up to the fantasy. These fantasies, rather than material realities, are crucial to an understanding of modern consumerism because they can never be fulfilled and are continually generating new 'needs', especially for consumer goods and services.

Although Weber saw the spirit of modern capitalism leading to rationalized, disenchanted capitalism, for Campbell the spirit of modern consumerism leads to romantic, enchanted capitalism. Weber's capitalism is a coldly efficient world virtually devoid of magic, and Campbell's 'romantic capitalism' is a world of dreams and fantasies. Although production is accorded central importance in rational capitalism, it is of secondary importance in romantic capitalism taking the form, for example, of the production of arts and crafts by Bohemians. What is of central importance for romantic capitalism (and for Campbell) is consumption. And, within the realm of consumption, Campbell accorded great importance to fantasies, especially the fantasizing of consumers. However, Campbell focused on the fantasies of individual consumers. I extend Campbell's work by focusing on the enchanted aspects of the new means of consumption. We will see that these are not only increasingly fantastic in themselves, but also are involved in generating fantasies about consumption among consumers.[9] Despite Weber's pessimism, enchantment persists. As Schneider (1993: x) puts it, 'Enchantment ... is part of our normal condition, and far from having fled ... it continues to exist ...'

I draw on both Weber and Campbell in my conceptualization of the cathedrals of consumption as not only rationalized and disenchanted, but also enchanted. Much the same thing could be said of the cathedrals associated with organized religions.

Other Theories of Enchantment, Rationalization, and Disenchantment

Perhaps religious structures seem rather removed from our concrete concern with the enchanted and disenchanted aspects of the new means of consumption. Much closer is work on the major precursors of the new means of consumption, such as the Parisian arcades and the French department store of the mid-1800s.

Walter Benjamin's work, especially what is known as the 'arcades project' (*Passagen-Werk*), is a major resource for thinking about the new means of consumption as being enchanted. This fragmentary, unfinished undertaking focuses on the nineteenth-century Parisian arcades which were seemingly as little grist for the scholarly mill as fast-food restaurants or discount department stores are today. However, Benjamin used the arcades as a lens to gain greater insight into not only the era in which they flourished, but also into the time in which he wrote (roughly 1920–1940). Benjamin's work on the arcades not only serves as a model for this work, but the arcades themselves were forerunners to many of the means of consumption discussed in this book (Buck-Morss, 1989).

One key difference between the two works is that Benjamin was looking back on phenomena (the arcades) that, by the time Benjamin wrote, had lost their central place in the process of consumption in France to later developments like the department store.[10] In contrast, in this work we are examining phenomena that have only recently attained center stage in the world of consumption or, in some cases (for example, cybermalls; see Chapter 7), are only beginning to acquire centrality. However, we should keep in mind that the newer means of consumption, like the arcades and even the department stores that eventually succeeded them, will eventually recede and be replaced by as yet unknown, even newer means of consumption.

The arcades were essentially privately owned covered city streets lined on both sides with shops of various sorts. The streets were closed to vehicular traffic allowing consumers to wander from shop to shop in order to buy or merely window shop. (Fremont Street in downtown Las Vegas has a new canopy that has made it into a kind of arcade except that it is lined more with casinos than shops.) Here is a description of the arcades used by Benjamin himself:

> These arcades, a recent invention of industrial luxury, are glass-roofed, marble-walled passages cut through whole blocks of houses, whose owners have combined in this speculation. On either side of the passages, which draw their light from above, run the most elegant shops, so that an arcade of this kind is a city, indeed, a world in miniature. (Benjamin, 1986: 146–7)

The arcades had their origin in Paris of the late 1700s. While London had broad streets with sidewalks that came to be lined with shops, Paris had narrow streets that lacked sidewalks and therefore could not easily accommodate shoppers. Hence the need in Paris for arcades which provided a public area for strolling and shopping. The first arcade, the Palais Royalem, developed in the 1780s; between 1800 and 1830 Paris saw the creation of seventeen arcades. Additional Parisian arcades were built in subsequent years and the arcade spread to other cities including London, Brussels, Milan (Galleria Vittorio Emanuele II), Berlin (Kaisergalerie), Moscow (GUM), and even Cleveland in the United States. Toward the end of the nineteenth century, the arcade disseminated still further to places like Melbourne, Johannesburg and Singapore.

As a neo-Marxian social theorist, Benjamin was not satisfied with merely describing the arcades as a new social phenomenon. Benjamin is critical of the arcades and what they represent and a critical perspective, while not mainly animated by a Marxian perspective, will also inform this chapter, at least in part. The following excerpt from a 1929 book (*A Walk in Berlin* by Franz Hessel) offers a critical, even nightmarish, view of Berlin's Kaisergalerie which was modeled after the Parisian arcades:

> I cannot enter it without a damp chill coming over me, without the fear that I might never find an exit. I am hardly past the shoeshine and newspaper stands under the lofty arches of the entrance, and I feel a mild confusion. A window promises me dancing daily and that Meyer without whom no party would be complete. But where is the entrance? Next to the ladies' hairdresser there is another display: stamps and those curiously named tools of the collector: adhesive pockets with guaranteed acid-free rubber, a perforation gauge made of celluloid. 'Be sensible! Wear wool!' demands the next window of me ... . I ... almost stumbled over the peep shows, where one poor schoolboy stands, his school bag under his arm, wretched, immersed in the 'scene in the Bedroom.' ...
>
> I linger over ... Knipp-Knapp cufflinks, which are certainly the best, and over the Diana air rifles, truly an honor to the goddess of the hunt. I shrink back before grinning skulls, the fierce liqueur glasses of a white bone cocktail set. The clowning face of a jockey, a handsome wooden nutcracker graces the end of the musical toilet paper holder ... .
>
> The whole center of the arcade is empty. I rush quickly to the exit; I feel ghostly, hidden crowds of people from days gone by, who hug the walls with lustful glances at the tawdry jewelry, the clothing, the pictures ... . At the exit, at the windows of the great travel agency, I breathe more easily; the street, freedom, the present! (cited in Buck-Morss, 1989: 38)

While the goods might be different today, a critic might offer a very similar description of more modern means of consumption such as the department store or the shopping mall. Such a critique might focus on such issues as the difficulty in getting out once one wanders in, the proliferation of useless commodities, and the orgy of consumerism to which today's means of consumption contribute.

Putting it in its broader Marxian context (and picking up on the theme of enchantment), Benjamin sees the arcade as 'the original temple of commodity capitalism' (cited in Buck-Morss, 1989: 83). It was the immediate precursor of other temples for the consumption of commodities – the department store and the international Exposition.[11] (The arcades themselves, of course, had predecessors such as the church – arcades were often shaped like a cross – and Oriental bazaars.) More importantly, they were the precursors of even later means of consumption, the modern temples of commodity capitalism that will concern us here. Also anticipating later developments, the arcades were not just about buying goods. They also offered food, drink, gambling, entertainment in the form of vaudeville and even prostitution.

What were originally confined to the arcades later burst out of those confines and flooded Paris 'where commodity displays achieved even grander, even more pretentious forms' (cited in Buck-Morss, 1989: 83). Benjamin accords an important role here to the architect Baron Georges-Eugene Haussmann, who created in Paris

> the new urban phantasmagoria ... railroad stations, museums, wintergardens, sport palaces, department stores, exhibition halls, boulevards – dwarfed the original arcades and eclipsed them. These once magical 'fairy grottoes' that had spawned phantasmagoria went into eclipse. (cited in Buck-Morss, 1989: 92)

Still later, of course, commodity displays came to inundate the rest of France and much of the developed world.

In focusing on the arcades, Benjamin was examining the debris or residue of the mass culture of the 1800s; these leftovers were the most mundane, the most banal of everyday sites. But he specifically chose such sites because they permitted him to relate an interest in the everyday world with more academic and political concerns.[12] Benjamin believed that the study of such phenomena would permit the 'dialectics of seeing' and lead to 'both metaphysical and political illumination' (cited in Buck-Morss, 1989: 23). And the latter, given Benjamin's Marxist orientation, would lead to historical awakening, social change and perhaps social revolution. In effect, Benjamin sought to do for consumers in the world of consumption, what Marx had hoped to do for the proletariat in the world of production. Involved in this is an implicit recognition by Benjamin of the fact that the essence of capitalism was already beginning to shift from production to consumption. Therefore, if a revolution was to be mounted, it had to be in the world of consumption and the consumer and not, as Marx believed, in the realm of production among the proletariat.

Paralleling Benjamin's work on the arcades, at least in part, this work seeks not only to illuminate the nature of the means of consumption

themselves, as well as the ways in which they interrelate and interpenetrate, but also to elucidate the consumerism (the 'fetishization of commodities') that increasingly goes to the heart of modern society. It is easy
to accept Benjamin's goal of illumination and even of social change,
although we must bear in mind that the modern world has produced
temples of consumption and a cornucopia of consumer goods and
services that would be the envy of the denizens of every other era in
human history. Yet, the means of consumption, as well as the consumerism that they help fuel, have more than their share of problems,
problems we will encounter throughout this book. Thus, at the mini-
mum, one might want to offer changes that retained the best of the
consumer society while coping with some of its worst excesses. One
thing, though, that is almost impossible to accept, in this postmodern era
following the death of communism, is Benjamin's Marxist-inspired hope
for social revolution.

However, Benjamin's major attraction to us in this context is the fact
that he not only sees the arcades as disenchanted, reified structures, but
also as enchanted storehouses of dreams and fantasies. The arcades
and their goods are seen as commodity fetishes, but ones that are used
to evoke dreams, especially the 'collective dream of the commodity
phantasmagoria' (cited in Buck-Morss, 1989. 271). In general, in the
process of commodificaton the 'wish image congeals into fetish' (cited
in Buck-Morss, 1989: 159). These wish images can also be said to pet-
rify or soldify into 'fossils', or in this case, commodities and the structures in which they are sold. More specifically, the arcades are seen as
'"houses without exteriors" ... themselves "just like dreams"' (cited in
Buck-Morss, 1989: 271). The arcades can be seen as having 'housed the
first consumer dream worlds'.[13] And more generally, Benjamin was
interested in the 'mass marketing of dreams within a class system'
(cited in Buck-Morss, 1989: 284).

The idea of a phantasmagoria is crucial to understanding the new
means of consumption as enchanted worlds. On the one hand, it
implies a cornucopia of goods and services that offers the possibility of
satisfying people's wildest fantasies. The dream here, and one that is
played to by most of the new means of consumption, is to be immersed
in a world filled with everything one could ever imagine, with all of
these things there for the taking. It is akin to the childhood dream of
finding oneself in a land in which everything is made of candy and all
of it is within reach.

On the other hand, phantasmagoria also implies a negative side of
enchantment – a nightmare world filled with specters, ghosts and a
profusion of things that seem simultaneously to be within one's grasp
and impossible to obtain. William Leach (1993: 15) describes the turn-
of-the-twentieth century means of consumption as 'the sometimes
dreamlike, sometimes nightmarish world of modern merchandising'.

More contemporaneously, the modern mall, for example, is both a dream world filled with a cornucopia of goods and services, as well as a modern nightmare for most of us since while we might be able to afford to buy a few of those offerings, most of them remain beyond our reach. Of course, this is far from the only nightmare associated with the mall. Another might be one in which we come to the realization that all of our needs and abilities have atrophied because of our single-minded effort to acquire all that the mall has to offer. Thus, just as we are destined to live out some of our dreams within the mall, we are also simultaneously doomed to nightmares involving frustration and failure. The same can be said of our involvement in all of the new means of consumption.

In integrating a concern with disenchanted material structures with enchanted dreams (and nightmares), Benjamin was influenced by the surrealists and their 'fascination with urban phenomena, which they experienced *both* as something *objective* and as something *dreamt'* (cited in Buck-Morss, 1989: 33; italics added). The surrealists questioned the prioritization of material reality by the realists and sought instead to focus on the subconscious, unconscious, irrational and dream-like (Fowlie, 1950). The vantage point of the surrealists also allows us another way of seeing that what are described as dreams can just as easily turn into nightmares. While the surrealists offered an attractive theoretical orientation, and one that is helpful in this chapter as well, Benjamin was critical of them for their lack of a practical interest in awakening people from the reverie that is being created for them by these structures.

This leads us to the point that while dreams are usually thought of in positive terms, they also can be interpreted negatively not only as nightmares, but also in the sense that they tend to lull people into a reverie that blinds them to the material realities that surround them. In other words, they can be conceived of as a kind of 'opiate' of the masses. Williams (1982: 67) uses such notions as 'numbed hypnosis' to describe consumers. Thus, the dreams created by the new means of consumption can be seen as creating a 'false consciousness' among consumers in much the same way that such a consciousness was created among the proletariat in the heyday of producer capitalism. Adrift in a dreamworld of consumption, people are unable to see what is happening to them as well as the realities of the economic system in which they are immersed.

To Marx, false consciousness applied not to individuals, but to a collectivity, especially the proletariat. Because of the nature of their propertyless position within society, the proletariat, unlike the capitalists, had the possibility of overcoming their false consciousness and attaining class consciousness. Among other things, this means coming to understand the way capitalism really operates and using that awakening as a basis to rally people to revolt against the capitalist system. While it is possible to see modern consumers as collectively suffering from false consciousness, it is difficult to see them achieving true consciousness and rising up against our commercial system. This is the case because, if for no other reason, unlike the proletariat, consumers do not have a class basis on which to build.

While Benjamin thinks of the means of consumption as phantasmagoria Rosalind Williams sees them as enchanted 'dream worlds'. She has focused on such things as the use of decor to lure customers to the early French department stores and to 'imbue the store's merchandise with glamour, romance, and therefore consumer appeal' (Williams, 1982: 70–1). The stores were in the business of enchanting and seducing their customers. In these settings, consumers could live out many of their fantasies by either purchasing goods or merely imagining what it would be like to own them. In other words, stores strove mightily to be enchanted worlds.

Although Williams has done relatively little with the rationalized, and therefore disenchanted, characteristics of the early French department stores, that issue gets much more attention in Michael Miller's (1981) study of Bon Marché. The early Bon Marché was a fusion of the emerging rationalized world with more traditional elements of French bourgeois culture; over the years it moved increasingly in the direction of becoming a rationalized, bureaucratized structure, that is, it encountered 'an incessant push towards greater efficiency' (Miller, 1981: 68). Among the rationalized elements of the store were its division into departments; its partitioning of Paris for the purposes of making deliveries; its files and statistics, records and data; its telephone lines, sliding chutes, conveyor belts, and escalators; and its '*blanc*', or great white sale, 'the most organized week of the store' (Miller, 1981: 71).

Taken together, the work of Williams and Miller indicates that the early French department store, like contemporary cathedrals of consumption, was both enchanted and disenchanted. Perhaps the most general conclusion to be drawn from this discussion is that enchantment and disenchantment are not easily distinguished from one another; one does not necessarily preclude the other. There is a reciprocal relationship. Fantasies draw people into the new means of consumption, and those fantasies can be rationalized in order to further draw people in and to reinforce the cage. The cage quality of the new means of consumption can itself be a fantasy – the fantasy of being locked into one of those cages with ready access to all of its goods and services. In fact, Campbell (1989: 227) concluded his work with just such an image: 'Modern individuals inhabit not just an "iron cage" of economic necessity, but a castle of romantic dreams, striving through their conduct to turn the one into the other.'

Marxian theory leads us to see the new means of consumption as oriented to, and based on, the control (and exploitation) of the consumer. Weberian theory points us toward some of the problems involved in being able to control consumers. Enchanted settings would seem to be well-suited to controlling consumers by luring them into a dream-like state so that it is easier to part them from their money. However, in the long run, in order to service and control large numbers of consumers, the cathedrals of consumption are forced to rationalize, and rationalization leads to disenchantment and the decline in the capacity to continue luring consumers or to create the dream-like states needed for hyper-consumption. The cathedrals of consumption, therefore, are faced with a seemingly unresolvable dilemma. However, a third, very contemporary resource – postmodern social theory – suggests a way out of this dilemma.

Postmodern Social Theory and Reenchantment   Postmodern social theory is a recent development in the social sciences (Ritzer, 1997). It is premised on the idea that in various ways we have moved beyond the modern world into a new, postmodern world that is very different socially and culturally from its predecessor. New, postmodern theories and ideas are required in order to analyze this new world.

Both modern social theory and modernity itself were closely tied to the idea of rationality. Theorists (including Marx and Weber) were urged to think rationally about that world, and when they did, they discovered that it was a world that was best characterized as being rational. Although acknowledging the advantages of rationality, they were also highly critical of it on various grounds. Postmodern social theory rejects the idea of rationality and is associated more with the ideas of nonrationality or even irrationality ...

Postmodern theory is of obvious relevance to this work because of its association with consumption and the idea that the postmodern world is defined by consumption (rather than production) (Bauman, 1992). As Eva Illouz (1997: 13) put it, we are dealing with a world 'in which economy has been transmuted into culture and culture into the transient and disposable world of goods'. We have already encountered Baudrillard's contribution to our conceptualization of the means of consumption and this is but a small part of his postmodern approach to consumption.

More important, postmodern thinkers also reject the idea that society is highly rational. Although postmodern society may have some rational elements, it is even more likely to be characterized by 'emotions, feelings, intuition, reflection, speculation personal experience, custom, violence, metaphysics, tradition, cosmology, magic, myth, religious sentiment, and mystical experience' (Rosenau, 1992: 6).

For example, to Baudrillard (1973/1975: 83), symbolic exchange involves 'taking and returning, giving and receiving ... [the] cycle of gifts and countergifts'. Baudrillard (1976/1993) developed his notion of nonrational symbolic exchange as a contrast, and alternative, to the highly rational economic exchange that characterized modern capitalist society. Thus, although economic exchange produces such things as goods and services, as well as profit, symbolic exchange is nonproductive. Economic exchanges tend to be limited to a specific exchange of, for example, goods and services for money, and symbolic exchanges occur continually and without limitation. In societies characterized by symbolic exchange, economic exchanges (considered of preeminent importance in modern societies) tend to be only a small portion of all exchanges.[14] Baudrillard prefers nonrational symbolic exchange and associates it with primitive societies. He uses the idea of nonrational symbolic exchange to criticize modern societies, which are dominated by rational economic exchange. Baudrillard argued that contemporary society was on the verge, or in the midst, of the transition to the postmodern. However, this newly emerging society to him offers powerful barriers to symbolic exchange. Although he develops a postmodern theory, Baudrillard ends up being a critic of both modern and postmodern society.

Two of Baudrillard's specific ideas – implosion and simulations – will play a prominent role in this discussion, as will other ideas closely associated with postmodern social theory such as spectacles, time, and space ... However, we must not forget that the greatest significance of postmodern social theory is its emphasis on enchantment, the lack thereof in the modern world, and the continuing need for it. For Baudrillard, the enchanted world of symbolic exchange continually haunts, and poses a threat to, the modern disenchanted world of economic exchange. There is no possibility of returning to the primitive society dominated by symbolic exchange, but there is the possibility of such exchange reasserting itself. In other words, postmodernists hold out the possibility of the *reenchantment* of the world.

Zygmunt Bauman (1993: 33) accords great centrality to this process of reenchantment:

Postmodernity ... brings 're-enchantment' of the world after the protracted and earnest, though in the end inconclusive, modern struggle to dis-enchant it (or, more exactly, the resistance to dis-enchantment, hardly ever put to sleep, was all along the 'postmodern thorn' in the body of modernity.) The mistrust of human spontaneity, of drives, impulses, and inclinations resistant to prediction and rational justification, has been all but replaced by the mistrust of unemotional, calculating reason. Dignity has been returned to emotions; legitimacy to the 'inexplicable,' nay *irrational* ... [15] the postmodern world is one in which *mystery* is no more a barely tolerated alien awaiting a deportation order ... We learn to live with events and acts that are not only not-yet-explained, but (for all we know about what we will ever know) inexplicable. We learn again to respect ambiguity, to feel regard for human emotions, to appreciate actions without purpose and calculable rewards.

To take a specific example, Baudrillard (1983/1990: 51) argued that 'seduction' offers the possibility of reenchanting our lives. Rather than the complete clarity and visibility associated with modernity, seduction offers 'the play and power of illusion'.

The introduction of the concept of reenchantment allows us to create an expanded model of Weber's theory. Weber offers a theory of the relationship among enchantment, rationalization, and disenchantment. We have seen that some neo-Weberians (Campbell, especially) allow for the possibility of enchantment in the contemporary world, but the postmodernists offer a stronger thesis. Postmodern thinkers such as Baudrillard tend to think of reenchantment as either a possibility within modern society or the basis of a future alternative to modern society and its numbing disenchantment. However, in this work, reenchantment will be viewed as an ongoing and very real development within the contemporary cathedrals of consumption. It constitutes the way out of the dilemma posed by the disenchantment of the world in general and of the means of consumption in particular. In order to continue to attract, control, and exploit consumers, the cathedrals of consumption undergo a continual process of reenchantment. Of course, those efforts at reenchantment may, themselves, be rationalized from the beginning. Even if they are not, with reenchantment the stage is set for the entire process to recur.

Postmodern theory offers us three other perspectives that are crucial to this analysis. First, postmodern theorists tend to see the contemporary world as both exhilarating and threatening. Most of the processes associated with the reenchantment of the cathedrals of consumption can easily be seen as quite exhilarating in reviving and reinvigorating those cathedrals. And many of those same processes are also quite threatening, even to the very existence of those cathedrals.

Second, postmodern theory offers a useful corrective on the idea that the means of consumption control and exploit consumers. Although there is control and exploitation in the sense that people are led to buy and to spend too much, the fact is that people are not, in the main, being coerced into doing so, but are quite eager to behave in these ways ... This is not only true of American consumers; much of the rest of the world seems intent on consuming like Americans. Most consumers do not see themselves as being controlled and exploited and would vehemently reject the idea that this is what is taking place. Whatever the objective realities (if one can even speak of such realities in a postmodern world) of prices paid and quantities purchased, most consumers seem willing to pay the prices and would, if anything, consume even more if they could.

There is an even stronger point to be made about postmodern consumers. Rather than having their consumption orchestrated by people like advertising executives and directors of cathedrals of consumption, it may be that it is consumers who are in control. It is the consumers who demand reenchanted cathedrals of consumption and those demands must be met if their business is to be retained. However, once one setting has been reenchanted, competitors must follow suit or risk the permanent loss of business. The means of consumption are in constant competition with one another to see which one can be most responsive to the demands of consumers for (re-)enchanted settings in which to consume. In fact, it could be argued that consumers are forcing the means of consumption into a reckless and potentially destructive war to see which one can offer the most (re-)enchanted setting. This is nowhere clearer than in Las Vegas today, where old hotels are being torn down and enormously expensive new ones are being constructed with ever more enchanted themes and settings.

Third, modern social theory tends to focus on agents and their intentions. Postmodern social theory, however, seeks to decenter the analysis by abandoning such a focus. This is one of the reasons why this analysis does not focus on consumers as agents, but rather the settings in which consumption occurs. In addition, this postmodern perspective leads us to the view that the processes involved in the reenchantment of the means of consumption are only in part a result of the intentions of the agents operating on behalf of the cathedrals of consumption.

In the end, this is not a work in postmodern theory, or any other theory for that matter. The goal is to gain a greater understanding of the new means of consumption and to that end theoretical tools that work will be employed, whatever their origin.[16] In order to create the theoretical framework for this analysis, I have borrowed the ideas of exploitation, control, rationalization, and disenchantment from modern social theory and the notion of reenchantment from postmodern social theory. This analysis offers what the postmodernists call a 'pastiche' of modern and postmodern ideas in order to analyze the cathedrals of consumption. The latter, of course, are themselves combinations of modern, postmodern, and even premodern elements. Both the subject matter and the theoretical perspective of this analysis stand with one foot in some of social theory's oldest ideas and the other in some of its most contemporary thinking ...

Linking Rationalization to Disenchantment

As we saw above, the process of rationalization leads, by definition, to the disenchantment of the settings in which it occurs. The term clearly implies the loss of a quality – enchantment – that was at one time very important to people. Although we undoubtedly have gained much from the rationalization of society in general, and the means of consumption in particular, we also have lost something of great, if hard to define, value.

Efficient systems have no room for anything smacking of enchantment and systematically seek to root it out of all aspects of their operation. Anything that is magical, mysterious, fantastic, dreamy, and so on is apt to be inefficient. Enchanted systems typically involve highly convoluted means to whatever end is involved. Furthermore, enchanted worlds may well exist without any obvious goals at all. Efficient systems, also by definition, do not permit such meanderings, and designers and implementers will do whatever is necessary to eliminate them. The elimination of meanderings and aimlessness is one of the reasons that rationalized systems were, for Weber, disenchanted systems.

As discussed previously, one major aspect of efficiency is using the customer as an unpaid worker. It is worth noting that all of the mystery associated with an operation is removed when consumers perform it themselves; after all, they know exactly what they did. Mystery is far more likely when others perform such tasks, and consumers are unable to see precisely what they do. What transpires in the closed kitchen of a gourmet restaurant is far more mysterious than the 'cooking' that takes place in the open kitchen of a fast-food restaurant, to say nothing of the tasks consumers perform in such settings.

The same point applies to employees of rationalized systems. Their work is broken down into a series of steps, the best way to perform each step is discovered, and then all workers are taught to perform each step in that way. There is no mystery in any of this for the employee, who more or less unthinkingly follows the dictates of the organization. There is little or no room for any creative problem solving on the job, much less any sense of enchantment.

Compare the efficient and mechanical preparation and consumption of food in the fast-food restaurant to the way food was cooked and eaten in the novel (and later movie) *Like Water for Chocolate*. Food was prepared lovingly over a long period of time:

> On Mama Elena's ranch, sausage making was a real ritual. The day before, they started peeling the garlic, cleaning the chillies, and grinding spices. All the women in the family had to participate ... They gathered around the dining-room table in the afternoon, and between the talking and the joking the time flew by until it started to get dark. (Esquivel, 1992: 10–11)

And the eating of the food had a magical effect on those who participated in the meal:

> The moment they took their first bite of cake, everyone was flooded with a great wave of longing. Even Pedro, usually so proper, was having trouble

holding back his tears. Mama Elena, who hadn't shed a single tear over her husband's death, was sobbing silently. But the weeping was just the first symptom of a strange intoxication – an acute attack of pain and frustration – that seized the guests ... (Esquivel, 1992: 39)

Or,

tasting these chillies in walnut sauce, they all experienced a sensation ... Gertrudis ... immediately recognized the heat in her limbs, the tickling sensation in the center of her body, the naughty thoughts ... Then she left ... All the other guests quickly made their excuses, coming up with one pretext or another, throwing heated looks at each other ... The newlyweds were secretly delighted since this left them free to grab their suitcases and get away as soon as possible. They needed to get to the hotel ...

Everyone else, including the ranch hands, was making mad passionate love, wherever they happened to end up. (Esquivel, 1992: 241–2)

With regard to *calculability*, in the main, enchantment has far more to do with quality than quantity.[17] Magic, fantasies, dreams, and the like relate more to the inherent nature of an experience and the qualitative aspects of that experience, than, for example, to the number of such experiences one has. An emphasis on producing and participating in a large number of experiences tends to diminish the magical quality of each of them. Put another way, it is difficult to imagine the mass production of magic, fantasy, and dreams. Such mass production may be common in the movies, but magic is more difficult, if not impossible, to produce in settings designed to deliver large numbers of goods and services frequently and over great geographic spaces. The mass production of such things is virtually guaranteed to undermine their enchanted qualities. This is a fundamental dilemma facing the new means of consumption. Take, for example, the shows that are put on over and over by the various new means of consumption – the 'Beauty and the Beast' show at Disney World, the sea battle in front of the Treasure Island casino-hotel in Las Vegas, or the night club shows on cruise ships. The fact that they must be performed over and over tends to turn them into highly mechanical performances in which whatever 'magic' they produce stems from the size of the spectacle and the technologies associated with them rather than the quality of the performers and their performances.

In any case, it could be argued that by its very nature fantasy has more to do with the consumer than with the means of consumption. Huxtable (1997a: 61), for example, has defined fantasy as a 'freeing of the mind and the spirit to explore unknown places', which she distinguishes from, for example, 'a handshake from some unconvincingly costumed actors in a totally predictable and humdrum context'. There are inherent limitations on the ability of rationalized settings to create fantasy for people.

No characteristic of rationalization is more inimical to enchantment than *predictability*. Magical, fantastic, or dream-like experiences are almost by definition unpredictable. Nothing would destroy an enchanted experience more easily than having it become predictable.

The Disney theme parks sought to eliminate the unpredictability of the midway at an old-fashioned amusement park such as Coney Island with its milling crowds, disorder, and debris. Instead, Disney World built a setting defined by cleanliness, orderliness, predictability, and – some would say – sterility. Disney has successfully destroyed the old form of enchantment and in its place created a new, highly predictable form of entertainment. As the many fans of Disney World will attest, there is enchantment there, but it is a very different, mass-produced, assembly-line form, consciously fabricated and routinely produced over and over rather than emerging spontaneously from the interaction among visitors, employees, and the park itself.

A similar point could be made about the 'new' Las Vegas. In the 'bad old days' when it was run by the 'mob', it was a much less predictable place and therefore, arguably, a far more enchanted one than it is today under the control of large corporations and their bureaucratic employees. What is true about Disney World and Las Vegas also can be said about fast-food restaurants, cruises, and so on.

Both *control* and the *nonhuman technologies* that produce it tend to be inimical to enchantment. As a general rule, fantasy, magic, and dreams cannot be subjected to external controls; indeed, autonomy is much of what gives them their enchanted quality. Fantastic experiences can go anywhere; anything can happen. Such unpredictability clearly is not possible in a tightly controlled environment. It is possible that tight and total control can be a fantasy, but for many it would be more a nightmare than a dream. Much the same can be said of nonhuman technologies. Such cold, mechanical systems are usually the antithesis of the dream worlds associated with enchantment. Again, it is true that there are fantasies associated with nonhuman technologies, but they too tend to be more nightmarish than dreamlike.

An interesting example of the replacement of human with non-human technology is currently taking place in Las Vegas. Shows in the old casino-hotels used to feature major stars such as Frank Sinatra and Elvis Presley. One could argue that such stars had charisma; they had an enchanted relationship with their fans. Now the emphasis has shifted to huge, tightly choreographed (that is, predictable) extravaganzas without individual stars. For example, the Rio Hotel and Casino features 'ballet dancers who bounce, toes pointed, from bungee cords, hooked into the casino ceiling ... [and] a mechanical dolphin that dives from aloft with a rider playing Lady Godiva' (Binkley, 1997: B1). The focus is on the nonhuman technology (which controls the performers) and not on the individuals performing the acts. The performers in such extravaganzas are easily replaceable; they are interchangeable parts.

The point of this section has been to argue that increasing rationalization is related to, if not inextricably intertwined with, disenchantment. However, there are aspects of rationalization that actually heighten enchantment.

Rationalization as Enchantment

There is no question that although rationalized systems lead in various ways to disenchantment, they paradoxically and simultaneously serve to create their own kinds of enchantment. We should bear in mind that this enchantment varies in terms of time and place. Because these settings are now commonplace to most of the readers of this analysis, few of them (especially fast-food restaurants) are likely to be thought of as enchanting. However, it should be remembered that they still enchant children, as they did us for some time (and, in many cases, may still); it is certainly the case that they enchanted our parents and grandparents; they are found enchanting in other societies to which they are newly exported. It is also worth remembering that there are degrees of enchantment; Disney World and Las Vegas are undoubtedly seen by most as more enchanting than Wal-Mart and the Sears catalog.

Reflect for a moment on the highly rationalized, and therefore presumably disenchanted, setting of Sam's Club and other warehouse stores. What could be more disenchanting than stores built to look like warehouses – comparatively cold, spare, and inelegant? Compare them to the 'dream worlds' of early department stores like Bon Marché. Great effort was made to make the latter warm, well-appointed, and elegant settings that helped inflame the consumer's fantasies – in a word, enchanting. Sam's Club has gone to great lengths in the opposite direction; it seems to have sought to create as rationalized and disenchanted a setting as possible. It comes strikingly close, in the realm of retailing, to Weber's image of the rational cage.

Yet this disenchanted structure produces another kind of fantasy – that of finding oneself set loose in a warehouse piled to the ceiling with goods that, if they are not free, are made out to be great bargains. It is a cold, utilitarian fantasy, but a fantasy nonetheless. As a general rule, disenchanted structures have not eliminated fantasies, but rather replaced older fantasies with more contemporary ones. The new, rationalized fantasies involve getting a lot of things at low prices rather than the fantasies associated with the older department stores that might involve imagining what it would be like to wear elegant clothing or to surround one's self with luxurious home furnishings.

People often marvel at the *efficiency* of rationalized systems; their ability to manage things so effectively can seem quite magical. For example, the ability of Disney World to process so many of us through the park, or to dispose of all the trash we produce is a source of amazement to many people.

As we saw in the example of Sam's Club, rationalized systems also often amaze on the basis of the large *quantity* of things they can deliver at what appears to be such a low cost. The cruise is another good example of this, especially the food that is available in great abundance and with great frequency and the bundling of lots of entertainment into one package: casino, spa, nightclub, visits to islands, and so on. Similarly, the continual expansion of Disney World makes it seem increasingly like a world that offers unlimited possibilities for entertainment.

The *predictability* of the new means of consumption can be astounding. This can range anywhere from amazement that the 'Big Mac' we ate today in New York is identical to the one we ate last week in London and will eat next week in Tokyo to being struck by the fact that today's sea battle at Treasure Island casino is identical to the one we saw on our last trip to Las Vegas.

Perhaps the ultimate in the capacity of the rationalization of the new means of consumption to enchant us comes from their advanced *technologies*. Although at one time enchantment stemmed from human wizards or magicians, it now stems from the wizardry of modern robotic and computerized technology. Ultimately, it is the technology of the modern cruise line, the Las Vegas casino, and Disney World that astounds us, not the humans who happen to work in these settings or the things they do.[18] Our amazement can stem from the technologies themselves or from what they produce. We can, for example, marvel over how McDonald's french fries always look and taste the same. Or we can be impressed by the fact that Wal-Mart's shelves are always so well stocked.

It is interesting that EPCOT Center in Disney World has run into difficulties in recent years, at least in part because its futuristic technologies have grown increasingly dated. It became more difficult for visitors to fantasize about the future in such obviously dated settings. As a result, EPCOT is undergoing a transformation and moving in the direction of becoming more like a conventional theme park ...

Are the contemporary fantasies associated with rational systems as satisfying as those conjured up in the past? This is a complex and highly controversial issue. Clearly, the huge number of people who flock to the new means of consumption find them quite magical. However, it is fair to wonder whether rationally produced enchantment is truly enchanting or whether it as enchanting as the less rational, more human, forms of enchantment that it tends to squeeze out. We might ask whether one of the *irrational* consequences of all of this is that these contemporary fantasies come closer to nightmares than did their predecessors. After all, it is far harder to think of a nightmare associated with an elegant department store than with a warehouse. In any case, it is clear that rationally produced enchantment is deemed insufficient as reflected in the many efforts at reenchantment that are the subject of the following sections.

Spectacle

The reenchantment of the cathedrals of consumption depends on their growing increasingly spectacular (Featherstone, 1991: 103). Spectacle itself is not new; it has been used throughout history to accomplish all sorts of objectives. Fairs, expositions, and the like are early examples of the use of spectacles to sell commodities. In fact, spectacle lay at the base of the success of one of the most important and immediate precursors of the new means of consumption: the department store. For example, of the French department store Bon Marché of the mid-1800s, Miller (1981: 173) said, 'Spectacle and entertainment, on the one hand, the world of consumption, on the other, were now truly indistinguishable.' The early American department stores used color, glass, light, art, shop windows, elegant interiors, seasonal displays, and even Christmas parades in order to create a spectacle (Leach, 1993). Similarly, at the turn of the twentieth century Coney Island relied heavily on the creation of spectacle to attract visitors. Over the years, the bar has been raised progressively, with the result that the display needs to be bigger and bigger in order to work. Furthermore, spectacles are no longer isolated events, spatially and temporally, but are increasingly ubiquitous.

The concept of the spectacle lies at the core of thinking of the French social thinker Guy Debord and his influential work *The Society of the Spectacle* (for more on this, see this volume Chapter 9). Debord (1967/1994: 16) said 'the spectacle is the *chief product* of the present-day society'. Central to the argument of his book, Debord (1967/1994: 16) argues that one of the functions of the spectacle is to obscure and conceal 'the rationality of the system'. I contend that the spectacle is used to overcome the liabilities, especially the disenchantment, associated with highly rationalized systems. Debord has argued that the spectacle associated with commodities is a kind of opiate that obscures the true operation of society (including its rationality). It also serves to conceal the fact that the goods and services purchased are ultimately dissatisfying.

The spectacle is closely linked in Debord's (1967/1994: 26) eyes to consumerism and commodities: 'THE WORLD THE SPECTACLE holds up to view is ... the world of commodity ruling over all lived experience.' Commodities and the spectacles that surround them have come to dominate not only the economy, but also the entire society. As a result, to Marx's alienated production it is necessary to add alienated consumption as a necessity imposed on the masses. That is, consumption is imposed from without and people are unable to express themselves in the process of consumption, or in the goods and services they obtain through it. Ultimately, Debord (1967/1994: 26) sees the emergence of a 'society of the spectacle, where commodity contemplates itself in a world of its own making'. People, as spectators, are not part of these contemporary spectacles; indeed they are alienated from them. People watch them because they are alluring, but the spectacles are put on *for* them; people are not an integral part *of* them.

David Chaney (1993) has done much to clarify the meaning of the spectacle by differentiating between two related but very different cultural orders: the early modern 'spectacular society' and today's 'society of the spectacle'.

In the past, spectacle tended to be an integral part of, and emerged from, everyday life (for example, a county fair). In contrast, in the contemporary society of the spectacle, drama is not an inherent part of everyday life. Rather, we travel to a Disney World where, far from our homes, we participate in various attractions in ways that are largely predetermined by the park's designers and not at all connected to our daily lives.

In addition, in the spectacular society, there were possibilities of excess and at least limited transgression (the 'carnivalesque' – Bakhtin, 1968; Stallybrass and White, 1986). An example might be illicit sexual relations in public. In the society of the spectacle, transgressions are likely to be systematically prevented from occurring by the control over, and close surveillance of, the spectators. Many of the spectacles that concern us have been systematically sanitized by those who create and control them.

Although these differences are important, we must not take them too far. It is impossible to draw absolute distinctions between past and present spectacles, to say nothing of the cathedrals of consumption in which they occur. Although Mardi Gras (and Carnival in Rio de Janeiro) have ancient roots, they continue today and they retain elements of transgression (for example, women showing their bare breasts in response to chants from the crowd). And transgression continues to occur in contemporary cathedrals of consumption, ranging from the mundane such as brawls in the stands of modern athletic stadia to the extraordinary periodic massacres that plague fast-food restaurants.

We should bear in mind that the new means of consumption create spectacles[19] not as ends in themselves but in order to bring in large numbers of people to buy more goods and services.[20] A mall, a casino, or a theme park that is empty, or only half full, not only has a smaller population to sell to but also does not generate the same excitement as a full house. Sparsely populated cathedrals of consumption generate less word of mouth appeal and are apt to fail as a result. People seem to be animated by the presence of large numbers of other people and that animation could be translated into increased sales of goods and services (Thompson et al., 1996).

Creating Spectacles with Simulations

The idea of simulations is so pivotal to understanding the enchanting aspects of the cathedrals of consumption that it must be discussed separately. In fact, if I had to choose only one term to catch the essence of the new means of consumption, as well as their capacity to create enchanting spectacles, it would be *simulations*.

Baudrillard (1983: 4) has argued that we live in 'the age of simulation'. This implies that we have left behind a more genuine, more authentic social world. Examples of simulation proffered by Baudrillard include:

- The primitive people the Tasaday, found in the Philippines. At least as it exists today, the Tasaday is a simulation because the tribe has been 'frozen, cryogenized, sterilized, protected *to death*' (Baudrillard, 1983: 15). It may at one time have been a 'real' primitive group, but today what exists is nothing more than an approximation of what it once was.
- The caves of Lescaux in France. The actual caves have been closed, but an exact replica, a simulation, is now open to the public.
- Disneyland. Baudrillard sees it as 'a perfect model of all the entangled orders of simulation' (Baudrillard, 1983: 23). One of Disney's classic attractions,[21] the simulated submarine ride to which people flocked in order to see simulated undersea life, is a good example. Many more went there than to the more 'genuine' aquarium just down the road (itself, however, a simulation of the not-too-distant sea).

The widespread existence of such simulations, in the world of consumption and elsewhere, contributes enormously to the erosion of the distinction between the real and the imaginary; between the true and the false. Every contemporary structure and event is at best a combination of the real and the imaginary. In fact, to Baudrillard, the true and the real have disappeared in an avalanche of simulations.

Las Vegas casino-hotels have a field day with the line between reality and unreality. The Bellagio, which opened in late 1998, is a simulation of the Italian region of the same name, but it also houses $260 million in original fine art by such masters as Renoir, Cézanne, and

Picasso. At about the same time, the Rio casino-hotel began hosting a six-month exhibit of treasures from Russia's Romanov dynasty. It includes Peter the Great's throne and a Fabergé pen used by Czar Nicholas to abdicate in 1917. These authentic artifacts are housed in a replica of the Russian royal galleries including 'a reproduction neogothic ceiling from high density foam'. King Tut's tomb in the Luxor hotel is called a 'museum' even though everything in it is a reproduction. However, its gift shop sells 'genuine ancient coins, 18th century Egyptian engravings, oil lamps and other artifacts'. Said an art critic, 'The museum had all fakes, and the gift shop had the real thing. It just summed up Las Vegas for me' (Binkley, 1998: B10).

Huxtable (1997a: 64, 65), following Umberto Eco (and Baudrillard), argues that the 'unreal has become the reality ... The real now imitates the imitation.' For example, the clearly simulated and unreal Disney World has become the model not only for Disney's town of Celebration, but many other communities throughout the United States. Seaside, Florida, and Kentlands, Maryland, are two examples of popular communities that have tried to emulate the ersatz small-town America that is championed by Disney World. Specifically, Huxtable (1997a: 3) has emphasized the growing importance of fake, synthetic, artificial, simulated architecture: 'Real architecture has little place in the unreal America.'[22]

Our environment has come to be dominated by entertainment and to emulate the theme park. Huxtable's (1997b: 1) architectural model of this is the casino, New York, New York, and more generally Las Vegas: 'the real fake reaches its apogee in places like Las Vegas ... The outrageously fake fake has developed its own indigenous style and life style to become a real place ... This is the real, real fake at the highest, loudest and most authentically inauthentic level of illusion and invention.' Huxtable (1997b: 40) has argued that visitors seem to find things such as the artificial rainforest, volcanos, and rock formations in Las Vegas far more impressive than the real thing. In fact, a spokesperson for the industry goes so far as to make the case *against* reality: 'You get a very artificial appearance with real rock.'

All of our environments are becoming increasingly spurious; Las Vegas is simply the extreme that defines the entire genre of simulated environments, especially those characterized by 'unreal' architecture. This is of great relevance because many of the new means of consumption are architectural spaces. In fact, Huxtable has examined several of the new means of consumption from this perspective. Among other settings scrutinized by Huxtable are Colonial Williamsburg (created in the 1920s, a forerunner and another model for Disney World and other settings), Disneyland as faux Americana ('expertly engineered, standardized mediocrity, endlessly, shamelessly consumerized, a giant shill operation with a Mickey Mouse facade'; Huxtable, 1997a: 50), Edmonton

Mall, with among other things its replica of Columbus's *Santa Maria* ('fantasy run amok'; Huxtable, 1997a: 101), and so on.

Not only are the new means of consumption simulations, but often so are the people who work within them and the interactions that take place between employees and visitors. The most blatant examples of simulated 'people' are the employees who dress up in a variety of costumes. McDonald's Ronald McDonald is obviously a simulated clown. The same is true of the characters – Mickey Mouse, Pluto, Snow White – that one encounters wandering the grounds of Disney World. Then there are the sports mascots such as the San Diego Chicken and the Baltimore Orioles' Bird.

Far more important, however, is the fact that most of the people we encounter in the new means of consumption are simulations, even if they are not wearing costumes. The entertainment director of the cruise ship, the blackjack dealer at a Las Vegas casino, the ticket taker at Disney World, the host on Home Shopping Network (HSN), the counterperson at McDonald's, and the cashier at Wal-Mart are all playing well defined roles. Their employing organizations have developed a series of guidelines about how they are supposed to look, speak, behave, and so forth. The result is that these positions can be filled by a wide range of individuals. There is little or no room for creativity or individuality. It could be argued that the blackjack dealer and the counterperson are simulations – they are fakes.

As a result of the same dynamic, the interaction that takes place between visitor and employee in a new means of consumption has a simulated character. For example, instead of 'real' human interaction with servers in fast-food restaurants, with clerks in shopping malls and superstores, with telemarketers, and so on, we can think of these as simulated interactions. Employees follow scripts (Leidner, 1993), and customers counter with recipe responses (that is, those routine responses they have developed over time to deal with such scripted behavior) (Schutz, 1932/1967), with the result that authentic interaction rarely, if ever, takes place. In fact, so many of our interactions in these settings (and out) are simulated, and we become so accustomed to them, that we lose a sense of 'real' interaction. In the end, all we have are the simulated interactions. In fact, the entire distinction between the simulated and the real is lost; simulated interaction is the reality.

Nowhere is this type of simulated interaction more obvious, or more inevitable than in our dealings with hosts of home shopping television programs. A typical 'interaction' on the part of one of those hosts: 'Thank you so, so, so much for calling in today ... We took a risk and brought out some new items. You responded with an outpouring of support – and we love you for it' (Waldman, 1995: 10). Did they really take a risk? Do they really love every member of their audience? All of this taking place in the medium that best exemplifies simulation: television!

Creating Spectacles through Implosion

The term *implosion* refers to the disintegration or disappearance of boundaries so that formerly differentiated entities collapse in on each other. The explosive growth in the new means of consumption has led to a series of such implosions.[23] There has been a kind of chain reaction: the collapse of one set of boundaries leads to the breakdown of a number of other frontiers. Boundaries between the cathedrals of consumption have eroded and, in some cases, all but disappeared. Borders between the means of consumption and other aspects of the social world similarly have been breached. In this way, we have witnessed the disappearance of many distinctions to which people had grown accustomed. The result is a re-enchanted world of consumption seemingly without borders or limits.

These imploded worlds represent a kind of spectacle that draws consumers into them and leads them to consume. For example, only a few decades ago people had to trek from one locale to another for various goods and services; now they can find that variety in a single mall. And it was not that many years ago that if one wanted to gamble, one went to Las Vegas, but if one wanted to visit a theme park one went to Orlando or Anaheim. Now one can go to the MGM Grand or Circus Circus in Las Vegas, for example, and find both a casino and a theme park on the hotel's grounds. The local Wal-Mart, or corner service station, might well encompass a satellite fast-food restaurant. REI in Seattle not only offers mountain climbing shoes but even a 'mountain' to practice on.

It is often the case that the conscious motiviation behind implosion has not been to create a spectacle. Entrepreneurs may be motivated by a variety of reasons such as economies resulting from having two or more means of consumption within one setting, the desire to offer consumers the conveniences associated with such imploded locales, and so on. Whether or not the motivation behind implosion is the creation of spectacle, the fact is that spectacle often results.

As with many other ideas in the previous discussion and this one, the idea of implosion, at least as it is used in this context, is derived from postmodern social theory, most notably the work of Jean Baudrillard. Baudrillard (1983: 57) defines implosion as the contraction of one phenomenon into another; the collapse of traditional poles into one another. To Baudrillard, all things are capable of dissolving not only into each other, but also into a single huge undifferentiated mass (a sort of 'black hole'). As an example outside of the cathedrals of consumption, contemporary television talk shows are dissolving into life and life is dissolving into talk shows. Consider the well-known case of a Jenny Jones talk show in which a gay admirer, Scott Amedure, expressed a homosexual interest in, and hugged, a straight male, Jonathan Schmitz, on the air. Schmitz (who expected to encounter a female admirer on the show) later killed Amedure (and was sentenced to 25–50 years in prison for it) in a case in which reality and television culture clearly imploded into one another.

We can get at this phenomenon in another way by distinguishing between differentiation and dedifferentiation. The modern world can be said to have been characterized by *differentiation* – that is, the creation of more new and different things. Throughout the industrial revolution more and more things were invented, created, produced, and distributed widely. This wide variety of products led to a parallel differentiation in the settings in which they could be consumed. Modernity, then, was characterized by highly differentiated and rigidly separated means of consumption: the butcher shop sold meat, the baker bread, the greengrocer fruits and vegetables, and so on.

Although such differentiation has not completely disappeared, post-modernists argue that today's world is increasingly characterized by dedifferentiation (Waters, 1996): a growing inability to differentiate among things and among places. They all are coming to interpenetrate, all imploding into one another. This is nowhere clearer than in the contemporary world of consumption in general and in the relationship among and between the new means of consumption in particular. The separate shops of the butcher, baker, and greengrocer have all but disappeared into the supermarket that has imploded into the supercenter into which a department store has also imploded. This dedifferentiation is spectacular and serves to draw consumers to these dedifferentiated entities.

Creating Spectacles through the Manipulation of Time and Space

The issues of time and space have received a great deal of attention from both modern and postmodern social theorists (Friedland and Boden, 1994; Lash and Urry, 1994). Among the modernists, best-known for his work on these issues is Anthony Giddens (1989); his entire theory concerns the analysis of institutions across time and space. To Giddens, the primordial human condition involves face-to-face interaction, in which others are present at the same time and in the same place. However, in the contemporary world, social relations and social systems extend in time and space, so we increasingly relate to others who are physically absent and more and more distant. Such distancing in time and space is facilitated by new forms of communication and transportation.

Such distancing has certainly taken place in several of the new means of consumption, especially the dematerialized ones based on the telephone, television, and the computer. In such cases, there is no face-to-face interaction, and those who communicate with the consumer can be quite distant physically. In fact, the consumer rarely has any idea, or cares, where such people are. In some cases, they may be distant in time as well. Information on a cybermall web site may have been loaded long before the consumer visits, and infomercials may have been taped for later broadcast. Giddens has argued that because of such distancing, place becomes increasingly 'phantasmagoric'. This is in line with the new means of consumption as being dreamlike, fantastic, and spectacular.

Also relevant is David Harvey's work on time–space compression. Harvey (1989: 284) believes that the compression of time and space characteristic of modernity has accelerated in the postmodern era, leading to 'an intensive phase of time–space compression'. While Harvey tends to have a negative view of this process as 'disorienting' and 'disruptive', the point being made is simply that the new means of consumption have tended to compress time and space. Indeed, it is their ability to do so that has helped make them so phantasmagoric, so spectacular. That ability, that spectacle, has enhanced their capacity to sell goods and services. If consumers stopped to think about it, they would be stunned by the fact that goods once available half a world away (say, French brie or Russian vodka) can now be purchased in local shops. They would be astounded by the fact that products that once took days or weeks to obtain can now be procured overnight, in hours, or in some cases even almost instantaneously (for example, by downloading over the Internet).

The notion of the compression of time and space has much in common with the idea of implosion, at least as it applies to time and space. In order to compress time and space, the barriers between various dimensions of time and space must be eroded. Indeed, another way of saying that time and space have been compressed is to say the differences within each have imploded. There is more to implosion than simply time and space compression, but the latter have certainly experienced implosion.

It is worth noting that space is not nearly as amenable to implosion as time. Time creates no barriers to those who seek to use it differently. Differences between day and night, one season or another, or even the past, present, and future (including past, present, and future incomes) can be overcome in efforts to sell more things to more people. Space, by definition, presents obstinate physical hurdles to those who want to use it in new and different ways. Most of these obstacles are not insurmountable, but they do tend to impede the revolutionary use of space more than they do that of time. In spite of the barriers, there have been enormous changes in the spatial characteristics associated with consumption. The spatial boundaries in and around consumption are imploding at an accelerating rate. In so doing, they create spectacles that, although not always intentionally manufactured by those in charge of the means of consumption, do serve to heighten consumption.

Time and space are being used to create spectacles. In terms of time, the speed with which we can obtain things in the new means of consumption often seems spectacular to the consumer. Examples include our ability to obtain a meal within seconds or minutes at a fast-food restaurant, or to obtain a book from Borders overnight. Many of the new means of consumption use a loss of a sense of time as a way to create a spectacle. For example, there are the 24-hour a day operations at Las Vegas, or better, on-line, casinos; the tendency to lose track of time on cruise ships, and the zombie-like behavior of consumers at shopping malls. Space is used to create spectacles in various ways, including the creation of a sense of infinite space (cybermalls and home shopping television), the sense that means of consumption are everywhere one turns (McDonald's and other franchises), and the sense of enormous space (superstores, Las Vegas casinos, cruise ships).

Disenchanted Enchantment: Where are we Headed?

Although some see signs of a waning of the consumer society (Gabriel and Lang, 1995), and others argue for the need for such a trend (Schor, 1998), there is no evidence in this analysis of any such decline. There appears to be a major expansion of consumerism under way in the United States and many other parts of the world. As long as the current economic boom continues in the United States (and many other nations with advanced economies), consumerism will continue to expand.

The same is even more true of the cathedrals of consumption. Virtually all of the specific means discussed here will continue to expand as will the means of consumption in general. The new means of consumption are enchanted, and they are in various ways quite spectacular, but above all they are highly effective selling machines. As effective as they are, through the process of 'creative destruction' (Schumpeter, 1950: 81–6) today's means of consumption will eventually be supplanted by even newer means that are infinitely more enchanted, spectacular, and effective as selling machines. Just as the Sands in Las Vegas succumbed to New York, New York, the latter will eventually be replaced. The future will bring with it unimagined palaces of consumption filled to capacity with a cornucopia of goods and services. And they will be incredibly effective selling machines that will bring with them an even further escalation of the consumerism that already is such a dominant reality in the contemporary world.

It is difficult to anticipate anything other than the continued growth of consumption and expansion of the cathedrals that service consumers, but there are some self-destructive trends that may threaten this expansion. The postmodern processes of reenchantment have generally been depicted throughout these pages as the salvation of the new means of consumption in the sense that they have allowed them to overcome the problems associated with disenchantment and to be attractive to ever-larger numbers of consumers. However, the implosion of the means of consumption into the home threatens the existence of many other means of consumption. Just as movie theaters were threatened by the arrival of television and later the VCR and video rentals, contemporary shopping malls, chain stores, super-stores and so on are endangered by the increasing ability to shop at home through home shopping television, cybermalls and shops, and the ubiquitous mail order catalogs. The latter are likely to grow in the coming years and other mechanisms for shopping at home are apt to come into existence. All of this is likely to come at the expense of some of the contemporary cathedrals of consumption. In fact, the latter have already been changing, becoming reenchanted, in response to this threat.

The point is that implosion, like most everything else about postmodernity, is both an opportunity and a danger. Some cathedrals of consumption have become reenchanted as a result of implosion, and others (such as cybermalls) have been made possible by it. However, still others are endangered by it and may well disappear. The increase in consumption shows no signs of ebbing, let alone disappearing. People will need to get what they want somewhere. The landscape formed by the cathedrals of consumption is constantly changing, but though it may encompass a different set of settings, it will still be filled with cathedrals ...

Another self-destructive aspect of the cathedrals of consumption is the ever-escalating need for spectacle. No matter how astonishing, consumers grow accustomed to extravaganzas. In order to attract their attention, let alone their business, the next spectacle must be even more spectacular than the last. Also contributing to this escalation is the competition among the cathedrals of consumption, each trying to put on an extravaganza that is more astonishing than that of its competitors. Of course, most of the costs are passed on to the consumers. More problematic is the need to keep coming up with extravaganzas that are innovative and spectacular enough to satisfy increasingly bored consumers.

At the same time, many of the spectacles discussed have little to do with the intentional actions of those who lead today's cathedrals. Various unforeseeable developments in the future will impel the cathedrals in the direction of being increasingly spectacular. For example, technological advances of various types will undoubtedly create innumerable possibilities for spectacle unimaginable today. Unforeseen implosions of various types will have a similar effect. Spectacles will also derive from further compression of time and space, as well as from as yet undreamt of uses of both.

Wary of grand narratives in this era of postmodern social theory, one must be ever-attuned to the possibility of developments that might disrupt or even derail the seemingly inevitable development of the means of consumption. For example, we could, I suppose, come to the collective realization that true happiness does not await us in the cathedrals and their goods and services. We could look elsewhere for satisfaction – family, work, the noncommodified realms of nature. Or the consumer could, perhaps even unwittingly, lure the means of consumption into disaster through unsupportable expansion or incur a level of indebtedness that could help to bring the economy down.[24]

However, the alternatives to consumption all seem like retrogressions into a past that is not likely to be resuscitated. As far as the economy may plunge in the midst of the deepest of recessions or depressions, it will recover and the consumer, as well as the means of consumption needed to help generate and satisfy the needs of the consumer, are likely to enjoy a rebirth that will make them even more central than they are today. Those who worry about consumer society, consumerism, the cathedrals of consumption, and the increasingly dizzying array of commodities have genuine concerns and many battles to fight, but the most immediate issue is how to live a more meaningful life within a society increasingly defined by consumption.

Notes

This chapter is derived from various places in *Enchanting a Disenchanted World: Revolutionizing the Means of Consumption*. Thousand Oaks, CA: Pine Forge Press, 1999. The discussion of the relevance of Walter Benjamin's work to the cathedrals of consumption is published here for the first time.

1   Thus, the focus is on structures and *not* on consumers as agents.

2   It is increasingly difficult to separate them. In many of the new means of consumption consumers produce their own consumption. For example, by pouring their own drinks or making their own salad, consumers are helping to produce their own meals.

3   Smith (1789/1994: 938) does not make this error, labeling what Marx calls the means of consumption 'consumable commodities'. Marx, like Smith, is really dealing with consumer goods and not with the kinds of structures that are discussed in this book as the means of consumption.

4   However, there is a sense in which we 'consume' means of consumption such as the fast-food restaurant.

5   As the reader will see, I will waffle a bit on whether the consumer is, like the worker, exploited.

6   Baudrillard also discusses the credit card, which is an important example of what can be termed 'facilitating means'.

7   It appears also in his writings on law. Weber (1921/1968: 895) argues, 'Inevitably, the notion must expand that the law is a rational technical apparatus ... and devoid of all sacredness of content.' In other words, law grows increasingly disenchanted.

8   This is so at least in the form of being emotional about not showing emotion.

9   Of course, they are successful to varying degrees. Some consumers may find a cathedral of consumption quite enchanting, whereas others will fail to see its enchanting qualitites. Most, of course, will stand somewhere in between.

10   Another key difference is that, unlike Benjamin, I am not for some collective unconscious that communicates to me through things and over time.

11   Following through on a religious theme, Benjamin (1986: 151) sees world exhibitions as 'the sites of pilgrimages to the commodity fetish'.

12   It is such an epistemological view that informs this work on the similarly mundane new means of consumption.

13   While Benjamin's thinking is very relevant to this work, one of the places I part company with him is over his belief that it is politically useful to study the past because a collective unconscious connects it with the present and communicates across generations.

14   Clammer (1997) offers a powerful critique of Baudrillard by demonstrating the continued importance of the gift, and thereby symbolic exchange, in contemporary Japan.

15   The reader might want to think of other aspects of the American society from this point of view. For example, this helps us understand the popularity of the television show and movie 'The X-Files'.

16   Illouz (1997: 17) does much the same thing.

17   As we will see, great spaces, large sizes, and the like can have, or be made to appear to have, a magical character.

18   This can be traced to the first Ferris Wheel at the 1893 Chicago Exposition, and perhaps even before that. But whatever its origins, we are amazed by the new technologies.

19   Although we often talk in this chapter as if the cathedrals of consumption act, it is clearly the case that it is those people who design, control, and work in them who take the actions. We must be wary of reifying the new means of consumption.

20   On the importance of crowds to consumption, see Clammer, 1997.

21   Unfortunately, for lovers of simulations, it has recently been closed, but there are many others to choose from at a Disney theme park.

22   Unlike Baudrillard, Huxtable (1997a: 3) does have a sense of the real as, for example, 'an architecture integrated into life and use'.

23   Like much else to do with the cathedrals of consumption, implosions are not new, although they have accelerated in recent years. For example, a century and a half ago the department store was created as a result of the implosion of boundaries separating a wide range of specialty shops.

24   These are what Baudrillard (1983) calls 'fatal strategies'.

7

ENSNARED IN THE E-NET: THE FUTURE BELONGS TO THE IMMATERIAL MEANS OF CONSUMPTION

There was a time in the not-too-distant past that consumption was almost completely dominated by a series of material realities. Embodied consumers walked or took conveyances of one sort or another to one of a wide variety of 'brick and mortar' shops where they paid 'flesh-and-blood' cashiers hard cash in exchange for which they received one or more of the innumerable available commodities. Although there were many other possibilities, especially the consumption of immaterial services as opposed to material commodities, this was the norm. However, as in many other areas of the economy, consumption is in the midst of a revolutionary change.

The newly emerging model is that of visiting a series of e-tailers via the Internet[1], paying with a credit card number, and buying books or downloading pictures, news, and the like. The most popular e-tailers at the moment, in descending order, are divisions of such brick and mortar businesses as Sears and J.C. Penney, CDNow (owned by Bertelsmann) and the embattled Amazon.com. The hot new development as I write is in the ability to buy and download music with high-quality sound. As a result, the recording industry is an uproar since the market for (material) compact disks is in jeopardy. Instead of buying CDs manufactured by the record companies, people have the capacity to download music at little or no cost directly from sites maintained by the musicians themselves. A seemingly fully nonmaterial process of consumption is beginning to replace its fully material (or, nearly so) forerunner.

Of course, most consumption today, and in the foreseeable future, involves some combination of material and dematerialized realities – going to the mall, buying a commodity, but paying with a credit card; shopping on line, ordering and receiving (often the next day) a book from Amazon.com delivered by Federal Express. Many of the material aspects of consumption are with us for some time to come and others will be with us forever, but the unmistakable trend is in the direction of the dematerialization of many aspects of the consumption process. Given the pace of change at the millennium it is almost impossible to anticipate what consumption will look like in 50 or 100 years, but it seems safe to guess that it will be far more immaterial than consumption today.

We can divide consumption into (at least) four dialectically related elements – the subject (consumer), the object (the commodity), the consumption process and the sites of consumption (Ritzer et al, 2001). This chapter will focus on the latter, as well as the means that facilitate their use by consumers, but there are obvious implications for the other elements of consumption. The objective here is to compare the dematerialized consumption sites[2] (and facilitating means) to their more material counterparts. We will see that the former have some striking advantages over the latter and pose a serious threat to the continued existence of many of them, at least in their present form. In the process, the dematerialized sites and their facilitators are serving to further ratchet up the already escalating level of hyperconsumption.

It should be clear that there is no definite dividing line between material and dematerialized sites of consumption (and facilitators). Rather, there is a continuum with the highly material consumption sites on one end and the highly dematerialized sites on the other. Thus, all sites of consumption (and facilitating means) combine elements of materiality and immateriality.

Before getting to a discussion of the more immaterial consumption sites, we need to clarify what we mean when we say they are 'dematerialized'.[3] In a sense, of course, consumption in cyberspace involves material structures like modems, the hard disks and circuit boards in RAM where electronic impulses are stored, as well as the computers in the hands of both buyers and sellers. However, cybertransactions and the sites through which they are conducted involve a series of dematerialized electronic impulses. While there is some materiality here, it is of a very different order from the materiality of traditional consumption processes and sites of consumption. Thus, the electronic impulses emanating from a cybermall are a far cry from the bricks and mortar of a shopping mall or a superstore. Furthermore, consumers deal with representations of cybermalls rather than the more material realities of traditional shopping malls. While hard drives, circuit boards and modems are closer to such material realities, consumption does not take place in them, but rather in the exchange of electronic impulses between the consumer's computer and the website of the seller; between the representations of the cybermall and the representations of the consumers (especially their credit card numbers).

Whatever the nature and degree of materiality of the new consumption sites, the consumer operating in cyberspace tends to view the process in general, and the sites of consumption in particular, as quite immaterial. The consumer can no longer locate the site of consumption in physical space. Furthermore, the site can be conjured up at any time or at any place consumers can gain access to a computer. Where they are, where the 'mall' is, where the goods are kept – none of this matters any longer. We would be hard pressed to say exactly where the transaction takes place.

Thus, the immateriality of the dematerialized sites of consumption is partly due to real differences between them and their material counterparts and partly a result of differences in perception on the part of consumers.

Whether perceptual or real, the differences between dematerialized and more material consumption sites have quite real material consequences. Not the least of these is the fact that people can consume more without ever leaving home. We will encounter other real consequences later in this chapter.

Just as the sites of consumption on the Internet are dematerialized, so too are other elements of consumption. The objects of consumption are less material (music over the Internet versus CDs), as is the entire circuit of activities involved in the consumption process. Consumers, too, are dematerialized, reduced to a series of numbers and letters transmitted in cyberspace – credit card number, password, and so on ...

The pace of change is so rapid that many of the new means of consumption are already being threatened by other, even newer, dematerialized means of consumption such as home shopping television (born in 1985) and especially cybercommerce of all types (made possible by the coming of the Internet in 1988, but exploding as I write these words). These combine a dematerialized form with the capacity to produce – and to a far greater extent – the phantasmagoria and dream worlds described above. Their greater immateriality (both perceptual and real) gives them enormous advantages over the material means of consumption both in terms of what they are able to do and the effect they are able to create. As a result, they pose a profound threat to several of the more material new means of consumption, especially shopping malls, megamalls and superstores.

Why venture out of the house, into one's car, onto the thruways, into those cavernous parking lots and those enormous and tiring consumption sites when one can obtain as much, and in many cases even more, from the comfort of one's sofa or seat in front of the computer? For example, Amazon.com's million-plus list of books is far larger than the stock in the largest of Border's and Barnes and Noble's book superstores. Instead of all of those physical acts required to get to and from the superstore, consumption can be accomplished with a few keystrokes. Many other new (and old) material means of consumption face a similar struggle in the future in luring customers out of their homes. Why fly to a Las Vegas casino-hotel, when one can play the slots and other games of chance on line? Why go to the racetrack when one can bet on the races over the Internet? Why go to a 'men's club' when one can view a private 'lap dance' on one's own computer screen?

More importantly, these new dematerialized sites of consumption, especially those associated with the Internet, have a far greater potential to produce phantasmagoria or dream worlds than their more material predecessors. In Chapter 6 of this volume I focus on various processes that serve to make the new means of consumption more spectacular, enchanting, dream-like, phantasmagoric. The fact is that, at least potentially, the dematerialized means of consumption have a far greater capacity to use these processes in order to create a fantasy world of great lure to consumers. In other words, greater immateriality is not only an advantage in itself, but also one that can be used to create still further advantages for dematerialized means of consumption.

For example, as we saw in the previous chapter, one of the ways that the new means of consumption create spectacles is through the implosion of once separate means of consumption into one setting – the Mall of America that is both a mall and an amusement park; the cruise ship encompassing a mall, a casino, and so on. Yet, because they are material structures, there are limits to what can be imploded into a mall or a cruise ship. People need to be able to physically navigate a mall or the deck of a cruise ship. If, in order to encompass more means of consumption, they grow too big, people will not be able to work their way through them. For example, it was found that if hypermarkets grew too large, customers, especially older ones, would be turned off by the need to walk so far to get a quart of milk.

There are no such limits in cyberspace. Cyberspace can be as big as the imaginations of those who create and view its various components. Of course, as cybersites and cyberspace grow larger, it does get harder and harder to get around, but this is where search engines and other technologies come in and do the work for the consumer. A more specific example of such a technology is a 'shop bot'; it roams through various e-tailers looking for a specific item. Thus, there is no need for consumers to switch from Amazon.com to BarnesandNoble.com in search of a specific book, the shop bot will do it for them. Consumers may get irritated by delays and problems finding what they want as the components of the Internet grow more numerous and diverse, but few of them will be winded by the process.

Many of the means of consumption, new and old, are collapsing into the Internet in one way or another. The incredible spectacle is that with a flick of a mouse button one can switch from shopping at the cybermall to gambling at the cybercasino to a virtual tour of Disney World.

As we have seen, another way in which the new means of consumption make themselves spectacular is through the creation of simulations more incredible than reality. Thus, the Las Vegas Strip encompasses a series of casino-hotels that are incredible simulations, including New York, New York, Bellagio, Venetian, Luxor, Excalibur, and Paris.

But, again as physical structures, casino-hotels must make do with the limitations imposed by their materiality. Thus, for example, New York, New York's attractions are not to scale and they are jumbled together indiscriminately. Furthermore, from the outside one never loses sight of the fact that one is looking at a simulation and inside one never loses the sense that one is in a casino-hotel. That is, one never 'really' feels that one is in New York.

Cybersites are by definition simulations. Furthermore, because they do not have the limitations of physical sites, they are freer to create simulations that are more spectacular and even in some senses truer to reality. Thus, a to-scale model of New York could, at least theoretically, be built in cyberspace. Once we have greater band width and the wedding of virtual reality and cyberspace, we will see even greater ability to place people in simulated worlds that closely approximate reality. They may even be more real than real; hyperreal. The point is that because they are not restricted physically, cybersites have a much greater potential to use simulations in order to create far more fantastic worlds than are possible in Las Vegas or the Mall of America.

Time and space are also manipulated in order to create spectacles in the new means of consumption. Las Vegas hotels freely juxtapose time periods. The Luxor of ancient Egypt stands next to Excalibur (the England of King Arthur) which stands adjacent to a mid twentieth-century New York, New York. Furthermore, the interiors of casino-hotels are designed so that gamblers have no idea what time it is. This is accomplished by, for example, allowing no clocks or windows in casinos. Space is manipulated by, for example, creating huge spaces designed to awe consumers. The Mall of America is large enough to encompass both a shopping mall and an amusement park. The Luxor has the world's largest atrium; one that can hold nine Boeing 747 airplanes. As impressive as these are, they pale in comparison to what can potentially be created in cyberspace where there literally are no limits on what can done with time and space. The entire universe and the entire expanse of time is at the disposal of the means of consumption that exist in cyberspace.

The means of consumption in cyberspace have enormous advantages over the more material means of consumption. There is no limit to the goods and services they can offer and they can be, at least potentially, infinitely more fantastic and spectacular. Another enormous advantage is that cybersites have the capacity to be far more McDonaldized than material means of consumption. (There are, of course, many more specific advantages such as the fact that cybersites and their links are capable of providing the consumer with much more information and the consumer has a far greater ability to engage in comparison shopping on the Internet.) In fact, such sites represent something approaching the ultimate in McDonaldization. They are highly efficient since virtually the entire process of consumption is handled in ways that have been carefully calculated to be the most expeditious way of getting from initial contact to final delivery. One can sense the dead hand of Frederick W. Taylor and his efficiency experts in every transaction with an e-tailer. The operation of the cyber-sites is totally predictable in that the computerized system handles every transaction in the same prescribed way. They are highly calcul-able in that costs and prices can be minimized and speed of handling and delivery maximized. And they represent the ultimate in the sub-stitution of nonhuman for human technology since humans are totally eliminated from the process (except for the customers placing orders) and far more control can be exercised over nonhuman than human technologies. The ultimate goal of any McDonaldized system, from this point of view, is the elimination of human beings from the process and this has been all but totally accomplished in cybercommerce (among the limited number of exceptions is the need for people to make or receive phone calls in case of problems).

Of course, as with all McDonaldized systems, there is the problem of the irrationality of rationality. For example, cybersites are dehuman-ized and dehumanizing worlds in which satisfaction from human action and interaction is all but impossible. They are part of what Knorr-Cetina (1997, 2001) calls the 'post-social world' where people interact more with nonhuman entities than with other human beings. In spite of such irrationalities, cybersites are growing in importance and popularity in a society increasingly accustomed to McDonaldized systems and their advantages and in search of ever-more McDonaldized ways of doing things.

A material means like a McDonaldized chain has rationalized the consumption process to a high degree, but it pales in comparison to what can be done in Internet commerce:

- Instead of getting to, through and home from the chain store, there is no need to leave the house at all. Thus one can visit the Gap web-site rather than one of its stores.
- Instead of dealing with scripted, robot-like workers, there is no need to deal with people at all. Put off by having to deal with the human robots at McDonald's, many are willing, even eager, to embrace the absence of humans in cyberspace.
- In a Gap outlet one must face the vagaries of dealing with human employees. No matter how scripted, the human employee can never be as controlled as the completely automated process in cyberspace.
- While the pair of Gap jeans is the same from one shop to another, conventional shoppers risk visiting a shop that is out of the style or size they want. However, the Gap website is far more likely to have whatever size or style one desires.

- While one may quickly get one's jeans at a Gap store, there are still vagaries associated with the time needed to get there and the time waiting because the clerks or cashiers may be busy. The rapidity with which one can order jeans from the website is far more predictable.

Given all of this, the term 'McDonaldization' now begins to appear quite quaint tied as it is to one of the material 'new' means of consumption that in terms of degree of rationalization pales in comparison to what can be accomplished on the Internet. Earlier, I argued that McDonald's may disappear and we may eventually need a term other than McDonaldization to describe the contemporary manifestations of the rationalization process. While McDonald's is alive and well, it appears that the incredible emergence of cybersites is making it necessary already to begin thinking of a new term to describe that process. I will reserve that for another time, but the need to do so is increasingly clear.

In any case it is now clear that McDonald's was a creature of the post-Second World War revolution in the United States that involved increasing affluence, suburbanization and the dramatic growth of the American highway system and interstate system of roads. It was a material structure (of course, it also has taken on great symbolic [immaterial] importance; it is a sign fraught with great meaning) that filled the material needs of Americans moving to those very material suburban communities and houses and driving their automobiles on those roads. In the 1990s and into the new millennium we have witnessed another revolution, but this one is taking place not on the highways and roads but in cyberspace. McDonald's was the paradigm of the revolution of the 1950s; it is certainly not the paradigm of the more recent revolution (although it helped set the stage for it). Its material existence on the roadside and the fact that its main business is material (and perishable) food products makes it ill-suited to the Internet. Maybe we will some day have the technology to ship hamburgers over the Internet, but it is hard for me to envision.

In any case, we need a new paradigm for this new revolution. At first, it seemed that Amazon.com was that new paradigm; a thought buttressed by the fact that *Time* (1999) magazine named its founder, Jeff Bezos, 1999 'person of the year'. It certainly played a key role in the early development of cybercommerce. However, Amazon.com, while it remains in business, has suffered much the same fate as other e-tail innovators and, in any case, it deals in largely material products (eg. books). A better paradigm is one that involves a totally immaterial process, at least from the perspective of the consumer, and the ones that suggest themselves are emusic.com or musicmaker.com. Through these addresses, consumers are able to purchase, download, and listen to music. (While it takes a variety of material forms, from consumers' perspective it only becomes material when it is downloaded onto a disk.) No entrepreneur has emerged as yet to control this dematerialized form of commerce, but when one does it may well be the McDonald's of its era and the new paradigm of the rationalization process. With its emergence, McDonald's and even Amazon.com will take their places as yet other precursors in the ongoing process of rationalization.

One can envision an ever-accelerating process of 'creative destruction' where new material means of consumption no more than a few decades old fall victim to the wrecking ball because they cannot compete with their even newer dematerialized counterparts. They will fail because they cannot offer as much, they cannot be as phantasmagoric, and they cannot be nearly as rationalized. Such failures will certainly occur (just as in professional sports perfectly good athletics stadia – really means for consuming sporting attractions – are being torn down after a few decades to be replaced by newer, state-of-the-art facilities), but even more likely is the fact that many other material means of consumption that exist only on the drawing boards or in some venture capitalist's fantasy world will never be built because of the move toward more dematerialized means.

Thus, newer and more sophisticated dematerialized means of consumption will progressively replace old and even new material means of consumption. Does this mean that eventually we will see the disappearance of most, or even all, material means of consumption as more and more of us do more of our consumption over the Internet (or through home shopping television)? An unqualifiedly positive answer to that question would be in the realm of science fiction; there will continue to be a role for the material means of consumption in the foreseeable future. Presumably, no matter how sophisticated the home-based technology becomes, no matter how far we have progressed into post-social society, at least some people will still want to get out of the house, if for no other reason than to have social relations with other people (those who accompany them on consumption jaunts, those they deal with when they consume things, the crowds in the consumption site). Further, it seems likely that no matter how incredible sites on the Internet become, there will still be spectacles that can only be created in the material means of consumption. People will be willing to put up with the comparative lack of McDonaldization in order to experience these kinds of things. Finally, many people will want to have hands-on relationships with the things they buy and for as far as one can see into the future this can only be had in the material world. I am conscious as I write these things that they are likely to seem naive in a few years when far more sophisticated computer technology gives characteristics and capabilities to Internet sites that cannot possibly be matched in the real world. Future generations may look at the ruins of the Las Vegas

Strip or the Mall of America and wonder why they were created or why anyone would have ever considered leaving their computers for such quaint and unappealing consumption settings in such remote places as the Nevada desert and the 'wilds' of (and in summer, mosquito-infested) Minnesota.

Paradoxically, it is perhaps immateriality that may save at least some of the newer (and even older) material means of consumption. That is, people go to these sites in order to connect with the sites themselves, the crowds and other individuals. A feeling is derived from being in those settings and with those people that cannot be obtained through the Internet and the television set. It is this 'feeling' rather than the material realities and offerings that may be the salvation of the material means of consumption. Unfortunately for them, the trend in the newer means of consumption is *away* from providing the kinds of feelings that could be their salvation. As pointed out above, the new means of consumption have grown increasingly McDonaldized. One result of that process is that instead of highly personal relationships with a waitress, short-order cook or bartender, customers are likely to either have to 'do it themselves' as more and more work is passed on to the consumer, or to interact with people who mindlessly follow scripts rather than interacting with customers in a personalized way. Such McDonaldized interaction is unlikely, to put it mildly, to create the kinds of feelings needed to lure people away from their computer screens. Of course, there are still those who accompany one on visits to sites of consumption or the crowds to be found in them.

Similarly, while simulated spectacles at material means of consumption may draw people for an initial visit or two, are simulated worlds going to provide the feeling needed to compete with the dematerialized means of consumption? In fact, scripted interaction is one form of simulation and it seems unlikely that endless repetition of the 'Have a Nice Day' script is going to be a great lure to many consumers. Similarly, how often will people be drawn to the fakery of the New York, New York casino-hotel in Las Vegas or one of the fake tropical islands operated by the cruise lines? If the choice is only between the simulations available on the Internet and those available in the new material means of consumption, why choose those that one has to venture outside in order to enjoy? Why choose the inferior simulation in a material means of consumption, when one can find a far superior one (at least in the future) on the Internet? It appears as if there is a contradiction between what the new means of consumption need to do in order to make themselves spectacular and what they need to do to compete with the dematerialized means of consumption. Simulations may make for spectacle, but they are not likely to create the feelings of awe at the sight of some natural wonder or the feelings of connection derived from relating to others at the mall or in a casino that will draw people away from their computer screens. In the face of the rise of the dematerialized means of consumption, material consumption sites may be guaranteeing their own destruction by moving away from the nonmaterial rewards that they are peculiarly able to offer.

As pointed out earlier, while it may sometimes have seemed as if a clear dividing line is being drawn between material and dematerialized means of consumption, the fact is that we are really describing a continuum with highly material means (the cruise ship) on one end and highly immaterial means (e-tailer) at the other end. In fact, all means of consumption combine materiality and immateriality in varying degrees.[4] On the one hand, by offering a spectacle, the highly material mega-mall seeks to create a feeling among those who shop there, a feeling that they will want to repeat by returning over and over. On the other, a visit to the cybermall will often end with the delivery by Federal Express of a quite material commodity. We should not ignore the nonmaterial aspects of material means of consumption, nor the material elements of dematerialized means.

The growing immateriality of the means of consumption is matched by the dematerialization of the facilitating means; those things that facilitate the use of the means of consumption. While material highways facilitate the use of McDonald's, the dematerialized Internet facilitates the use of Amazon.com. Perhaps the most important facilitating means in the past was cold, hard cash. Not too long ago it was nearly impossible to shop at the mall or gamble in the casino without cash. However, today cash is being progressively replaced in many consumption settings by credit cards, debit cards, and other more contemporary facilitating means (see Chapter 5 in this volume). In a sense, a credit or debit card is at least as material a reality as paper money or coins. However, it is not really the card itself that is important,[5] but rather the numbers that identify it. This is clearest when credit (and other) cards are used to facilitate the use of consumption sites on the Internet (and on home shopping television). The physical card is of no use here; one merely needs the numbers. While transmitting these numbers may lead to the delivery of some material goods, in other cases it can lead to totally immaterial transactions such as debits to your credit account being translated into numbers of shares on your brokerage account (shares rarely physically change hands these days) or a number of plays on a cyber-slot machine. Consumption in the age of the Internet will often be nothing more than one set of numbers being translated into another set of numbers.

The dematerialization of the means of consumption and the facilitating means is not only an important change in itself, but perhaps more important for what it augers for the future of consumption in general. Because dematerialized means and facilitators are quicker and easier to use than their material counterparts (Slater, 1997: 195), we are likely to see an enormous increase in what already can only be described as hyperconsumption. The immateriality of Internet consumption sites eliminates virtually all temporal and spatial barriers to consumption. One can shop any hour of the day or night, every day of the year. And it is of no consequence where the site is physically located; all physical locations are the same on the Internet. This obviously permits much more consumption than is the case in more material means of consumption where one is limited by the times when malls and shops are not open, or by the need to travel great distances to get to them. Also contributing to hyperconsumption is the fact that a far greater number and variety of things are available in cyberspace than in any material site, even one as large as the Mall of America.

The dematerialization of the means of consumption has also contributed to hyperconsumption by breaking down the barriers between home and consumption. Indeed, as I argue in *Enchanting a Disenchanted World* (1999), the home can now be seen as a consumption site. With a few exceptions (the Sears catalog, the traveling salesman, the telemarketer), people in the past had to leave their homes physically, and sometimes travel great distances, to shop. Now, of course, there is far less need to leave home and soon, if not already, it will be possible to buy everything one needs from the comfort of one's home. A good example is a cyberservice like Peapod that does supermarket shopping for consumers. Still in their infancy, such services will get better at what they do, more widespread (they are only in limited geographic regions at the moment), and more diverse (Canedy, 1999). However, the key point from the perspective of this discussion is that people can consume more, engage in hyperconsumption, because no more time and energy is lost leaving home and traveling to consumption sites.

Just as people can now shop at home, the growth of dematerialized means of consumption now allows them to shop while at work. Since increasing numbers of people will be working in front of computer consoles, it will be very easy for them to switch from a work-related application to something like Peapod where they can order the week's grocery needs. Of course, supervisors and surveillance systems will be on the lookout for such violations, but they will be hard to catch and to eliminate. Again, the key point is that this opens up more time and opportunity for consumption and therefore is another contributor to hyperconsumption.

More generally, with portable computers, one can consume anywhere – in the car, en route to Europe by plane, at the beach, even at the top of Mount Everest.

Also contributing to accelerating hyperconsumption is the dematerialization of the facilitating means. In the past, consumption was limited because people were restricted to cash on hand or in the bank. One could get loans or credit, but it was a cumbersome process requiring many quite material steps. With credit cards, often several of them, and high and expandable credit limits, the consumer is free to spend all available funds *and* then, in effect, by running up credit card debt, to spend income that will not be earned until well into the future. Even maximum limits are often fictions since as the consumer approaches those limits, they are automatically raised by the credit card firms (or, more accurately, their computers programmed to do so). Thus, credit cards serve to greatly expand the amount of money that can be spent on consumption.

The immateriality of credit cards, or more accurately the numbers associated with them (credit 'limit', balance, etc.), makes it easier for people to spend money and consume. Since people find it easier to spend using credit cards, as well as similar instruments such as debit cards, it is clear why they contribute to hyperconsumption. They give people access to far more money, money that people find easier to part with (at least until the overdue and delinquent notices begin arriving).

Another aspect of credit card expenditures that contributes to hyperconsumption is the fact that people find it far harder to keep track of how much they are spending when they use credit cards than when they use a shrinking wad of cash or a diminishing checkbook balance. People spend more because they have no ready indicator that they are spending more. As a result, many people are surprised at the size of their credit card bills at the end of the billing cycle.

Another half-hidden aspect of credit cards deserves attention. In a sense, the credit card companies are in the business of creating money. They do not print material currency or mint even more material coins, but rather create non-material credit limits. However, it is just as easy, in fact increasingly easier, to spend those credit limits than cash. By creating money in this way, the credit card companies have greatly increased the amount available to people for consumption. And, they have not only done this in the United States, but throughout the world. Thus, the credit card companies are independent global entities, part of Appadurai's (1990) finanscape. As such, they are funding and stimulating the worldwide trend toward hyperconsumption. There is no legal limit in the United States on how much credit the credit card companies can create, and this is certainly true throughout the world since the credit card companies operate transnationally and are not subject to the controls of any particular nation.

Of course, this is also true of all of the consumption sites in cyberspace. They are beyond the control of any given nation as reflected by the periodic uproar over the consumption of pornography over the Internet. However, the broader problem from the point of view of this chapter is that there is no way of controlling the devices and mechanisms put into place by cyberspace-based consumption sites in order to induce and increase hyperconsumption. It often appears that every new development in cyberspace is just another excuse to create new venues for advertisers. Clearly, the non-material means of consumption and facilitating means are impossible to control and this is a serious problem if one considers accelerating hyperconsumption to be a threat and a danger.

Debit cards contribute to hyperconsumption in a slightly different way. In common with credit cards, debit card expenditures are less real, more immaterial than cash expenditures. However, there is no escalating credit limit here; one is bound by the balance in one's account, although the banks have sought to loosen consumers up by offering them overdraft protection that allows them to go beyond the balance in their debit card (and checking) accounts. While not the contributor to hyperconsumption that credit cards are, debit cards play their role by making it difficult for the consumer to know how much they have spent and how much they have left to spend. Again, people spend more in this ambiguous situation, at least in comparison to those who are faced with a declining stash of cash.

Of course, many other dematerialized and easily accessible credit instruments have been created to foster hyperconsumption. For example, many checking accounts have convenient lines of credit associated with them so consumers can easily spend beyond the balance in their accounts. Electronic funds transfers allow, as the name suggests, funds to automatically be transferred into (for example, automatic deposits of pay checks) and out of (automatic bill payment) people's accounts. Through things like automatic check deposit, funds get into accounts faster and can therefore be spent faster. More generally, the speed with which money is used has accelerated greatly and greater speed permits more consumption.

It could be argued that it is the immateriality of these new credit instruments, especially the credit card, that has made possible the current explosion of consumption. To continue to facilitate the insatiable need of the economic system for ever-increased consumption we can expect to see the expansion of the use of current credit instruments and the creation of newer, more immaterial, faster and even more seductive ones.

Virtually all of the discussion to this point has focused on the means of consumption and facilitating means. What of the other key elements of consumption – the consumer, the commodity and the consumption process?

The consumer ceases to be an embodied figure in dealings with the dematerialized means of consumption. Rather, the consumer as subject is reduced to such abstractions as a credit card number and/or a password. The proprietors of cybermalls (themselves nameless, faceless, and formless) deal with similarly disembodied consumers; ones they have no need of ever seeing or ever knowing more about than a credit card number, an e-mail address, and maybe a snail mail address.

The consumers do physically need to enter some selections and some needed numbers, but for their part the proprietors can computerize the entire operation from that point on. Orders are filled, acknowledgments made, billing completed, and in the case of dematerialized products, orders delivered with no human intervention. All of this is quite alienating from the point of view of the human consumer, but it is perhaps the ultimate in rationality from the perspective of the cybermall's proprietor. The disembodiment of both consumer and merchant is a natural extension, and perhaps the ultimate expression, of the dehumanization inherent in progressive rationalization.

Material commodities will be handled through cybercommerce and they constitute a natural limit on its dematerialization. However, the forte of cybercommerce will be the delivery on non-material goods and services such as digital newspapers, books, medical diagnoses, legal advice, and the like. In fact, this capacity will lead merchants to transform more and more goods and services into digital forms that can be delivered over the computer. Of course, there are limits to this – digital shoes or condoms will not do people much good. However, within those outer limits we will see the increasing dematerialization of things consumed over the Internet.

And, of course, the increasing dematerialization of consumer sites, facilitating means, consumers and consumer goods, means that the process of consumption will grow increasingly dematerialized.

One of my preferred ways of thinking about the modern world in general, and the new means of consumption in particular, is as Weberian iron cages. How does such an image fare in an era in which dematerialized means of consumption are steadily replacing the material means of consumption that lend themselves better to such an image? In one sense, the idea that there is no escape, the image works quite well. In fact, in the age of dematerialized means of consumption, it is far harder to escape than when consumption was dominated by material means. With consumption now worming its way into the home and into the workplace, it is harder and harder to find a safe haven from consumption and the means needed for it. Thus, from the point of view of escape, the new dematerialized means of consumption are far stronger iron cages.

However, such an imagery is awkward when thinking about the dematerialized means of consumption. After all, Weber's paradigm was the quite material bureaucracy and mine was the similarly material fast-food restaurant.[6] We clearly need a better metaphor for the greatly controlling, but more nonmaterial character, of the dematerialized new means of consumption and the world of hyperconsumption that they are playing such a large role in creating. We could think of them as 'e-nets' – electronic networks that ensnare us in invisible, but no less difficult to escape, nets.

In what sense are we increasingly enmeshed in these e-nets? After all, we are free not to buy computers, not to subscribe to Internet providers, not to enter the Internet, and not to enter an e-tailer's site, let alone actually buy anything. While all of these things are true, it is the case that more of us will be doing these things more of the time. We will be drawn by their increasing popularity, their rationality and the magic that is associated with journeys through cyberspace.

Once in cyberspace and visiting the wide range of consumption sites, we will find it hard to leave. We are likely to behave like the 'mall zombies' one finds in shopping malls (Kowinski, 1985), or the gamblers who find it impossible tear themselves away from the slot machines or gaming tables. However, there will be a huge difference. Unlike traditional malls and casinos, the cybermalls and cybercasinos are in our homes, our offices and on vacation with us. As a result, many of us are destined, some would say doomed, to be far more ensnared in these e-nets than we were ever imprisoned in the iron cages of the material means of consumption like the mall and the casino.

Clearly, a 'brave new world' of consumption is being put in place as I write. It will be a world of unprecedented plenty, but it will also be a world of ever-escalating hyperconsumption. Can we truly find happiness wandering in cyberspace in search of the latest product or service? Can the world handle the heightened ecological threats posed by such hyperconsumption? Can we live with the growing gap between the haves able to freely explore cybercommerce and the have-nots largely excluded from it and its rewards (and costs)? Few are asking such questions in their rush to lose themselves in the joys of consumption in cyberspace.

Notes

The material in this chapter is published here for the first time. It is based on a paper presented at the conference 'Sociality/Materiality: the Status of the Object in Social Science', Brunel University, Uxbridge, England, 9–11 September 1999.

1   This chapter was written before the decline experienced by many e-tailers in 2000. Stock prices had gotten far ahead of business realities. The pioneering e-tailers took the risks and made the innovations that established firms will learn from and build upon. I retain the view that for the reasons outlined in this chapter, in the long-run e-tail will become an increasingly important presence and competitor to 'bricks and mortar' business which, themselves, will develop much more of a presence online.

2   Slater (1997: 193–5) has discussed other aspects of the dematerialization of consumption, including the increasing importance of nonmaterial goods (e.g. services), the greater immaterial aspects of material goods (increasing importance of their design and advertising), the increasing immateriality of the mediation of goods (we encounter them in the form of representations in ads), and the increasingly nonmaterial nature of production and labor (e.g. knowledge, science).

3   I would like to thank Doug Goodman for his help in clarifying this issue.

4   The same point is to be made about the facilitating means to be discussed below.

5   Of course, in the case of money, it is not the bill or coin that is important, but the implicit backing of the government.

6   However, it is true that we were both thinking about the nonmaterial processes of rationalization and McDonaldization.

8

GLOBALIZATION THEORY: LESSONS FROM THE EXPORTATION OF McDONALDIZATION AND THE NEW MEANS OF CONSUMPTION

Recent dramatic increases in the transnational flows of capital, people, goods, information, and culture have transformed the world. The consequences of these far-reaching economic, political, demographic, and cultural changes have elicited increasing political and civic interest in globalization – as evidenced in 1999 in the mass protests against the World Trade Organization in Seattle and in the Spring of 2000 against the World Bank and International Monetary Fund in Washington, DC. Globalization theory, which seeks to construct theoretical models to address these realities, emerged both from the social changes that it seeks to explain and internal developments in social theory, most notably as a reaction to earlier perspectives such as modernization theory and its western bias (although some globalization theorists, for example, Galtung, 1997; Giddens, 1990; Hall, 1997, retain this bias). It is not surprising, therefore, that globalization theory has emerged as one of the most widely discussed and hotly debated perspectives in contemporary social theory.

Given the vast expanse of globalization theory, it would be impossible in a single chapter to address the full range of perspectives that it encompasses (for a sampling, see Lechner and Boli, 2000). Nevertheless, although globalization theorists differ on a number of issues, they focus primarily upon the world as a whole and devote most of their attention to global processes that transcend or operate more or less autonomously from individual societies or nations. Theories of globalization can be classified on the basis of their emphasis on cultural, economic, political and/or institutional factors, on the one hand, and whether they stress homogeneity or heterogeneity, on the other.

At the extremes, the globalization of culture can lead either to a trend toward common codes and practices (homogeneity) or to a situation in which many cultures interact to create a kind of pastiche or a blend leading to a variety of hybrids (heterogeneity). The trend toward homogeneity is often associated with cultural imperialism (see below). There are many varieties of cultural imperialism, including associating it with American culture (Smith, 1990), the West (Giddens, 1990), or core countries (Hannerz, 1990). Robertson (2001), although he doesn't use the term, seems to be describing a series of hybrids when he talks about the interpenetration of the universal and the particular, as well as in his discussion of the 'glocal'. Garcia Canclini (1995), Pieterse (1995), and others talk specifically about hybrids; Featherstone and Lash (1995), Abu-Lughod (1997), and Friedman (1994) describe a world characterized by a cultural pastiche. The pastiche may include a 'global culture' (the world of jet setters and of international board rooms) that becomes yet another component of world culture.

Theorists who emphasize economic factors tend to focus on homogeneity (Harvey, 1989; Piore and Sabel, 1984; Wallerstein, 1974). They generally see globalization as the spread of the market economy throughout the world. In a recent, more specific example, Chase-Dunn et al. (2000) have focused on the globalization of trade. While those who focus on economic issues tend to emphasize homogeneity, most acknowledge that some differentiation (heterogeneity) exists at the margins of the global economy. Other forms of heterogeneity involve, for example, the commodification of local cultures and the existence of flexible specialization that permits the tailoring of many products to the needs of various local specifications.

A political/institutional orientation, too, either emphasizes homogeneity or heterogeneity. Meyer et al. (1997), for example, focus on the nation-state, more specifically, the existence of worldwide models of the state and the emergence of isomorphic forms of governance. Keohane and Nye (1989) focus on the global influence of a multiplicity of institutions. Hobsbawm (1997) and Appadurai (1996) see transnational institutions and organizations greatly diminishing the power of both the nation-state and other, more local social structures to make a difference in people's lives. This is the phenomenon that Barber (1995) has termed 'McWorld', the antithesis of which is 'Jihad' – localized, ethnic, and reactionary political forces (including 'rogue states') that involve an intensification of nationalism and lead to greater heterogeneity (Barber, 1995; also Appadurai, 1996).

Given the great scope of globalization theory, and the rate at which the literature is growing, we will not be able to address it in anything approaching its entirety in this chapter. To make this discussion manageable we will focus on a recent statement by one of its foremost practitioners, Roland Robertson (2001). Robertson is associated with the cultural approach to globalization, and while he reaffirms that position in this chapter, he also seeks to deal with the significance of economic and political/institutional factors. In this context he seeks to identify and discuss the key problems in globalization theory. Here we will examine several of Robertson's ideas from the point of view of related processes that Ritzer (1998, 2000; Alfino et al., 1998; Smart, 1999) has termed 'McDonaldization' and the emergence of the 'new means of consumption' (Ritzer, 1999). This will allow us to analyze some of the strengths and weaknesses of globalization theory, at least as Robertson presents it.

While an important development, globalization theory is often presented as a series of broad generalizations that are not embedded in specific details of the social world. One of the things that the study of McDonaldization and the new means of consumption allows us to do is to examine some of the premises and assertions of globalization theory within the context of a specific set of developments about which much is known. It allows us to 'test', at least in a very rough sense, some of the basic tenets of globalization theory. We will see that while globalization theory has much to offer to our understanding of McDonaldization and the new means of consumption, the specifics of these processes make it clear that some of globalization theory's basic tenets need to be both tempered and made far more specific.

McDonaldization and the New Means of Consumption

Before proceeding to a discussion of the relationship between globalization, McDonaldization and the new means of consumption, we need a brief introduction to the latter two (to parallel the brief sketch of globalization theory offered above) in order to orient the ensuing discussion.

McDonaldization This is the process by which the principles of the highly successful and revolutionary fast-food restaurant are coming to dominate more and more sectors of American society and an increasing number of other societies throughout the world. The principles of the process are *efficiency, calculability, predictability*, and *control*, particularly through the *substitution of nonhuman for human technology*; also associated with McDonaldization are the seemingly inevitable *irrationalities of rationality*. The basic concept, as well as its fundamental dimensions, is derived from the German social theorist Max Weber's (1921/1968) work on formal rationality. Weber contended that the modern western world was characterized by an increasing tendency towards the predominance of formally rational systems. Thus, the process of McDonaldization obviously predates the establishment and proliferation of McDonald's restaurants (Weber, 1927/1981). However, the McDonald's franchise system and the principles upon which it has so successfully spread throughout the world represent the exemplar (as was the bureaucracy in Weber's model) of the contemporary development of rationalization. While the fast-food restaurant is the paradigm of this process, the process of McDonaldization has by now affected most, if not all, social structures and institutions in the United States, and has penetrated most nations (at least those that are reasonably developed economically) in the world. Thus, the term McDonaldization is not restricted to the fast-food industry or to the United States. Rather, it refers to a wide-ranging and far-reaching, but distinctive, process of social change.

The McDonaldization model has been applied well beyond the fast-food restaurant and even everyday consumption to such disparate phenomena as higher education ('McUniversity') (Parker and Jary, 1995), vegetarianism (Tester, 1999), theme parks (Bryman, 1995, 1999a; Ritzer and Liska, 1998), southern folk art (Fine, 1999) and politics (Beilharz, 1999; Turner, 1999). (Bryman (1999b) has even recently proposed a process of 'Disneyization' as a complement to McDonaldization.) McDonaldization is a broad social development. Even the processes surrounding birth and death increasingly conform to its principles (see Ritzer, 2000: Chapter 8).

Of course, not all systems are equally McDonaldized; McDonaldization is a matter of degree, with some settings having been more McDonaldized than others. However, few contemporary social settings or institutions have been able to escape its influence altogether.

The relevance of the McDonaldization thesis to issues of globalization should be apparent, for, both implicitly and explicitly, it asserts that social systems in contemporary society are becoming increasingly McDonaldized and, more important, that the basic principles of efficiency, calculability, predictability, and control through the substitution of nonhuman for human technology that undergird it have been exported from the United States to much of the rest of the world. To the extent that these principles have been adopted and become defining features of institutions in other nations, they can be said to be undergoing the process of McDonaldization.

It is worth noting that when they have addressed the McDonaldization thesis and related ideas, some globalization theorists (for example, Robertson, 2001), especially those committed to the idea of heterogeneity, have tended to be critical of McDonaldization's focus on processes emanating from the United States and for its emphasis on its homogenizing impact on much of the rest of the world. Instead, they focus on diversity, the multi-directionality of global flows and the existence of global processes that are relatively autonomous of specific nation-states. While all of these processes exist and are significant, it is also the case that *some* aspects of globalization are best described as flowing from the United States and having a largely homogenizing effect on much of the rest of the world. We will return to the relationship between McDonaldization and globalization at a number of points in the ensuing discussion.

The thesis that the United States is undergoing a process of McDonaldization and that it is actively exporting manifestations of that process to much of the rest of the world is obviously a global perspective, but it is both less than and more than globalization theory. On the one hand, McDonaldization does not involve anything approaching the full range of global processes. For example, many of the economic, political and institutional aspects of globalization are largely unrelated to McDonaldization. On the other hand, McDonaldization involves much more than an analysis of its global impact. For example, much of it involves the manifold transformations taking place within the United States, the source and still the center of this process. Thus, McDonaldization is not coterminous with globalization, nor is it solely a global process. Nonetheless, McDonaldization has global implications and can thus be a useful lens through which to examine globalization theory, or at least some of Robertson's perspectives on it.

The New Means of Consumption   There has been an almost dizzying creation and proliferation of settings that allow, encourage and even compel us to consume innumerable goods and services. These settings, the new means of consumption, have come into existence, or taken revolutionary new forms, in the United States since the close of the Second World War. Building upon, but going beyond, earlier settings, they have dramatically transformed the nature of consumption.

Although all of the new means of consumption are highly McDonaldized (and McDonald's, fast-food restaurants, and franchises are such new means) – that is, the underlying principles that we have enumerated above are essential to their operations – there is much more to these settings than simply their McDonaldized characteristics. The exportation of these new means of consumption must be considered, along with McDonaldization, in the context of a discussion of globalization.

The development and growth of the new means of consumption in the United States and their exportation to much of the rest of the world is also a global process. However, like McDonaldization (and for many of the same reasons), the exportation of the new means of consumption is, at once, more than and less than globalization and it, too, offers an important perspective through which to view globalization theory.

With this background, we will address the issue of the relationship between globalization, McDonaldization, and the new means of consumption. To explore this relationship we will adopt as a framework, at least in part, some of the issues raised by Robertson (2001) about globalization. First, what are the driving forces of, and most important factors in, globalization? Second, what are the relationships between the global and the local and between homogeneity and heterogeneity? Third, does globalization imply the decline of the nation-state? Finally, is there any evidence of local and international resistance to globalization?

Key Factors in Globalization

Robertson is often accused by other globalization theorists of under-estimating the importance of economic factors as driving forces in globalization. He acknowledges this and admits to downplaying their significance. While he continues to adhere to a view that emphasizes cultural factors, he concludes that globalization has no single motor force; such forces (politics is a third factor) will vary from one histori-cal situation to another and must be studied empirically. Thus, the question of the relative importance of motor forces can only be answered empirically in cases like McDonaldization and the exporta-tion of the new means of consumption.

The interaction of culture and economics is obviously central to the origins of McDonaldization. While Ritzer, like Robertson, emphasizes the importance of cultural factors (for example, the fit between a culture that values efficiency and acceptance of McDonaldized sys-tems), in the end he concludes that *material* – that is, economic – factors (especially profitability within a global capitalistic market) are the motor forces behind the spread of McDonaldization. Since McDonaldi-zation involves a far more specific set of processes than globalization, it is possible to identify its driving force more precisely. For example, if we look at the paradigm for the process – the McDonald's restaurant – it is clear that no given restaurant, nor the entire chain itself, would exist were it not for the search for profits and that these enterprises are, and continue to be, profitable.

The spread of the McDonald's chain throughout the world repre-sents the kind of specific empirical case suggested by Robertson. That is, it is an instance where one can study in historical detail the forces that caused, and continue to cause, the international expansion of the chain and assess the relative weight of economic, cultural, political (and other) factors. Robertson suggests the importance of comparative empirical research and one could even do such a study comparing the origins of McDonald's to those of other chains that developed in the United States, or to chains that have emerged more recently in many other nations. One point to be made about the latter is that McDonald's itself has become a motor force in the rise of those chains. That is, it is the success of McDonald's, and the methods by which it achieved that success, that have facilitated the development of indigenous chains.

Perhaps the most important point, however, is that, just as Robertson views his work on globalization as part of the 'cultural turn', the work on McDonaldization is of much the same genre. That is, even if economics is the motor force behind McDonald's, the process of McDonaldization is much more important culturally than it is economically (although, as Robertson points out, the two are increasingly difficult to distinguish from one another – the economic is becoming cultural, the cultural economic); the process of McDonaldization is transforming not only the culture of the United States, but also the cultures of much of the rest of the world.

The most notable and more directly visible cultural impact is the way McDonald's is altering the manner in which much of the rest of the world eats. What and how people eat is a crucial component of almost all, if not all, cultures, but with the spread of the principles of McDonaldization virtually *everyone* in McDonaldized societies is devouring french fries (and virtually every other kind of food) and doing so quickly, often on the run (we will discuss some exceptions to this below). Of course, not just food, but many other sectors of many societies (health care, politics) are being McDonaldized and as a result the cultures of those societies, the way people live many aspects of their lives, are being transformed.

Much the same thing could be said about the new means of consumption. Each one of them, as well as the new means of consumption taken collectively, offers the possibility of an empirical test of the relationship between cultural, economic, political (and others) factors. The motor force is once again clearly economic – new means of consumption would not be created or survive were they not successful economically, and they would not be exported internationally were they not economically rewarding to the largely American corporations of which they are part. Yet, what is critical about all of the new means of consumption is that they are powerful reflections of American culture and they all bring that culture to any nation to which they are exported. A good example is Disney World, which has been exported to Japan and France with other foreign ventures planned or in the discussion stage. On the one hand, Disney World is clearly a product of American culture, or at least Walt Disney's romanticized 'Main Street' vision of that culture circa 1900. On the other, it brings American culture and some its most famous icons (Mickey Mouse, Donald Duck) to those areas of the world to which it has been exported. Like most of the other new means of consumption (and McDonaldization), Disney has been welcomed by many in other countries, but its establishment abroad has also elicited extremely negative responses from critics concerned about its impact on national cultures. For example, at the opening of Euro Disney, a French politician said that it will 'bombard France with uprooted creations that are to culture what fast-food is to gastronomy' (Riding, 1992: A10).

Both McDonaldization and the exportation of the new means of consumption tend to support Robertson's emphasis on cultural factors in the process of globalization. However, it is clear that neither process would have been begun without the expectation of economic rewards and both continue because they are enormously profitable. Nevertheless, the specifics of such case studies illustrate that there are other forces involved (such as McDonald's own success) as important factors in the international spread of McDonaldization. Much the same could be said for many of the other new means of consumption. For example, Disney is a similarly important international icon and its success has led to the creation of clones of its various enterprises throughout the world.

The Relationship between the Global/Local and Heterogeneity/Homogeneity

The relationship between global/local and heterogeneity/homogeneity is an area where there are fairly substantial differences between McDonaldization and the exportation of the new means of consumption and globalization, although they are mainly matters of emphasis. Robertson (2001) is at pains to argue that 'globalization is not an all-encompassing process of homogenization but a complex mixture of homogenization and heterogenization'. Featherstone (1990: 2) writes of global culture 'in terms of the diversity, variety and richness of popular and local discourses, codes and practices which resist and play-back systemicity and order'. Far from giving us a universally homogenous culture, globalization defines a space in which the world's cultures rub elbows and generate new, heterogeneous meanings and understandings. Featherstone and Lash (1995: 2) delineate a world in which 'international social, political and cultural (for example, the media) organizations are standing alongside and beginning to replace their national counterparts'. They see every national culture in the mix, so that it is possible to discuss Americanization, Europeanization, Japanization – and even Brazilianization. Of more direct relevance to this discussion, Robertson (2001) argues: 'the frequent talk about the McDonaldization of the world has to be strongly tempered by what is increasingly known about the ways in which such products or services are actually *the basis for localization*', and he cites approvingly James L. Watson's *Golden Arches East: McDonald's in East Asia* (1997a). Given its centrality to Robertson's argument, and to the larger issue of homogeneity/heterogeneity, Watson's book, a series of essays on the impact of McDonald's on a number of Asian cities, represents an appropriate place to begin to deal with the relationship between globalization and McDonaldization and the new means of consumption. Watson (1997a: 6) contends that 'East Asian consumers have quietly, and in some cases stubbornly, transformed their neighborhood McDonald's into local institutions'. McDonald's adapts to each distinctive cultural context and, as a result, is so modified that it is ultimately impossible to distinguish the local from the foreign. Thus, in China, McDonald's is seen as much a Chinese phenomenon as it is an American phenomenon. In Japan, McDonald's is perceived by some as '*Americana as constructed by the Japanese*' (Ohnuki-Tierney, 1997: 173). In Watson's terms, it is a 'transnational' phenomenon. Rather than being monolithic, McDonald's, in Watson's view, is a 'federation of semi-autonomous enterprises'. We begin with the evidence in support of this position (heterogeneity) and then turn to a discussion of the alternative view that McDonaldization is an imperialistic force (homogeneity).

McDonald's as a Local Phenomenon　There is no question that McDonald's (and other McDonaldized systems) adapt to local conditions, realities and tastes. In fact, the president of McDonald's International says that the goal of the company is to 'become as much a part of the local culture as possible' (Sullivan, 1995: 1). Thus, while its basic menu remains intact, McDonald's has added local foods in many nations.

Even more adaptive in terms of foods are the smaller American food franchisers (Big Boy, Dairy Queen, Schlotzky's Delicatessen, Chesapeake Bagel) that have followed McDonald's and the other American giants overseas. In 1998 alone, these mini-chains opened 800 new restaurants overseas and as of that year there were more than 12,000 of them in existence around the world (Frank, 2000). However, such mini-chains are far weaker than McDonald's and therefore must be even more responsive to local culture. Thus, Big Boy sells things like 'country-style fried rice and pork omelette' and has added sugar and chili powder to make its burgers more palatable to its Thai customers. Because it caters to many European tourists, it has added Germanic foods like spatzle to its menu. Said the head franchiser for Big Boy in Thailand: 'We thought we were bringing American food to the masses ... But now we're bringing Thai and European food to the tourists. It's strange, but you know what? It's working' (Frank, 2000: B4).

McDonald's (as well as the mini-chains) also adapts to the local environment in the way it operates its outlets. In Beijing, the menu is identical to that in America, but the food is eaten more as a snack than as a meal. In spite of perceiving the food as a snack, Beijing customers (and those in other nations, as well) often linger for hours rather than eating quickly and leaving or taking their food with them as they depart the drive-through window, which undermines one of the principal dimensions of McDonaldization – efficiency. Perhaps the biggest difference, however, is that in Beijing McDonald's seeks to be more human by consciously presenting itself as a local company, as a place in which to 'hang out' and celebrate important events and ceremonies (for example, children's birthday parties) rather than simply a place to get in to and out of as quickly as possible. Personal interaction is emphasized by employing five to ten female receptionists, who are referred to as 'Aunt McDonalds' (similarly, Ronald McDonald is known as 'Uncle McDonald' in Taiwan), whose main tasks involve dealing with children and talking to parents.

Instead of discouraging the lingering of children, McDonald's in Hong Kong (and Taipei) tends to encourage it, especially for children on their way home from school. As in Beijing, McDonald's in Hong Kong is a more personalized setting where customers take about twice as much time as Americans to eat their food. It is a teenage hangout from 3 to 6 in the afternoon and McDonald's makes no effort to limit table time. Overall, McDonald's feels more like 'home'.

Also in Hong Kong, McDonald's employees rarely smile at customers, but instead display the traits valued in that culture – 'competence, directness, and unflappability' (Watson, 1997b: 91). Those who eat in Hong Kong's McDonald's do not bus their own debris. In addition, napkins are dispensed one at a time because if they were placed in a public dispenser, they would disappear quickly. In Taipei, McDonald's is also a hangout for teenagers and more generally is treated as a home away from home; it is 'familiar and indigenous' (Wu, 1997: 125). The same customers return over and over and come to know one another and the employees quite well.

Although there is considerable evidence that McDonald's (and other McDonaldized systems) adapts, and this adaptation has helped it to succeed overseas, an important question is whether this adaptation constitutes a threat to McDonald's because it goes against the very basis of the success of the system – its standardized foods and methods of operation (Barboza, 1999). That is, if McDonald's adapts too much, 'goes native', and loses its identity and uniformity, will it undermine the very source of its worldwide success? If local McDonald's around the world go their own way, will they eventually cease to be identifiable as McDonald's? Will the company itself (or at least its international operations) eventually be undermined, and perhaps destroyed, by such local adaptation? Moreover, will its surrender to these local practices that obviously undermine the efficiency that it achieves in the United States make it economically unprofitable?

McDonald's as Cultural Imperialism In contrast to those who emphasize the local adaptation of American imports, others argue that McDonaldized systems are imposing themselves on local markets in other societies and in the process transforming local economies and cultures. The enormous expansion of such systems in the international arena is one indication of this cultural imperialism. Second, while McDonald's may adapt to local realities in terms of the food and the way it runs its operations, the fact remains that not only the basic menu, but also – and more important – the fundamental operating procedures remain essentially the same everywhere in the world. Third, in many ways, it is not the existence of American chains (and other new means of consumption) in other countries that is the most important indicator of the spread of McDonaldization, but rather the existence of indigenous clones of those McDonaldized enterprises. After all, the importation of American products in other countries could simply be a manifestation of an invasion of isolated and superficial elements that represent no real and fundamental threat to the underlying realities of those countries. However, it is clear that the emergence of local variations on American consumption mechanisms reflects an underlying change – the McDonaldization of those societies.

The power of McDonald's to transform local restaurants is evident in Moscow. The initial success there of McDonald's restaurants, which were greeted with great fanfare and long lines (Ingwerson, 1997: 1), led to the development of many imitators, indigenous enterprises such as Russkoye Bistro that now has over 100 outlets and serves 35,000 to 40,000 customers per day. Said Russkoye Bistro's deputy director, 'If McDonald's had not come to our country, then we probably wouldn't be here.' And further, 'we need to create fast-food here that fits our lifestyle and traditions ... We see McDonald's like an older brother ... We have a lot to learn from them' (quoted in Hockstader, 1995: A13). That is the central point: innumerable institutions throughout the world feel that there is much to learn from McDonald's and what is critical are the basic principles that the process of McDonaldization embodies.

In China, local restaurants copied the McDonaldized imports. For example, Ronghua Chicken and Xiangfei Roast Chicken emulated Kentucky Fried Chicken. The Beijing Fast-Food Company has almost a thousand local restaurants and street stalls that sell local fare. Several of the company's executives are former employees of KFC or McDonald's, where they learned basic management techniques. They are applying the methods of those McDonaldized systems to the preparation and sale of local cuisine. Government officials and those from the restaurant and catering businesses often tour McDonald's restaurants. Even 'the most famous restaurant in Beijing – Quanjude Roast Duck Restaurant – sent its management staff to McDonald's in 1993 and then introduced its own "roast duck fast-food" in early 1994' (Yan, 1997: 75).

In Japan, the strongest competitor to McDonald's is Mos Burger (with 1,500 outlets), which serves 'a sloppy-joe-style concoction of meat and chili sauce on a bun' (Ohnuki-Tierney, 1997: 165). In Taipei, local establishments have become 'fast-food-style restaurants' (Wu, 1997). In Seoul, competitors to McDonald's include Americana and Uncle Joe's

Hamburger (the inventor of the *kimchi* burger featuring an important local condiment – spicy pickled cabbage).

However, the impact of McDonaldization is much more pronounced than minor changes in the operations of local restaurants alone; indeed, McDonaldization is likely to lead to changes in the customs of society as a whole. In Korea (and Japan) the individualism of a meal at McDonald's threatens the commensality of eating rice that is cooked in a common pot and of sharing side dishes. As in the United States, McDonald's in Hong Kong has helped to transform children into customers. Immigrants to the city are given a tour that *ends* at McDonald's! The clear implication is that this is the very best Hong Kong has to offer. In Japan, McDonald's is described as a new 'local' phenomenon. One of the pieces of evidence for that is that a Japanese Boy Scout was surprised to find a McDonald's in Chicago; he thought it was a Japanese firm (Watson, 1997a).

From our perspective these cultural transformations, like the development of indigenous McDonaldized settings, exemplify the power of McDonaldization. Its impact is far greater if it infiltrates a local culture and becomes a part of it than if it remains perceived as an American phenomenon superimposed on a local setting. As local residents come to see McDonaldized systems as their own, it seems certain that the process of McDonaldization will continue to expand and embed itself ever more deeply into the cultures and everyday realities of societies throughout the world.

This discussion of cultural transformation points to another important difference with the position taken by Robertson and other globalization theorists. In rejecting the idea of cultural imperialism and McDonaldization, Robertson argues that globally few goods and services are standardized. While this may be true, of far greater importance are the standardized *principles* by which McDonaldized systems, both global and local, operate. Thus, it is far less significant that in Russkoye Bistro blinis rather than hamburgers are sold than that the cooking, serving and sale of both is based on a very similar set of standardized principles.

Consider Yan's conclusion to an essay on McDonald's in Beijing: 'It is ... tempting to predict that, twenty years from now, the "American" associations that McDonald's carries today will become but dim memories for older residents. A new generation of Beijing consumers may treat the Big Mac, fries, and shakes simply as local products' (Yan, 1997: 76). The author takes this to mean that the local will triumph over McDonaldization, Americanization and globalization, but to us it represents the strongest possible evidence of the triumph of all three over the local.

Ohnuki-Tierney (1997) seems to take consolation from the fact that McDonald's has not really altered Japanese dinners or even lunches, and this is true elsewhere in Asia, as well. As we have seen, McDonald's food is viewed there more as snack food than as a meal. Yet Ohnuki-Tierney also recognizes that something of great cultural importance – the way people eat – *is* being altered. For example, the traditional Japanese taboo against eating while standing has been undermined by the fast-food restaurant (the valuable real estate in Japan necessitates standing; in the United States larger restaurants that permit more seating can be built comparatively inexpensively). Also subverted to some degree is the cultural sanction against drinking directly from a can or bottle. She claims that the norm against eating with one's hands is holding up better (the Japanese typically eat their burgers in the wrappers so that their hands do not touch the food directly). Nevertheless, that deeply held norms are being transformed by McDonald's is evidence of the profound impact of McDonaldization.

While those who accept the cultural imperialism argument tend to emphasize the negative effects of McDonaldization on local customs, we must not forget that the imperialism of McDonaldized systems brings with it many advances over local ways of doing things. For example, in both Hong Kong and Taipei McDonald's virtually invented restaurant cleanliness and served as a catalyst for improving sanitary conditions at many other restaurants in the city.

While we argue in favor of the cultural imperialism position, at least in the case of McDonaldization, it is impossible to offer a single generalization that applies equally well to all nations. For example, in Korea, unlike other East Asian locales, there is a long history of anti-Americanism (co-existing with pro-American feelings) and there is great fear among Koreans of encroaching Americanism and the loss of Korean identity. Thus, one would anticipate greater opposition there to McDonaldization than in most other nations.

Finally, while a general threat to indigenous culture exists, there are counter-examples that demonstrate that McDonaldization has instead contributed to the revitalization of local traditions. For example, while fast-food restaurants have boomed in Taipei, they have helped lead to the revival of indigenous food traditions, such as the eating of betel nuts. More generally, in his book, *Jihad vs. McWorld*, Benjamin Barber (1995; see also, Friedman, 1999) argues that the spread of 'McWorld' brings with it the development of local fundamentalist movements ('Jihads') deeply opposed to McDonaldization.[1]

The New Means of Consumption, Localism, and Imperialism   Many of the same points apply to the new means of consumption more generally. For example, many have adapted to local cultures by altering what they sell and how they sell it. While many of the new means of consumption succeeded in entrenching themselves in many other countries, they have also given rise to indigenous versions that have adopted most of their underlying principles and methods of operations. Thus, for example, Europe has its own superstores that represent serious competition to the successful exportation of Wal-Mart and Costco. European television carries its own varieties of televised home shopping, obviously influenced by the American innovators in this area. American e-tailers and cybermalls are available throughout the world, but so are local clones of both. From our perspective, it makes little difference whether people utilize American-based or indigenous versions of superstores, home shopping networks, or e-tailers. While indigenous versions may manifest a variety of inputs, by far the most powerful are those that emanate from the American pioneers and leaders in this area.

Take the case of Latin America's Rock in Rio Cafe. Its developers are very cognizant of American theme restaurants (eatertainment) and have made it clear that they have taken the lead from them in creating a spectacular chain of restaurants that include entry via monorail, changing projected imagery on the walls, and indoor fireworks (Friedland, 1997). While Rock in Rio has its local touches, it is clearly heavily influenced by American theme restaurants. Its spread throughout Latin America may be expedited by those local touches and local ownership, but it is still bringing with it a very American approach to restaurants and eating with little emphasis on the nature and quality of the food and much on the spectacular nature of the setting. In some sense it matters little whether those in Rio de Janeiro eat in Rock in Rio or in Planet Hollywood since both are new means of consumption. But, in another sense, the seemingly local character of the former obscures its American roots and therefore poses an even greater threat to indigenous culture.

The more general point is that the American pattern of consumption – what may be termed hyperconsumption – accompanies and undergirds both the exportation of the new means of consumption and the opening of indigenous versions of these American imports. These settings encourage people around the world not only to consume more, but also to consume more like Americans. That is, more and more people engage in mass consumption, spend most if not all of their available resources on consumption, and increasingly go into debt in order to support such a consumption pattern.

It is not just how much people consume that is being changed; it is also the ways in which people consume. Instead of paying cash for the things they consume, increasingly large numbers of people around the world follow large numbers of Americans into debt by using credit cards.

The credit card (a mechanism that facilitates the use of the new means of consumption rather than itself being such a new means), which had its origins and still has its base in the United States, is also an American export (Ritzer, 1995). Instead of the traditional method of shopping at a variety of local shops and stands, people around the world are increasingly embracing the American pattern of one-stop shopping at supermarkets, hypermarkets, superstores and shopping malls. Instead of visiting shops where clerks and shopkeepers perform various tasks for consumers, people are increasingly following the American pattern of doing more and more things relating to consumption for themselves. Perhaps most important, the American pattern of making consumption less social is being adopted throughout the world. For example, instead of interacting with familiar shopkeepers on a regular basis, many are doing things for themselves in vast stores and malls, interacting only briefly and anonymously with robot-like clerks, or, in the most extreme case, interacting with nothing more than television and computer screens. Whether or not they consume in American-based means of consumption, others around the world are increasingly consuming like Americans. As with the case of McDonaldization, there is great variation in this from one locale to another, and the success of the new means of consumption is likely to lead to local counter-reactions and perhaps even to a revival of traditional consumption settings. Nevertheless, it seems safe to say that the exportation of the new means of consumption, and the development of indigenous copies of these settings, are leading to a worldwide movement in the direction of American-style patterns of consumption. Thus, the cases of the exportation of the new means of consumption and McDonaldization point much more to cultural imperialism and homogeneity than they do to localism and heterogeneity.[2]

Globalization and the Nation-State

Robertson (2001) contends that, as a consequence of globalization, 'the nation-state is being simultaneously weakened and strengthened'. From the broad perspective of globalization theory, this is certainly accurate. However, when looked at through the lens of McDonaldization and the exportation of the new means of consumption, at least at this point in their historical development, two points are clear. First, both of these processes operate transnationally with little interference from the state. Such transnational flows serve, at least to some degree, to undermine the power of the state. To take one example, for obvious reasons the Chinese government may want to keep McDonald's or other new means of consumption out, but the public demand for them has made that impossible. By allowing in McDonaldized systems based in the United States (and elsewhere), China is both admitting its weakness and further increasing that weakness. Chinese citizens and observers around the world see the inability of the Chinese to resist McDonaldization and they strive to further exploit that weakness. This is even clearer in the case of the Internet, and the cybermalls and e-tailers that are such an increasing presence on it. Unable to keep the Internet out, the Chinese are therefore unable to keep out these new means of consumption and the types of consumption and consumer goods associated with them.

Second, while overall McDonaldization and the new means of consumption suggest the weakness of the state, they indicate again, at least at this point in history, the power of a *single* state – the United States. McDonald's, the process of McDonaldization it helped spawn, and the new means of consumption are distinctive products of American society, and their spread throughout the world enhances the global reach and power of the United States. Furthermore, a significant portion of the profits earned abroad return to American shores and some find their way into the American treasury. However, while McDonaldization and the exportation of the new means of consumption work to the interests of the American state, it is also the case that the corporations involved in these processes operate largely independently of the US government. In that sense, they can be said to undermine the power of the American state and the nation-state in general.

Thus, the study of McDonaldization and the new means of consumption points to the growing power of the corporation over the nation-state in the globalization process. Corporations have long operated at least semi-autonomously and to the detriment of state power, but this seems to be reaching new heights in contemporary corporations, especially those involved with McDonaldized systems and the new means of consumption. Increasingly, the corporation, not the state (even the American state), has become the most important actor on the world stage and the gap between these two entities is likely to grow in the future. This reality is captured in an anecdote that Friedman reports about a former US ambassador to Israel who officiated at the opening of the first McDonald's in Jerusalem while wearing a baseball hat with the McDonald's golden arches logo:

> An Israeli teen-ager walked up to him, carrying his own McDonald's hat, which he handed to Ambassador Indyk with a pen and asked: 'Are you the Ambassador? Can I have your autograph?' Somewhat sheepishly, Ambassador Indyk replied: 'Sure. I've never been asked for my autograph before.'
>
> As the Ambassador prepared to sign his name, the Israeli teen-ager said to him, 'Wow, what's it like to be the ambassador from McDonald's, going around the world opening McDonald's restaurants everywhere?'
>
> Ambassador Indyk looked at the Israeli youth and said, 'No, no. I'm the American ambassador – not the ambassador from McDonald's!' Ambassador Indyk described what happened next: 'I said to him, "Does this

mean you don't want my autograph?" And the kid said, "No, I don't want your autograph", and he took his hat back and walked away.' (Friedman, 1999: 43–4)

Such actions challenge Robertson's (2001) assertion that 'the nation-state remains the central and most formidable actor in world affairs generally'.

On the other hand, the perspective that we are arguing is also at odds, at least in part, with the view of some globalization theorists, most notably Appadurai (1996), that what is most significant about globalization is the existence of global processes that operate independently of, and free of ties with, any given nation. While our previous discussion of the independence of corporations tends to support such a stance, the overall thrust of this chapter is to stress the persistence of ties to the United States and American culture. Thus, while it is undeniable that there are global processes that operate free of any nation-state, one nation-state remains disproportionately important in globalization. The nation-state may, as Robertson (2001) suggests, not be as formidable as it once was, but, at least in the realms being discussed here, the United States remains a powerful presence.

Local and Global Resistance

One of the issues highlighted by the specifics of McDonaldization and the exportation of the new means of consumption is the nature of the resistance to them. Robertson (2001) discusses such resistance in terms of anti-global movements that themselves involve globalization. Once again, the specific issues of concern here allow us to examine the nature of this resistance much more concretely.

The global reach of McDonaldization and the exportation of the new means of consumption have given rise to reactions against these processes that are similarly transnational. For example, the exportation of McDonald's led to the infamous McLibel trial in Great Britain[3] and, more important to a global McLibel movement against McDonald's, franchises, as well as many other new means of consumption (Vidal, 1997). Several million copies of the leaflet that led to the trial, 'What's Wrong With McDonald's: Everything They Didn't Want You to Know', have been distributed around the world and it has been translated into a number of languages. More important, a site dedicated to opposing McDonald's and related phenomena (http://www.mcspotlight.org/), was created on the World Wide Web and it reported an average of 1.75 million 'hits' a month, a total of 65 million hits by March 1999. It acts as the repository for information on actions taken against local McDonald's throughout the world. It has become the heart of a worldwide movement in opposition to McDonald's, as well as other aspects of our McDonaldized world. For example, in one month it reported efforts to block the opening of new McDonald's restaurants in Surrey, England; Kerikeri, New Zealand; Torquay, Australia; and Edmonton, Canada. Among 'McSpotlight's' other targets is the Body Shop, which is accused of using its 'green' image to conceal the fact that its products are detrimental to the environment, that it pays low wages, and that it encourages consumerism.

Another reaction against McDonaldization has been The Slow Food movement, which was initiated in the mid-1980s by an Italian food critic against the opening of a McDonald's in Rome. It is opposed to the homogenization of food styles and takes as its mission 'to give voice to local cooking styles and small-time food producers'. In addition to its anti-McDonald's stance, more recently it has taken on 'fending off the homogenizing effects of European Union regulations on regional culinary treasures' (Richman, 1998: M1). Its objective 'to provide members from all different countries with an identity and [to propagate] convivia throughout the world' (*Slow*, 1998) reflects its anti-McDonaldization animus. It has over 400 chapters (called Convivia) and a membership of 40,000 people, mostly in Europe, but also in 35 other nations. Among other things, the movement has a website (www.slowfood.com), publishes a handsome journal (*Slow*), and held its first biennial meeting, 'Salone del Gusto: World Flavours in Piedmont', in Turin, Italy in late 1998.

This is clearly a movement of a very different order from the McLibel group. The impoverished targets of the McDonald's libel suit are a far cry from the mainly well-heeled gourmets drawn to Slow Food. The Slow Food movement focuses on the issue of the poor quality of food (and, implicitly, almost all other products) in McDonaldized restaurants and food emporia, while McLibel focuses on threats to health (as does another movement, National Heart Savers), the environment and workers. While there are differences in goals, methods, and in the social class backgrounds of most of the participants, these two groups share hostility to the McDonaldization of society (and the new means of consumption), and they are global in their reach.

Turning to other new means of consumption, Sprawl-Busters (info@sprawl-busters.com), founded by Al Norman, grew out of his successful effort to keep Wal-Mart out of his home town, Greenfield, Massachusetts. Now the organization offers consulting services to local communities that want to keep McDonaldized superstores and chains out. For his efforts, the TV program '60 Minutes' called Norman 'the guru of the anti-Wal-Mart movement'. Among the services offered by the organization to local communities is help with overseeing media operations, raising money, referenda, data searches, and the like. Beyond Wal-Mart, organizations on Sprawl-Buster's 'hit list' include

Super Kmart, Home Depot, CVS, and Rite-Aid. The main objective is to keep out such superstores and chains – prime examples of the new means of consumption – in order to protect local businesses and the integrity of the local community.

Thus, this analysis suggests that while McDonaldization and the exportation of the new means of consumption are global in reach, they generate opposition movements that are similarly global. It is unlikely that these opposition movements will defeat the largely American-based forces that they oppose, but they are likely to force them to ameliorate their worst excesses.

Although there is general accord between Robertson and the perspective offered here on the global nature of resistance, one key difference is that while he sees the United States as the '*home of opposition and resistance to globalization*', movements such as McLibel based in England and Slow Food in Italy indicate that in the specific case of McDonaldization opposition has emerged outside of the United States, as well.

However, in our rush to focus on global opposition to these global changes, we must not lose sight of the wide variety of local and individual opposition efforts (although, as Robertson (2001) points out, these cannot be clearly separated from global processes) both within the United States and throughout the world. Thus, towns as widespread as Sanibel Island in Florida and Hove in England have succeeded in keeping out McDonaldized chains. Other towns and cities throughout the world have forced such chain restaurants to mute their structures and alter their menus. Beyond the local, there is individual opposition which can take such forms as refusing to patronize McDonaldized settings and new means of consumption, fleeing to areas free of such settings, or even escaping into a fantasy world free of these systems.

Thus, there are many ways to oppose the forces of McDonaldization and the new means of consumption. A discussion of these techniques highlights the global nature of some of them, but such a global perspective might lead us to ignore other more local and individual efforts. As is true of globalization in general, a focus on specific forms of opposition reveals much more than airy generalizations about this opposition. There is much more to the changing nature of the world than is caught by globalization theory and even by the globalization process.

Conclusion

The objective in this chapter has been to examine several of the basic tenets of globalization theory from the perspective of the processes of McDonaldization and the exportation of the new means of consumption. The most general point is that while there is a role for broad generalizations about the nature and consequences of globalization, they need to be closely examined in case studies that focus on specific aspects of that process. Globalization has innumerable strands and interrelated developments; we have only been able to focus on two of them here. However, even the examination of these two processes has made it clear that generalizations about globalization need to be tempered and specified. What is true about some aspects of globalization is not necessarily true of other aspects of that process.

We have focused here on four issues related to globalization theory derived, at least in part, from the recent work of one prominent globalization theorist, Roland Robertson. By looking at these issues through the lenses of McDonaldization and the new means of consumption, we have found some support, some lack of support, and in all cases a need for greater specificity.

First, the processes of McDonaldization and the exportation of the new means of consumption support Robertson's assertion that globalization is multi-factorial, with economic and cultural factors being of prime importance. The evidence from these processes indicates that although they must be profitable to be undertaken and maintained, it is really their cultural character and cultural implications that are of utmost importance and significance. That is not to say that culture is the most important aspect of all elements of globalization. For example, the global financial system, and its many sub-components, are undoubtedly far more important economically than they are culturally.

Second, our greatest disagreement with Robertson is over the issue of homogeneity/heterogeneity or cultural imperialism/localism. While Robertson emphasizes heterogeneity and the coexistence of the global and the local, the cases of McDonaldization and the new means of consumption indicate the centrality of homogeneity, cultural imperialism and the triumph over the local. Our evidence points much more to homogeneity than heterogeneity, even though in those cases where McDonaldization and the new means of consumption have been most successful in embedding themselves in indigenous cultures, elements of heterogeneity, the glocal and the local survive and may even be stimulated into reasserting themselves by the success of these imperialistic efforts. Again, however, other elements of globalization might well demonstrate the reverse. We need to look at what *each* of these aspects of globalization show and not be satisfied with generalizations about the process.

Third, our examination of McDonaldization and the new means of consumption adds nuance to Robertson's assertion that globalization simultaneously weakens and strengthens the nation-state. McDonaldization and the exportation of the new means of consumption serve to weaken, and to demonstrate the weakness of, the nation-state in that most are powerless to resist their incursion. However, these two processes serve to strengthen the *American* state through increased tax revenues generated by overseas successes and by furthering the proliferation of American culture throughout the world. Ultimately, however, these processes demonstrate the growing importance of the corporation *vis-à-vis* the state. It is really the corporations – the multinational and transnational entities that lie at the base of McDonaldization and the new means of consumption – that benefit most from their success. These corporations operate largely on their own, free of state control. They are little interested in the success of their state of origin or of the other states in which they do business. In the end, distinctively American products such as McDonald's, Disney, Wal-Mart, the Gap, Amazon.com, and the like will remain based in the United States only so long as it suits their interests and bottom line to do so. When, and if, it makes more economic sense to base their operations elsewhere, or to sell out to some foreign-based conglomerate, they will do so without giving a second thought to the implications of these acts for the United States. What the cases of McDonaldization and the new means of consumption suggest is that it is the corporation, not the state, that is key actor on the world stage today.

Finally, the specific cases of McDonaldization and the new means of consumption illustrate the emergence of various types of resistance to them at the individual, local and global levels. Theorizing about resistance to globalization at a general level is useful, but we learn a great deal more about resistance, and much else, if we look at the specific forms that they take in reaction to specific dimensions of globalization.

Notes

This chapter was co-authored by Liz Malone and was published previously in *American Studies*, 41: 2 (Summer), 2000. © Mid-America American Studies Association, 2000.

1   However, it is worth noting that in the end Barber concludes that McWorld will win out over Jihad; to succeed on a large scale, fundamentalist movements themselves must begin to use highly rationalized, McDonaldized systems (for example, e-mail, the Internet, television).

2   However, we should reiterate that the realities of these cases do not contradict the idea that other global processes are producing greater heterogeneity around the world.

3   McDonald's sued two impecunious young people associated with London Greenpeace for passing out anti-McDonald's pamphlets. In what became the longest libel trial in the history of Great Britain, McDonald's won on most counts, but suffered an expensive public relations disaster (Vidal, 1997).

9

THE NEW MEANS OF CONSUMPTION AND THE SITUATIONIST PERSPECTIVE

Nothing is surprising anymore, there's the rub! (Raoul Vaneigem, *The Revolution of Everyday Life*)

One non-revolutionary weekend is infinitely more bloody than a month of permanent revolution. (Situationist graffito)

The new means of consumption are best understood as part of a broader change in capitalism that has rippled across the social world. This change is characterized by both a shift in focus from production to consumption and the rise of the postmodern phenomena that are characteristic of late capitalism, such as simulation and ephemerality. Though Marx's writings contain important conceptual tools for understanding the exploitative nature of consumption – especially the idea of commodity fetishism – there is a sense that nineteenth-century capitalist exploitation stopped at the factory gate. Beginning with Lukács and continuing with the Frankfurt School, however, Marxian theory was updated to capture the pervasiveness of commodity relations in the twentieth century. More recently, postmodern theorists have described a new stage in capitalist social relations: 'The relatively stable aesthetic of Fordist modernity has given way to all the ferment, instability, and fleeting qualities of a postmodernist aesthetic that celebrates difference, ephemerality, spectacle, fashion, and the commodification of cultural form' (Harvey, 1989: 156). The new means of consumption embody these changes in capitalism; they represent the greatly amplified effort of capital to sell its product through, and resulting in, a range of postmodern processes.

The ideas of the Situationist International (SI) are compatible with a theory and critique of the new means of consumption. This group, known chiefly through the work of Guy Debord, developed during the 1960s a critique of spectacular society. Recently, the SI has received attention as an important antecedent of postmodern social theory (Best and Kellner, 1997; Plant, 1992). Its adherents argued that capitalism had extended its reach so that commodity relations not only affected workers in the realm of production but also reached into all facets of life through the dominance of the spectacle. By way of the culture industry, consumer society and the media, capitalism conspires to control individuals and alienate them from social life by creating ever more distracting and phantasmagoric spectacles and by commodifying all spheres of social life. The situationists criticized the passive and bored consumption of spectacles and argued that they prevented people from actively creating their own lives.

The power of situationist theory is located in its ability to transcend theoretical categories. On the one hand, the situationists can be considered critical theorists: 'Debord and the situationists can thus be interpreted as an attempt to renew the Marxian adventure under historically specific conditions' (Best and Kellner, forthcoming). Like the Frankfurt School, the situationists update Marxism to deal with emergent conditions in capitalism. On the other, the situationists are early cartographers of the now familiar territory of postmodern phenomena. The concept of spectacular society refers to the same proliferation of seductive and phantasmagoric commodities, extravaganzas and signs that occupy Baudrillard. Moreover, situationist irony and subversion mirror postmodern techniques. As a result, the situationists remain a valuable resource for theorists who want to critically engage postmodernity.

The ideas of the SI can make several contributions to understanding the new means of consumption. First, the idea of a spectacular society puts the new means of consumption into context as a part of a broad change in capitalist methods of domination. Second, the SI argues that an individual who is confronted with spectacular society is rendered alienated and bored, conditions that can counteract false consciousness because the promises made by consumer society often excite desires it cannot fulfill. This theory of the contemporary consumer allows for agency without overestimating the role, or freedom, of the consumer. Third, as a revolutionary group, the SI develops a novel theory of resistance and transcendence that, even now, still carries a powerful subversive message. Finally, a reformed 'science of the spectacle' is suggested to consider the multiple sites of contemporary spectacularization.

Contextualizing the New Means of Consumption

Situationist theory provides a framework for understanding the position of the new means of consumption in the changing field of capitalist social relations. The SI contends that the economic structures of capitalism first described by Marx have been extended by the expansion of commodity relations into all aspects of social life through new systems of technology. When alienated relations of production are disseminated through capitalist society, culture, knowledge and leisure are produced as commodities. Debord developed the concept of the spectacle to address the effects of capitalist domination in the realm of consumption.

Debord borrows ideas and phrases from a number of theoretical sources. His immediate influences include Weberian Marxism

(Lukács), existential Marxism (Lefebvre), and surrealist writings applied to the moment when capitalist domination shifted from production to social reproduction. Modifying Lukács' idea of reification, the spectacle describes the alienating (yet transfixing) thing-like quality of the culture industry and consumer society. From Lefebvre, the SI took a pair of ideas – everyday life and unalienated festivity – and applied them as a critique of a reified spectacular society, arguing that despite the strong grip of the spectacle, individuals can retreat to everyday life for real unalienated experience (Lefebvre, 1971; Poster, 1975). From the surrealists, the SI appropriated their subversive techniques including irony, pastiche, *detournement*[1] and *derive*[2] (Ball, 1987; Gray, 1974; Plant, 1992).

Assembling all of these ideas, Debord built a theoretical model explaining the origin of the abundance of commodities and images in contemporary life and enumerating their effects. The spectacle corresponds to the Frankfurt School's culture industry critique (Berman, 1990–91). What becomes important in spectacular society is the desirable surface of images and signs, as opposed to the problematic cultural objects of earlier days, the active construction of one's own experience, or the critical evaluation of knowledge and culture. In this world, domination becomes objective, universal, rational and productive: it is diffused throughout social life in a comprehensive and ceaseless barrage of images and commodities. Aimed at an attentive audience who view its predigested content passively, the spectacle satu- rates social life, displacing lived experience with glamorous images to facilitate social reproduction.

The spectacle creates the appearance of a unity or totality in spite of generalized differentiation, separation and fragmentation. In other words, the dissolution of social life, social interaction, and community in late capitalism is masked by the false unity of the attention-grabbing spectacle. For example, in the United States we are convinced of our own unity by television commentators who tell us certain events (show trials, impeachment hearings and Senate trials, spectacular invasions, elections) are of grave importance to the American people. Such reports distract individuals from the socially destructive aspects of contemporary American culture where television has displaced conversation and commodities mediate relationships.

Echoing Debord's assertion that everyday life has been mediated by commodity culture, Don Delillo explores the effects of spectacular society on family relationships in his novel *White Noise*. Professor Jack Gladney feels alienated from his family until they take a trip to the mall together:

People swarmed through the boutiques and gourmet shops. Organ music rose from the great court. We smelled chocolate, popcorn, cologne; we smelled rugs and furs, hanging salamis and deathly vinyl. My family gloried in the event. I was one of them, shopping, at last. They gave me advice, badgered clerks on my behalf. I kept seeing myself unexpectedly on some reflecting surface. We moved from store to store, rejecting not only items in certain departments, not only entire departments but whole stores, mammoth corporations that did not strike our fancy for one reason or another. There was always another store, three floors, eight floors, basement full of cheese graters and paring knives. I shopped with reckless abandon. I shopped for immediate needs and distant contingencies. I shopped for its own sake, looking and touching, inspecting merchandise I had no intention of buying, then buying it. (Delillo, 1985: 83–4)

About the only time the Gladney's function well as a family is during their periodic orgies of consumption. Debord says the unity that a family like the Gladney's feels on a shopping excursion is a false and perverse unity because the family comes together in the service of consumer imperatives. His point is the forms of social cohesion (structures such as families and communities) that once brought order to everyday life, require consumable goods to cement their relationships in late capitalist society. In other words, everyday social life is *mediated* by consumer society.

Many of the new means of consumption create such a sense of unity. The best example is the virtually self-contained world of the cruise ship which offers everything everyone wants and can even imagine. Las Vegas hotel-casinos are a similar totality, at least as far as the gambler is concerned, and increasingly from the point of view of other family members as they encompass more and more sites and activities. As Disney attractions proliferate, and ancillary attractions around the resort mushroom, the entire Orlando region takes on more and more of the feel of a totality. Mega-malls offer a similar sense of totality, as do superstores that offer the unity of everything one could want of a particular kind of commodity. A more specific example is Disney's town of Celebration and the many similar towns that have been inspired, at least in part, by Disney. In the luxury gated community the gates are there not only to keep outsiders away, but also to help provide a sense that the community is a self-contained world. Caught up in the seeming unity of any of these totalized means of consumption, the consumer loses sight of the fact that the larger society is so fragmented.

Though the spectacle simulates unity, it actually mediates social life through images, technology and the commodity system. Large art exhibits nowadays almost always offer a personal headset tour of the show. There are scores of people walking around the National Gallery of Art who are wearing headphones and milling about – a situation that captures the isolating nature of technology and the way in which it is employed by the new means of consumption. According to Debord (1967/1994: 28), 'Isolation underpins technology, and technology isolates in its turn; all goods proposed by the spectacular system, from cars to televisions, also serve as weapons for that system as its strives to reinforce the isolation of "the lonely crowd"'.[3] Individuals are linked to the spectacle in a one-way relationship while maintaining their isolation from one another. As a result, individuals (or spectators) find themselves alienated from each other and subordinated to the spectacle.

Of course, isolation, alienation and subordination to the spectacle characterize other cathedrals of consumption as well. Take, for example, the drive-through window at the fast-food restaurant that guarantees the most fleeting of relationships with employees. Even when consumers enter a fast-food restaurant, their interaction with employees is almost always brief and dominated by the scripts followed by employees. There is unlikely to be any interaction with 'diners' at other tables and, in their haste to eat and depart, there may even be little interaction with those accompanying the customer. Isolated and alienated, consumers are there to take part in the spectacle produced by the McDonaldized cooking and distribution of the food, the carnival-like atmosphere, and so on. The spectacle is not only the chief product of spectacular society, it also serves as its ideology and justification. 'In form as in content the spectacle serves as the total justification for the conditions and aims of the existing system. It further ensures the permanent presence of that justification, for it governs almost all time spent outside the production process itself' (Debord, 1967/1994: 6). The power of this ideology is such that it encompasses almost all that is to be seen; it becomes, in effect, reality. Put simply, spectacular society lacks the reflexivity to ask whether a particular product or spectacle is necessary. Instead, we tend to accept the system's justifications – Hollywood blockbusters, giant theme parks, and Christmas, each asking you to believe your dreams have come true. The commodity system functions as an ideological proclamation of the affluence and justness of the system as well as a means of domination – mediating, controlling, and seducing.

Disney World dominates and controls us in similar ways. For example, it controls our immediate actions while we are in the park. And, it controls our future actions by helping to inculcate a continuing desire for Disney products. Disney ideology stresses the need to have fun and that that fun can be best found in commodified settings like Disney's parks, cruise lines, and clubs. One is pushed to spend time in these settings and this, in turn, is designed to lead to a heightened desire for the vast array of goods associated with the Disney line.

Why the spectacle? Spectacular society is premised on a shift from production of goods to social reproduction. For Marx, the problem of social reproduction took the form of reproduction of labor power (involving the housing and feeding of workers) as necessary for the continuation of the capitalist system. The spectacle, in contrast, reproduces itself through the production of signs and images. Consumption of spectacular signs and images, exclusive of others, validates the dominant mode of production and ensures its continued survival.

Marx's concept of commodity fetishism, the domination of society by things that are perceptible as images and signs but, at the same time, mask the social relationships that produce them, reaches its apex in spectacular society which replaces social life with images that appear superior to that world. In other words, the poverty of social life caused by the dominant mode of production – exploitation, alienation – is covered up by the abundance of fetishized commodities and reified settings in which they are purveyed. Spectacular society is not qualitatively different from Marx's fetishism of the commodities, rather, the discrepancy is located in a more extensive and intensive role for commodity production (and their settings): 'The spectacle corresponds to the historical moment at which the commodity completes its colonization of social life. It is not just that the relationship of commodities is now plain to see – commodities are now all that there is to see; the world we see is the world of commodities' (Debord, 1967/1994: 42).

Spectacular society manufactures a desirable world of commodities shimmering and glimmering around the spectator. Spectacular commodities alienate spectators not only from each other, but simultaneously from the commodity thereby isolating individuals and conquering social life. The reign of the commodity is achieved in numerous ways, including 'the ceaseless manufacture of pseudo-needs'; the marketing of fully equipped blocks of time; the manufacture of mass pseudo-festivals; and the construction of 'distribution centers'. Each of these relates very well to the cathedrals of consumption and we will look at each in turn.

The success of the spectacular economy is predicated on replacing the satisfaction of primary human needs with 'a ceaseless manufacture of pseudo-needs, all of which come down in the end to just one – namely, the pseudo-need for the reign of the autonomous economy to continue' (Debord, 1967/1994: 34). Radio, television, film, and all forms of advertising manipulate desire and socialize individuals into commodity culture. Through these media, the spectacle creates an enchanted world that seduces the spectator into facilitating and reproducing spectacular society and boundless economic development with each purchase. The creation of pseudo-needs is the métier of the cathedrals of consumption as exemplified by, for example, the production by Disney of the strong need of many to visit its theme park and purchase its debris, such as mouse ears and suitably embossed T-shirts.

The spectacular society also controls leisure time through the marketing of fully equipped blocks of time; 'a complete commodity combining a variety of other commodities' simulating actual leisure

(Debord, 1967/1994: 111). Actually, leisure time is molded into time for the 'work' of consumption. Spectacular housing, 'all-inclusive' purchases, collective pseudo-travel, cultural consumption, and an expanding variety of leisure activities are portrayed as events and moments we are supposed to look forward to but are, in the last analysis, only heightened versions of the spectacle – highly rationalized, passive, standardized, commodity-infested time. A good example of a fully equipped block of time is a cruise ship vacation. An event to be saved for and looked forward to (like any cyclical consumption time), the cruise ship vacation is a floating orgy of commodity consumption. Highly structured eating schedules, entertainment schedules, on-shore shopping excursions and leisure times are coupled with a simulation of the posh gluttony of early twentieth-century ocean liners. Bound for nowhere, these cruises are ceaselessly repeated for new batches of passive, relaxed vacationers.

The frequently recurring pseudo-festivals of our era – Christmas, the Fourth of July and TGIF (Thank God It's Friday) – do not qualify as 'true' festivals for Debord. Like the marketing of fully equipped blocks of time, mass pseudo-festivals are publicized as times to which people are supposed to look forward with great anticipation. Parodying gift exchange, inciting excessive spending, and creating disillusion, pseudo-festivals are pale imitations of true festivals, times when a community participates in a 'luxurious expenditure of life'. A true festival needs actual social relations unmediated by commodities; a condition that is unavailable in spectacular society. Little needs to be said about the creation of pseudo-festivals in this context since the cathedrals of consumption are such festivals and/or they are likely to contain them.

'Distribution factories – giant shopping centers created *ex nihilo* and surrounded by acres of parking' (Debord, 1967/1994: 174) replace the urban environment[4] with a homogenized world of perfect monotony. The current 'Disneyfication' of Time Square in New York involves the invasion of this kind of homogenized world into a city that one would think would be highly resistant to it. Shopping malls are strewn across the country, replacing organic urbanism with an anesthetized, surveillanced, and rationalized commodity-selling machine. Virtually all of the means of consumption are distribution centers for commodities. Worth mentioning is the increasing rationalization of distribution within the conventional material means and, especially, the great increase in that rationalization with the arrival of the dematerialized cathedrals of consumption (see Chapter 7).

The end result of these techniques of the spectacular economy – manufacture of pseudo-needs, marketing of fully equipped blocks of time, mass pseudo-festivals, and distribution factories – is the domination of social life by commodities. This domination has several consequences.

First, the spectacle (like McDonaldization) replaces quality with quantity. Spectacular society emphasizes the immensity of spectacles in terms of both numbers and size, preferring the technology of mechanical reproduction and mass production to craftsmanship or artistic production (the shift in Las Vegas from the star system (for example, Frank Sinatra) to the techno-extravaganza is a good example of this). The problem here is that these goods contribute to a culture of 'augmented survival' where poverty, in terms of a lack of leisure or human creative development, still applies. In a formulation that owes something to Marx's concept of species being, Vaneigem (1967/1984: 8) asks, 'Who wants a world in which the guarantee that we shall not die of starvation entails the risk of dying of boredom?' The predigested content of commodities serves the ends of mass production by contributing to inoffensive and homogenous spectacles intended to be sold in Albany, Indianapolis, and Denver.

Second, the spectacular economy necessitates the concurrent development of a service economy. Though the production process has become increasingly automated, the portion of the service sector responsible for distributing and publicizing the commodities of the moment has grown. Thus, the problematic for late-capitalism is found in the tension between the productivity and the disposal of the product (Baran and Sweezy, 1966). Spectacular society becomes a 'selling-machine' to keep the wheels of capitalism turning.

Third, the loss of quality in products and the development of intensive systems of publicity and distribution are accompanied by the spread of the spectacle over space. The spectacle turns the whole planet into a single market. Even in developing countries – Paraguay, China, Madagascar and Romania – the spectacle reaches the population through the growth of the worldwide media and advertising, the appearance of new means of consumption, and the spectacular images associated with all of them. Products like Coca-Cola, McDonald's, Michael Jordan and Mercedes Benz sedans have become universalized commodities and images as familiar to an old woman in New Delhi as to a student in Boston. Not far behind is the universalization of the new means of consumption and their images. Because of uneven development, citizens of developing countries might not yet be able to be fully fledged consumers, but they are already being prepared to do the job.

In sum, Debord supplies us with a powerful critical analysis of contemporary consumer culture. He delineates the techniques and consequences of the growth of the spectacle, demonstrating Vaneigem's (1967/1984: 236) formulation, 'The repressive unity of Power is threefold: constraint, seduction, and mediation are its three functions.' The spectacle has achieved one of its peaks in the new means of consumption. Here the process of consumption becomes a pseudo-event representing the implosion of the four techniques of the spectacle reviewed above. The new means of consumption are at once distribution factories, pseudo-festivals, fully equipped blocks of time and generators of pseudo-needs. The combination of spectacular techniques in the new means of consumption is, thus, a totally integrated version of spectacle and the paradigm for the spectacular society of the twenty-first century. An analysis of shopping malls illustrates the heightened unity of the spectacle, the ubiquity of fully equipped blocks of time and the transformation of the pseudo-festival.

Though malls perhaps began as mere 'distribution factories', they have clearly outgrown this role: once a place to shop, the mall has grown into the mega-mall as a festive, fully equipped destination. Entertainment and merchandising are combined in a mind-boggling dream world of glamour and 'fun'. A trip to the mall is an enchanting respite from mundane everyday life, a chance to stroll about in the land of the brand-new, the cutting edge, and the must-have. Today's somnambulants roam stores like Nature Company, Sharper Image, and Learning Store that target curiosity to sell their products. Like raccoons, people are attracted to shiny things.

The new shopping mall represents the heightened unity of the spectacle. Although the situationists are prescient in describing a totally commodified world, they could not have anticipated the *microcosmic worlds of commodities* that shopping malls and other new means of consumption have become. Hotels, food courts, dentists' and optometrists' offices, the DMV, movie theaters and a wide variety of entertainment are all found inside. No longer can the spectacle be described as colonizing social life, rather, the spectacle is building its own society within the walls of the shopping malls and other new means of consumption. This society is premised on commodity consumption that is homogenous, rationalized, functional, impersonal, productive, under constant surveillance, and utterly spectacular. The situationist nightmare realizes its true potential in the totally integrated shopping mall.

Furthermore, malls around the world offer the same stores, the same products and what amounts to the same experience. The unity of the spectacle grows in intensity when France, China, and America look alike (as they do increasingly in terms of commodities and the settings in which they are sold). The new means of consumption seduce the world into craving the same goods and images, jettisoning much of locality and difference in the process.

Similarly, because the intensification of the spectacle has fully equipped all of time, we can no longer speak of merely marketing fully equipped blocks of time. Debord's concept and our specific examples – the mall and the cruise ship – are incommensurate with the extent of today's spectacle where all times and all places are accessible to variegated and compulsory consumption. For this reason, pseudo-festivals cease to be cyclical; that the pseudo-festival is available any time is a key element of the new means of consumption and their enormous success. Today's shopping malls emphasize their festive atmosphere all year round, not just for cyclical festivals. They are holiday and vacation destinations, places to stop after work, places to take the kids, places to get a bite, and places to go for a walk. Food courts, museums, movie theaters, atriums, carnival rides, and musical performances make shopping an event and an experience. The new means of consumption routinize the carnivalesque by offering a festive atmosphere, awash with people and extravagance, all day, every day. As such, they have replaced the traditional rhythms of collective life with a new and monotonous rhythm of consumption. Our days, seasons, and lives are punctuated with purchases 'appropriate' to the festival at hand.

The new means of consumption can be understood in terms of the evolving integration and rationalization of the spectacle (as we saw in Chapter 6 rationalization itself can be spectacular). Resources are marshaled and technologies employed for concentrated experiments in refining the spectacle. As veritable laboratories of spectacular techniques, the new means of consumption create novel recipes of simulation, extravaganza, pseudo-interaction and abundance to hone the seductiveness and legitimacy of the spectacle. As the spectacle becomes more rationalized, techniques once applied intermittently (like the marketing of fully equipped blocks of time and cyclical pseudo-festivals) are sustained permanently in order not to miss any time that might be spent consuming.

Shopping malls, cybermalls, superstores and theme parks, among others, compete as elements of the dominant fraction of the spectacle. Out-dazzling each other, the new means of consumption push the spectacle to dizzying heights of glamour and gloss. Simultaneously, the new means of consumption gain competence at controlling, mollifying, and co-opting individuals. Resistance to early spectacular images may have been possible but individuals find it increasingly difficult to avoid, let alone resist, the omnipresent and potent images deployed by the new means of consumption. One need only compare the lure of an early means of consumption like the department store to more contemporary means of consumption like the mega-mall to fathom the increasingly intensive and extensive spectacularization and commodification of our society.

On the other hand, spectacularization has been with us for so long that people may grow numb to its effects or get wise to the game. The SI believe this to be the case. In the next section we will consider the situationists' ideas on the consumer in relation to the new means of consumption.

A Theory of the Consumer

The new means of consumption is a decentered concept. In *Enchanting a Disenchanted World* the gaze does not fall mainly on individuals but rather on the settings of consumption. This strategy has the advantage of concretely describing macro-objective social phenomena (the new means of consumption as structures) without imputing any perspectives or motives to the consumer. Instead, the approach attempts to understand the conscious and unconscious objectives of the new means of consumption: enchant the setting in order to lure the consumer and thereby to sell more products. By using this approach, *Enchanting a Disenchanted World* seeks to steer clear of the sticky debate over the role of consumers in consumption.

An appropriate theory of the consumer could, however, result in a deeper understanding of the processes underlying the evolution of the new means of consumption (see Chapter 4 for more on the consumer in McDonaldized settings). A dialectic of enchantment and boredom reconciles the continual renovation of the new means of consumption with the situationists' consumer. As such, it links the macro-sociological idea of re-enchantment with a compatible micro-level social psychology. This, of course, is not the only way to look at the consumer, but it is the one to be employed here.

Gabriel and Lang (1995) detail an extensive list of types of consumers. Theorists' assumptions about what consumers are like will influence their views on consumer society. The Frankfurt School thought that consumers were manipulated fools and consequently believed that consumer culture offered illusions of freedom, choice and pleasure and integrated individuals into a system of exploitation by encouraging them to define desires and identities in terms of commodities (Slater, 1997: 121). Another version casts the consumer as a hero able to navigate the marketplace rationally in pursuit of self-interest (Slater, 1997: 33). This view is taken by economic liberals who see consumption as an act of individual self-determination, rational calculation and social advancement. A third view is offered by the postmodernists who describe the consumer as 'ironic and knowing, reflexive and aware of the game being played' (Slater, 1997: 197). In contrast to the mass society view, the postmodern consumer has the awareness, cultural capital and wealth to navigate commodity culture, to make meaning of, and to interact playfully with its signs. It would be unnecessarily reductionistic to insist that a single view is correct. Rather, it is likely that there are multiple types of consumers and they will be more or less likely to be taken in by advertisements, to build fantasy lives through purchases, or to become enchanted with the new means of consumption depending on their creativity, sophistication, and thriftiness. Though the situationists, perhaps because they were French, disaffected, young, and artistic and wrote for an audience of their peers, believed that most consumers are alienated and bored, their political program requires only that *some* consumers be alienated and bored.

In the situationist view, consumers are confronted with a culture industry and commodity culture similar to the edifice described by the Frankfurt School. Moreover, this edifice has produced a culture similar to that described by the postmodernists for whom image is also paramount. The difference from both the Frankfurt School and the postmodernists is that rather than being taken in (duped) or not, indoctrinated or creative, knowledgeable or imaginative, the SI argue the individual confronted with consumer culture will, above all, feel estranged and bored.

The SI diagnose a disconnect between culture and individuals because objective culture – the spectacle produced by capitalist social relations – tends to inhibit active participation by the subject.[5] Individuals are alienated non-participants in the abundance of non-intersubjective culture generated by media, technology, and productive processes. Transposed to commodity culture, this disconnection is characterized as alienation from the creation of a spectacle in the commodity form. In other words, creative production of one's own social life is by and large displaced by the profusion of commodities and their settings. As such, individuals are likely to feel bored by the simulated life they live but, paradoxically, cannot participate in making. 'You can't lose: two fridges, a VW, TV, a promotion, time to kill ... but then the monotony of the images we consume gets the upper hand, reflecting the monotony of the action which produces them' (Vaneigem, 1967/1984: 25).

This is not to say that there is no possibility of creativity or agency in the situationist program. Their most novel contribution (to be discussed more thoroughly below) is their ideas about resisting the spectacle. On the one hand, individuals can decontextualize and disrupt the dominant meanings of images and consumer products, a technique called *detournement*, by interpreting images and using products in new ways. On the other, individuals can *avoid* the spectacle, a process called *derive*, and try to find areas of everyday life as yet uncolonized by the spectacle. Nevertheless, the recognition of a gut feeling of boredom with the insufficiency of the spectacle remains the first step toward resistance.

The concept of boredom integrates conventional Marxist notions of false consciousness with Weber's idea of disenchantment. From the Marxist perspective, the consumer engages in fetishistic consumption in a misguided reification of the system of objects. But, the consumer is wise enough to feel discouraged and disenchanted, unfulfilled by commodity culture. The monotony of being involved in spectacular society causes the boredom that leads to critical consciousness (valuable because rationalization is, for Weberian Marxists, a tool of capitalism, not a one-way ticket to the iron cage). This fusion results in a situationist consumer who is smarter and better able to recognize the insufficiency of spectacular society than the consumer in either the liberal economic or the critical perspective.

Although the SI argues that boredom precipitates class consciousness, the concept of the cathedrals of consumption creates a dialectic between the potentially bored spectator and the spectacle. The boredom intrinsic to spectatorship requires the continual re-enchantment[6] of the new means of consumption. In this reformulation, the monotony of the spectacle – intrinsically rationalized and commodified – induces boredom. The spectacle, accordingly, adapts (or at least the spectacles' creators adapt; assuming there are creators) by creating a higher level of spectacle, remystifying and re-enchanting in an effort to dazzle the spectator in perpetuity. Ergo, postmodern characteristics like ephemerality, transience, and instantaneity become part and parcel of spectacularization and should be read as the flailings of a system trying to keep the attention of its increasingly bored and restless audience.

Both seductive and alienating, the spectacle concurrently enchants while prohibiting any truly human participation. Because of this contradiction, there is a special dialectical relationship at work in the new means of consumption making for extreme sensitivity to the law of diminishing returns. Spectators cannot remain enchanted by a particular spectacle, image, or cathedral of consumption forever. Any particular spectacle will ultimately become tedious. Visited often enough, even Disney World or Las Vegas loses its luster. This relationship is true in the particular and the universal: the whole of spectacular society can become humdrum. Therefore, re-enchantment is necessary to the continuation of the spectacular society and the new means of consumption. If they succeed in adapting, the new means of consumption can reproduce themselves indefinitely. If not, they will be condemned to the dustbin of history.

The concept of re-enchantment has grave implications for situationist theory. The situationist hope for class consciousness via boredom is limited by the counter-efforts of the spectacle to re-enchant itself, becoming once again dazzling, seductive and new. Though the spell of the Hard Rock Cafe, Planet Hollywood, and the Rainforest Café will one day be broken, they are likely to be replaced by cathedrals of consumption producing even more magical spells. Hope rests in the routinization of novelty. As ever more dazzling spectacles are produced at preprogrammed intervals, doubtless, consumers will also become bored by them.

Resisting the New Means of Consumption

The SI became famous in France for its role as propagandists and provocateurs in the events of May '68, when their slogans helped motivate the students to take to the streets ('Underneath the cobblestones, the beach'). Like all good Marxists, the SI developed, along with its theoretical work, a theory of revolutionary praxis and transcendence.[7] In this section we will analyse this, their most novel contribution, in relation to the new means of consumption. First, we will show the SI argued that the spectacle is at once dominating and, at the same time, an image of a better society. Then, we will contrast radical subjectivity with traditional Marxist praxis. Last, we will outline three ways of resisting the spectacle – *derive, detournement* and the construction of situations.

Though the spectacle represents the domination of the individual by the image and the commodity, it is possible to identify within it the seeds of transcendence. The SI claimed the promise of the spectacle – dazzling abundance, festivity, leisure and pleasure – can be taken literally to inform revolutionary praxis. This position is analogous to the strategy of American reformists who measure the promises of the Constitution against the reality of life (the style of criticism that informed the Civil Rights and Woman's Rights movements). Instead of a foundational text, the SI bases an immanent critique on the spectacle's contradictions – its promise and its reality. They place their bets on, 'A creative, imaginative, and sensuous subjectivity, it takes the promises of the spectacle literally, willing the end of all separation and refusing to perpetuate the sacrifices, deferrals, and endless layers which mark its relationship to the world' (Plant, 1992: 38). This subjectivity is expected to defy the objectivity of the spectacle. Vaneigem's positing of radical subjectivity as a revolutionary agent is a contrast with more traditional Marxist accounts of universal history that proffer an objective view of history – the 'inevitability' of the proletarian revolution. When the situationists were active, a century after Marx, it must have been difficult for any critic of capitalism to accept the notion of 'inevitability'.

Though it dominates us in its constraining, seductive, mediated form, the spectacle is potentially a participatory utopia when released from the commodity form and capitalist social relations. Advertisements, media, and the new means of consumption offer a transcendent vision of happiness and abundance, but rarely deliver the goods. Indeed, creativity, desire, and spontaneity go un-nourished in a spectacle-induced poverty of the soul. The SI believe that this contradiction will be seized upon by individuals, providing the impetus to create a new intersubjective spectacle: picture a ruthless king being overthrown by oppressed peasants who subsequently move into his immensely beautiful castle.

The notion of radical subjectivity is quite distant from more traditional notions of praxis. The SI chose it because they were impatient with the idea that careful theory is the essential ingredient of revolution. Debord believed that the 'science of revolutions' had become too conservative, 'consciousness now always came on the scene too soon, and needed to be taught' (Debord, 1967/1994: 55). The scientific-determinist character of Marxian theory underestimated praxis. In Lukács' work, for example, revolutions develop when conditions are ripe and class consciousness depends on the dissemination of scientific knowledge among the proletariat. What results is a structuralist-like despair of objective social relations in the capitalist system (again the Frankfurt School is the exemplar). The SI pin its hopes on the possibility of individual critical consciousness and a consciousness of desire. Individuals can become aware of spectacularization and have the volition to take their lives back. As such, radical subjectivity balances Marxian structuralist-determinist analyses with strong agency. In contrast with the Marxists, the SI believes an individual can easily gain the critical consciousness needed to conduct his or her own rebellion.

The situationist perspective has risks. The immanent critique of spectacular society and the subjectivity from which it arises offer no guarantees of scientific correctness, of success, or of its vision for the future. Because any person can revolt against the spectacle, there are any number of possible outcomes. This revolution is as likely to result in barbarism as utopia – another of the fears of the Frankfurt School and of other, more contemporary, thinkers such as Bauman. With subjectivity, the SI trades Marxist teleology for uncertainty of the goals and outcomes of a revolutionary project. Marx's vision placed its trust in class consciousness, something which would come in time, but the SI believes the time is now: people can become conscious of their desires and rebel against the spectacle.

An inter-subjective spectacle (as compared to one imposed by, for example, the cathedrals of consumption) is built by individuals acting creatively without having their desires influenced by spectacular society or their relationships mediated by commodities. This spectacle will be everyday life and unalienated festivity to the hilt, with radical subjectivity realizing its potential in love, poetry and play (Vaneigem, 1967/1984).

By invoking such terms as love and poetry, the SI distinguishes its theoretical stance from traditional Marxism. The novelty of the position is the recognition that capitalist relations of domination had shifted from the realm of production to the realm of consumption and the revolution too needs to take place there. Having shifted the battlefield, the SI updated revolutionary rhetoric to match the characteristics of late capitalism. By defining techniques of resistance based on the subversive misuse of commodities, images and culture, the SI developed an enormous variety of subjective challenges to the spectacle, three of which are considered below.

Derive – or drifting – is a tactic borrowed from the surrealists (Spector, 1997). An individual or small group would stroll through everyday life, trying to find the spaces and places where the spectacle was in crisis or the dominant mode of living was not enforced. Drifters witnessed all manner of vandalism and play; behaviors they treated as instances of rebellion. They approached this work as a scientific enterprise (psycho-geography) and even drew maps of the contours of the spectacle and the points of crisis and lack of enforcement.

> One evening, as night fell, my friends and I wandered into the Palais de Justice in Brussels ... As we wandered through the labyrinth of corridors, staircases and suite after suite of rooms, we discussed what could be done to make the place habitable; for a time we occupied the enemy's territory; through the power of our imagination we transformed the thieves' den into a fantastic funfair, into a sunny pleasure dome, where the most amazing adventures would, for the first time, be really lived. In short, subversion is the basic expression of creativity. Daydreaming subverts the world. People subvert, just as Jourdain did with prose and James Joyce did with *Ulysses*, spontaneously and with considerable reflection. (Vaneigem, in Gray, 1974: 150)

This technique holds promise for changing the new means of consumption. Consumers could and should unfix their gaze from products and prices and take a look around: a couple steals a kiss between the clothes racks, some kids spray-paint a wall, two oldsters argue at the top of their lungs. These cracks in the periphery of the spectacle are evidence that real life exists: sexual urges, destructive feelings, death, signs of crisis in the system. And these impulses are sometimes even directed against the spectacle itself, as when rioters tip over cars and break into shops, challenging the order of commodities. Any act of rebellion against the spectacle and any evidence of unalienated social life could spark the consciences of others, so drifters bolster the situationist belief in the will of individuals to resist the spectacle.

This brings us to another sense of *derive* – the seeking out of movements by actors other than those pre-designed by the environment. Many of the cathedrals of consumption are structured, both subtly and not so subtly, to get people to move in certain ways and not in others. Supermarkets tend to put the basics (meat, dairy, vegetables, bread) on far walls so that consumers must traverse the entire store in order to get them. Another major example is Disney World with its paths, methods for dealing with long lines, its 'weinies' (Walt Disney's term for attractions to which visitors will be drawn thereby leading them to move in the way the system wanted them to), and its Main Street through which visitors must enter and exit.

Clearly, the cathedrals of consumption would be altered greatly if people chose to move about in ways other than those pre-set by the designers and could be eventually brought to their knees if many people totally rejected the dictates of the system. Disney World is able to survive and prosper because of its ability to move people about in predetermined ways. If visitors refused to pass through Main Street and found a way around it, the businesses there would close and a significant source of revenue would be lost. If tourists refused to follow the paths and struck out on their own through bushes, over grassy areas, and through attractions that stood in their way, chaos would ensue. The Disney system would be destroyed by the simple act of refusing to queue at each attraction. Similarly disruptive would be efforts to find one's own way through attractions rather than riding in the various vehicles that move people through them. People clambering through and over the attractions at 'It's a Small World', rather than sitting quietly and passively in the designated conveyance, would be a phenomenon that the Disney organization, with its fetish for control, could not bear. Practicing *derive* in these and other ways would force at least a radical restructuring of Disney World and, more likely, lead to a shuttering of the park.

Derive at Disney World would not, in itself, pose a threat to consumer society, but if it was practiced routinely at the more mundane means of consumption, it would. Take the fast-food restaurant and the following subversive acts:

- Refusing to enter through the front door, but entering through the side door.
- Instead of queuing, consumers simply storm the counter.
- Backing into the queue at the drive-through window or entering it from the opposite direction.
- After exiting the drive-through window, parking one's car, and then returning to the restaurant to put one's debris in its receptacles.
- For those who eat in the restaurant, eating one's food while standing in the middle of the restaurant.
- Bringing additional debris to one's table (perhaps even trash brought from home) rather than gathering everything up after one eats and depositing it in the appropriate trash can.

Acts such as these would clearly have a dramatic effect, to put it mildly, on the fast-food restaurant. More generally, if acts of this kind were repeated in superstores, malls, and the like, there would be dramatic changes in the way we consume on an everyday basis and perhaps on the way we live our lives on a daily basis.

The situationists developed another technique, called *detournement*, which advocates the deliberate and subversive misuse or misunderstanding of images and objects. For the SI, plagiarism and misinterpretation are forms of political resistance to the over-determined meanings of the code. One way Vaneigem put *detournement* into action was by recaptioning cartoons. Among the first to employ this technique, well-known from such films as Woody Allen's *What's Up Tiger Lily?*, situationists would take an ordinary cartoon and re-write the script using their own subversive rhetoric. In this way, the SI hoped to re-situate objects, freeing them from the domination of their spectacular context.[8] Critical-creative consciousness never takes objects at face value, it imagines what they could be. A similar technique might be employed in the new means of consumption. As Best and Kellner (forthcoming) note, the spectacle has in recent years become interactive, allowing and demanding participation. Nevertheless, the spectacle determines the form and extent of participation. Phenomena like interactive television, virtual reality games and the Internet are participatory but only in a patterned way. Almost any interaction with an employee at Disney World is scripted and tightly monitored. *Detournement* indicates non-conformist participation could be a useful way to challenge the hegemony of the spectacle. The goal would be to break the rhythm and order of the system of commodities. One might, say, take the free pretzel sample and hurl it across the shopping mall's food-court – it's not food, it's a projectile!

Direct challenges to the new means of consumption like pretzel-tossing are in our estimation inappropriate techniques for non-revolutionaries. First, remember the 'access points' to the new means of consumption are peopled by exploited service workers. To challenge the new means of consumption in this way causes problems for these people, not the spectacle or the dominant fraction. Second, the new means of consumption not only demand our attention, they also watch us. They are under heavy surveillance and they will prosecute to the fullest extent of the law.

Although these more radical applications of *detournement* may be off-limits to some, as technologies of resistance, they still have their uses. As communication, *detournement* denies definitive interpretations and precise meanings – it is the 'fluid language of anti-ideology' (Debord, 1967/1994: 208). Anticipating Lyotard, the situationists envision *detournement* as a non-coercive discourse – free association and play with language, interpretation and objects stimulate creative subjectivity and challenges the legitimacy of the spectacle and sanctioned culture.

In addition to *derive* and *detournement*, the situationists proposed the construction of real, uncommodified, unmediated situations as counterpoint to the spectacle. The SI wants to create opportunities for people to engage in social interaction unmediated by commodities, the spectacle, and dominant culture:

What we consider to be a truly meaningful experiment lies in setting up, on the basis of desires which are already more or less clearly conscious, a temporary field of activity which is favourable to the further development of these desires. This alone can lead to the further clarification of those desires which are already conscious and to the first chaotic appearance of new ones. (IS, in Gray, 1974: 13)

A typical situation might involve gathering a number of old friends in an appropriate setting, some interventions (surprises – hopefully, everyone can bring a surprise) and some strangers to join in. The simple enactment of 'true' desires, repressed but available to us in dreams and imagination, will challenge the functional, boring spectacle with a participatory spectacle. If you are a consumer, the situationists want you either to avoid or subvert the new means of consumption in favor of creating your own spectacle. It is especially important not to be coerced into consuming or be pacified by the new means of consumption. Thus, resistance to the new means of consumption might simply entail doing something fun and out-of-the-ordinary.

Conclusion

The new means of consumption are a paradigmatic example of what the spectacle has become and where it is heading in the future. The spectacle will continue to integrate and dazzle, homogenize and pacify. The new means of consumption are also at the nexus of system-wide developments in capitalism – the vanguard of commodification, technological development and spectacularization. Within their walls – material or virtual – glamorous images pique desire, pacify individuals and mystify, legitimate, and reproduce social relations.

Because of rapidly changing social relations within the dominant mode of production, studies of the cathedrals of consumption are extremely important. Social scientists, theorists, and revolutionaries alike would be wise to consider the internal logic of the spectrum of spectacles. It is imperative that spectacles be identified and their techniques exposed in order to raise consciousness. We need more information on the techniques, trajectories, manifest and latent consequences of these relatively new phenomena. In short, we need an expanded 'science of the spectacle'.

The problems with situationist theory are similar to those of Lukács' Weberian Marxism. Eager to identify opportunities for transcendence and relying heavily on Marx, Lukács' theory oversimplifies reification. Rather than seeing multiple logics of reification, as Weber might analyze the various rationalities employed by institutions, Lukács reduces all rationality to the service of capitalism and commodification. Similarly, reification is seen as a unity and possibilities for transcendence are posited against such a unity.

The situationists fall into a similar trap. Not all spectacles take the commodity form. Political spectacles like the Monica Lewinsky scandal, technological spectacles like the John Glenn shuttle launch, and military spectacles like the Gulf War each have their own internal logic worthy of study. Situationist theory is uniquely equipped to cope with the multiple logics of multiple spectacles because it does not truly require any concept of totality for the transcendence of radical subjectivity. However, we should not lose sight of the fact that there are commonalities among all of these spectacles and that they act together to pacify people.

Thus, the work of the SI is incomplete. An expanded science of the spectacle should study the multiple logics of fractions of the spectacle. At the same time, it should probe for weakness in its structures and identify possibilities for resistance. Last, it should disseminate this information to as wide a readership as possible. This is not expert discourse, but essential knowledge for anyone confronted with spectacular society.

This chapter attempts to delineate, in all its specificity, one type of spectacle. It captures the character of the new means of consumption as controlling, exploitative, legitimating and spectacular. Furthermore, the goal has been to be both pragmatic and accessible to lay-people. As such, the goal is to inform efforts to resist the hegemony of the spectacle. Other work, on topics like the spectacularization of politics and the media, are also badly needed.

Some Reservations

While this discussion has focused on the utility of the situationist approach, it has its limitations. The major problem is traceable to the focus on 'situations' and just what is meant by that term. The situationists see a dialectical process in which people are both products of situations and create those situations. Since they are products of situations, it is necessary for people to produce truly human situations. Relatedly, since people are defined by their situations, they must create situations worthy of their desires. Thus, the free and playful construction of situations is an especially revolutionary moment as far as the situationists are concerned. We are enjoined to 'construct the situations in which we live' (Plant, 1992: 32). This is all well and good as long as we think of situations in microscopic terms. We can rather easily play with and reconstruct our interactions with friends, acquaintances, even strangers. Thus, within the shopping mall we can engage in little conspiracies with our friends, jest with acquaintances and act in unexpected ways toward strangers.

However, the situation is more complex when we think of larger scale phenomena in these terms. For example, Plant discusses shopping malls (and similar cathedrals of consumption) as situations that have been constructed for us. Thus, the mall is a large-scale situation that encompasses many more microscopic situations and is, itself, enmeshed in even more macroscopic situations. Staying with the mall, Plant makes it clear that it manipulates people, their experiences and their actions. Given this power, it is clear that it will be far harder to reconstruct the situation that is the mall. It has a structure that will resist such efforts and it employs social control agents who perform a similar function.

Further, malls are larger and more distant from us than face-to-face situations and this, too, makes it much harder to reorder them. Thus, the situationist approach fits small unstructured situations best, as well as small, face-to-face situations within larger situations. It does not work well when the concern is the restructuring of larger social phenomena.

It might be argued that changes in micro-situations will eventually culminate in the alteration of a macro-situation such as the mall. This seems far-fetched, but the real problem is that no mechanism is specified, no scenario is outlined, that could take us from tossing pretzels to bringing the Mall of America to a standstill and eventually altering its fundamental structure (for example, turning it into a stadium in which pretzel-tossing contests are held).

Notes

This chapter is published here for the first time and was co-authored by Todd Stillman.

1   *Detournement* is the recontexualization of images and objects to subvert their dominant meanings.

2   *Derive*, or drifting, is a systematic search for 'situations'. Situationists would roam the city looking for or creating examples of unalienated everyday life erupting despite the spectacle.

3   All references to *The Society of the Spectacle* record the numbered aphorism rather than page number.

4   The city is considered by the SI to be a setting in which human beings can interact to form non-commodified ways of life. Of course, this is obviously a city not yet Disneyfied.

5   Although in some settings, especially the new dematerialized locales, consumers are quite active.

6   Commodity fetishism and re-enchantment are conceptual cousins. The former involves a mystification of commodities while the latter posits the mystification of rationalized structures. When commodities and rationalized structures become intertwined in Lukács' concept of reification, Debord's concept of spectacle, or the new means of consumption, reenchantment and commodity fetishism are two sides of the same coin.

7   This section takes into consideration some of the SI's more novel ideas about resistance. We have refrained from taking up Debord's oft-critiqued advocacy of workers'

councils as a form of socialist government chiefly because it does not apply to the new means of consumption.

8   This facet of situationist theory works with a post-structuralist paradigm. The fixed meanings of signs, encompassing all commodities produced by the spectacular economy, can be made contingent and uncertain by re-contextualizing the signs. The SI understood the role of signs but they believed these were consequences of the dominant mode of production. Thus, Baudrillard's hyper-reality is a condition endemic to capitalism, not an inalienable mode of being. For the situationists, contingent meanings and the production of new meanings in everyday life challenge the dominance of the code. In Debord's words, '[It] is not structuralism that serves to prove the transhistorical validity of the society of the spectacle; but, on the contrary, it is the society of the spectacle, imposing itself in its massive reality, that validates the chill dream of structuralism' (Debord, 1967/1994: 202). (For opposing interpretations of the affinities between Baudrillard and the SI, see Plant, 1992 and Crary, 1984).

10

THORSTEIN VEBLEN IN THE AGE OF HYPERCONSUMPTION

Thorstein Veblen has always had a small, but significant, following in the social sciences. However, his influence has increased recently because his famous work on 'conspicuous consumption' anticipates the growing importance of consumption (absolutely and in comparison to production) in American society and much of the rest of the world, as well as the increasing academic interest in sociology (and other fields) in consumption.[1] Yet, the irony is that Veblen was very much a product of his times (late nineteenth- and early twentieth-century America) and, as a result, he shares with the other classical theorists of the day a focal interest in issues relating to production. Before we rush to give Veblen too much credit as a theorist of consumption, we must recognize that the vast majority of his work is devoted to production; his ideas on consumption are embedded in, and subordinated to, his thinking on production. Thus, one objective here will be to outline Veblen's once familiar, but now far less well known, theory of production so that we may better understand his thinking in general as well as its relationship to his perspective on consumption.

A second objective will be to revisit Veblen's ideas on consumption from the point of view of today's world of hyperconsumption. Clearly, the social world in general, and the world of consumption specifically, have changed dramatically since Veblen's time. We need to examine and assess how well his ideas on consumption, especially his famous notion of conspicuous consumption, fare when they are examined from the point of view of a new and very different world of consumption.

Veblen's Theory of Production and How it Relates to his Theory of Consumption

One of the places in which Veblen's 'productionism' is manifest is in his basic assumption that humans have a primary instinct of workmanship. That is, people instinctively make efficient use of available means and seek to adequately manage available resources. This instinct involves 'practical expedients, ways and means, devices and contrivances of efficiency and economy, proficiency, creative work and technological mastery of facts ... a proclivity for taking pains' (Veblen, 1922/1964: 33).

It is manifest at the micro level in terms of the technical efficiency of the individual worker and at the macro level in the technological proficiency and accomplishments of the community as a whole (the 'industrial arts', see below). The instinct of workmanship is found throughout the social world in domains as diverse as the arts, religion, and law. In a way, it relates to all ends since it is concerned with achieving ends in the best possible way.

Veblen sees the industrial arts, or technological knowledge, as 'a common stock, held and carried forward collectively by the community' (Veblen, 1922/1964: 103); a historical product, that is continually changing. However, the new additions are slight in comparison to the total body handed down from the past. The efficiency of individual workers, as well as the community as a whole, is a function of the state of the industrial arts. Efficiency is apt to be high when these arts are well developed and it is likely to be low when they are underdeveloped. This background on the instinct of workmanship and the industrial arts helps us to better understand Veblen's most general productivist concern throughout his career – the conflict between business and industry. While to our way of thinking these terms seem closely related, to Veblen there is a stark contrast, in fact an inherent conflict, between them: 'The material interest of the underlying population [largely those associated with industry] is best served by maximum output at a low cost, while the business interests of the industry's owners ['business'] may best be served by a moderate output at an enhanced price.' The instinct of workmanship and the industrial arts relate to output maximization in industry. That is, more efficient workers and well-developed industrial arts lead to higher output. Veblen clearly values all three (the instinct, the arts, and output maximization) and is critical of business to the degree that it inhibits any and all of them.

Veblen details a historic change in the nature of business and business leaders. The early leaders tended to be entrepreneurs who were designers, builders, shop managers and financial managers. They were more likely than contemporary entrepreneurs to have truly earned their income because, at least in part, it was derived from their direct contribution to production. In other words, Veblen positively values the early business leaders because they functioned more like industry. Today's business leaders are almost exclusively concerned with financial matters and therefore, at least in Veblen's view, they are not earning their income since finance makes no direct contribution to industry. A further development involved the routinization of financial matters and the rise of financial organizations (for example, investment bankers) to handle them. As a result, the business leader is left as an intermediary between industry and finance with little concrete knowledge of either.

It is business that tends to define production in Veblen's day. The 'captains of industry'[2] as well as the 'captains of solvency' (the investment bankers, financiers who come eventually to control the captains of industry) have a business orientation (and are members of the leisure class). A business orientation is defined by a pecuniary approach to economic processes; that is, the dominant interest is money. (This also turns out to be true in consumption, as well, since the business leaders make up a significant proportion of the leisure class and they bring their pecuniary orientation to their leadership position in consumption.) The focus is not on the interest of the larger community but rather on the profitability of the organization and the income of the business leader. Relatedly, business is oriented to acquisition and ownership, not production, and it serves the interest of invidious rather than non-invidious interests. By being highly profitable, business leaders seek to be the envy of their peers. (Again, this notion of invidious distinction also plays a prominent role in Veblen's thinking on consumption, especially conspicuous consumption.) Since it is non-productive (as is conspicuous leisure and conspicuous consumption), Veblen (1919/ 1964: 69) sees a business orientation as parasitic and exploitative: 'the chances are that the owner has contributed less than his per-capita quota, if anything, to that common fund of knowledge on the product of which he draws by virtue of his ownership, because he is likely to be fully occupied with other things – such things as lucrative business transactions, for example, or the decent consumption of superfluities' (here is a clear reflection of the relationship of all of this to consumption). Instead of production, business leaders focus on 'sharp practice', '"cornering the market"' and '"sitting tight"' (Veblen, 1923: 34).

Veblen gives the business leader credit for increasing productive capacity, but Veblen's (1904) most distinctive contribution here is to see such leaders as being at least as much involved in 'disturbing' production and in restricting capacity as they are in increasing it. Veblen not only associates business leaders with the waste of material resources, equipment and manpower as a result of the restriction of capacity, but of other ills as well. (As we will see, since business leaders are also part of the leisure class they are guilty of waste in *both* production and consumption.) Business people are responsible for the unproductive and wasteful expansion of 'salesmanship' ('little else than prevarication'; Veblen, 1919/1964: 69) and the attendant sales costs that are passed on to the consumer. In addition, Veblen attributes to business people the production of unnecessary and useless products (and, as members of the leisure class they consume products that are useless and unnecessary) and the dislocation of industrial processes through sabotage.

Veblen sees the modern corporation as a type of business. As such, its interests are in financial matters like profit and in sales and not in production and workmanship. As he puts it, 'the corporation is always a business concern, not an industrial appliance. It is a means of making money, not of making goods' (Veblen, 1923: 85).

Industry has to do with 'the apprehension and coordination of mechanical facts and sequences, and ... their appreciation and utilisation for the purposes of human life' (Veblen, 1899/1934: 232). An industrial orientation is associated with those involved in workmanship and production. It is the working classes that are most likely to be involved in these activities and to have such an orientation. Unlike business's pecuniary orientation which leads to a personal standpoint (that is, their own profits), the industrial orientation leads to an 'impersonal standpoint, of sequence, quantitative relations, mechanical efficiency, or use' (Veblen, 1899/1934: 239).

Unfortunately, industry is controlled by the captains of industry who have little or no understanding of it (Veblen, 1919/1964: 89). In fact, the main interest of those leaders is to restrict production, restrict the free operation of the industrial system, in order to keep prices (and therefore profits) high. The result, to Veblen, is that the main task of the business leader is to obstruct, retard and sabotage[3] the operation of the industrial system. Without such obstructions, the extraordinary productivity of the industrial system would drive prices and profits progressively lower. This would be a boon to the community as a whole, but adversely affect business.

Veblen also calls those associated with a business orientation 'vested interests', or those with the 'marketable right to get something for nothing' (Veblen, 1919/1964: 100). While they may be getting something for nothing, they cost the larger society a great deal. These costs stem from three business activities aimed at increasing profit – limitation of the supply of products, obstruction of their traffic, and publicity. All of these are aimed at salesmanship, not workmanship. They add nothing to production and, as a result, are viewed by Veblen as waste.[4] He argues that although it may benefit the pecuniary interests of the captains of industry, the work that salesmen (and accountants) perform 'is, on the whole, useless or detrimental to the community at large' (Veblen, 1904: 63). To the costs associated with these activities, Veblen adds illegal business activities such as fraud. Not only are the captains of industry parasites, but Veblen (1904: 64) describes entire industries – advertising, military equipment, and those involved in 'turning out goods for conspicuously wasteful consumption' (thus conspicuous waste is a problem in *both* production and consumption) – as parasitic.

The increasingly tightly interlocking industrial system lends itself to cooperative undertakings, but this characteristic makes it increasingly vulnerable to the efforts of business and national leaders to sabotage it. This may be done consciously or as a result of the business leader's increasing ignorance of industrial operations (Veblen (1921: 64) writes of the 'one-eyed captains of industry'). In either case, it results in hardship to the community in the form of unemployment, idle factories, and wasted resources. Veblen (1904: 213–14) even goes so far as to imply that business leaders are consciously responsible for depressions; they reduce production because under certain market conditions they feel they cannot derive what they emotionally consider to be a 'reasonable' profit from their goods:[5]

> Industrial depression means that the business men engaged do not see their way to derive a satisfactory gain from letting the industrial process go forward on the lines and in the volume for which the material equipment of industry is designed. It is not worth their while, and it might even work them pecuniary harm. Commonly their apprehension of the discrepancy which forbids an aggressive pursuit of industrial business is expressed by the phrase 'overproduction'.

To Veblen, there is no such thing as overproduction from the point of view of the larger community. However, even with the activities of the business leaders, including the creation of depressions, the industrial system is still so effective and efficient that it yields returns far beyond that required to cover costs and to give reasonable returns to owners and investors.

These additional returns are the source of what Veblen calls 'free income'. Most generally, free income is that 'income for which no equivalent in useful work is given' (Veblen, 1923: 126). This free income is attributed by business leaders to intangible assets of the firm such as possession of trade secrets, trademarks, patents, and monopolies. The problem is that these intangibles produce *nothing*. Rather, the free income that goes to the captains of industry and their investors is the result of the constraints that these intangible assets place on the free operation of the industrial system. In addition to harming industrial efficiency, these intangibles also adversely affect the entire community because far less is produced than could be. Veblen (1919/1964: 76) sees an analogy between the operations of business leaders and 'blackmail, ransom, and any similar enterprise that aims to get something for nothing'.

The free income earned by the captains of industry has been capitalized by the firm and this results in pressure on the firm to keep prices and profits high. Capitalization of the firm is no longer just the cost of the plant, but also the 'good will' of the organization including 'established customary business relations, reputation for upright dealing, franchises and privileges, trade-marks, brands, patent rights, copyrights, exclusive use of special processes guarded by law or by secrecy, exclusive control of particular sources of materials' (Veblen, 1904: 139). The problem with all of these things is that they 'give a differential advantage to their owners, but they are of no aggregate advantage to the community. They are wealth to the individuals concerned – differential wealth; but they make no part of the wealth of nations' (Veblen, 1904: 139–40).

Veblen traces many of the problems within the economy to the operation of the price system. For example, he argues that the nature of the price system and the need to maintain prices so that a reasonable profit may be earned and business recession prevented makes it necessary for the captains of industry to sabotage production through 'peaceable or surreptitious restriction, delay, withdrawal, or obstruction' (Veblen, 1921: 4). The 'problem', again, is that the industrial system is so productive that business leaders must sabotage it to some degree or else prices and profits will plunge.

Veblen sees the relationship between the price system and business leaders in much the same way that Marx sees the relationship between the capitalist system and the capitalists. (There are, as should be obvious, many other similarities between the theories of Veblen and Marx. For example, the basic conflict between capitalist and proletariat is transformed by Veblen into that between business and industry.) That is, both the price system and the capitalist system are seen as structures that are constraining on actors. Thus, in Veblen's case, even if a business leader wanted to ignore profits and concentrate on producing more goods so that the larger community might benefit, that business leader would quickly be pushed to the brink of bankruptcy. More generally, Veblen (1921: 14) sees business people as 'creatures and agents' of the price system.

Overall, the business leaders (and the leisure class to which they belong), and their pecuniary orientation, are associated with 'waste, futility, and ferocity' (Veblen, 1899/1934: 351). In encouraging such things, business (and the leisure class) tends to stand in opposition to the needs of modern, industrial society.

Given this brief overview of Veblen's thinking on the relationship between business and industry and his critical orientation to business, let us now turn to his famous ideas on consumption and how they look from the perspective of developments in the last century in consumption and in theorizing about consumption. Bear in mind that many of the ideas that we have discussed under the heading of production – instincts, a pecuniary orientation, invidious interests, consumption of 'superfluities', waste (especially conspicuous waste), and so on – are also related to Veblen's thinking on consumption. Also bear in mind that Veblen's primary goal throughout much of his life was to create and refine a production-based theory of the conflict between business and industry; his theory of consumption was a secondary, although not unrelated, development.

Veblen's Theory of Consumption in the New Millennium

Textual interpretation of *The Theory of the Leisure Class* must be sensitive to the dimensions of time and space. Veblen wrote this text one hundred years ago in the Midwest. This was a time before the advent of mass consumption; before mass advertising and the mass media; before credit cards and the Mall of America. America, especially the Midwest, was rural and Protestant; cities were gradually being built and the work ethic was strong. Veblen himself grew up on a farm in rural Minnesota, reared in a Norwegian Protestant family (Dorfman, 1934/1966). Veblen's 'habitus' needs to be understood in order to get an adequate sense of the meaning of conspicuous consumption (and leisure), as well as his critique of those who partake in it.

Conspicuous Consumption and Conspicuous Leisure

As we have seen, Veblen praises workmanship throughout his writings, and this must be taken into account when interpreting his thinking on consumption. While the term conspicuous consumption is generally defined as the ostentatious display of wealth, the value Veblen places on workmanship, or productive work, is evident in the way he defines conspicuous consumption as the 'unproductive consumption of goods' (Veblen, 1899/1934: 69). This meaning of conspicuous consumption is derived from Veblen's discussion of leisure as the 'non-productive consumption of time' (1899/1934: 43). The element of waste is common to both conspicuous consumption and leisure: 'From the foregoing survey of the growth of conspicuous leisure and consumption, it appears that the utility of both alike for the purposes of reputability lies in the element of waste that is common to both' (1899/1934: 85). Veblen (1899/1934: 91, 96) claims that both conspicuous consumption and leisure conform to the 'fundamental canon of conspicuous waste' and that in order for an expenditure 'to be reputable it must be wasteful'. As workmanship and productive efficiency became ignoble pursuits for the business/leisure class, they were relegated to technology and the working class. Simultaneously, their antithesis – waste – became increasingly valuable to the business/leisure class. Veblen is careful to explain what he means by waste and he attacks it in much the same way he criticizes business: 'It is here called "waste" because this expenditure does not serve human life or human well-being on the whole, not because it is waste or misdirection of effort or expenditure as viewed from the standpoint of the individual consumer who chooses it' (1899/1934: 97–8).

In order for one to participate in conspicuous waste one must first have the pecuniary orientation and the means to engage in such activity. The leisure class is the class that in Veblen's America had the means to engage in both conspicuous leisure and consumption; to waste time and money.

In the evolutionary model that Veblen elaborates in *The Theory of the Leisure Class*, conspicuous consumption eventually replaces conspicuous leisure as the primary means of displaying pecuniary strength. In modern societies, characterized by a high degree of anonymity and mobility, it is very difficult to display a conspicuous waste of time. It is far easier to be conspicuous on the basis of the goods one has purchased. Strangers passing each other on the street have no other option but to judge one another's reputability or worth by observing the consumer goods each is displaying: 'In order to impress these transient observers, and to retain one's self-complacency under their observation, the signature of one's pecuniary strength should be written in characters which he who runs may read' (Veblen, 1899/1934: 87). The most visible way to show that one has wealth is to conspicuously consume goods; to demonstrate that one has enough money to waste it on useless or overly expensive goods. Social worth or honor is above all based on wealth – something the leisure class accumulates far more of than any other class in society. As Veblen (1899/1934: 26, 29) states, 'the possession of wealth confers honor; it is an invidious distinction', and 'property becomes the most easily recognized evidence of a reputable degree of success'. Thus, 'it becomes indispensable to accumulate, to acquire property, in order to retain one's good name'. In this sense, social standing or status is not intrinsic to the actual consumer object itself (Marx's use value), but from the expensiveness of the consumer object (exchange value).[6] The qualities of the consumer object itself are superfluous; what is important is the wealth and status it signifies.

The Motive of Emulation

Perhaps the most important way Veblen utilizes the concept of conspicuous consumption is to explain the relationship between emulation and consumer behavior. According to Veblen, the motive behind ownership in general and consumption in particular is emulation. The leisure class wants to be emulated; the other social classes emulate it (although they, too, want to be emulated). Veblen's thinking here is based on his view that emulation is another crucial instinct: 'Men are moved by many impulses and driven by many instinctive dispositions. Among these abiding dispositions are a strong bent to admire and defer to persons of achievement and distinction, as well as a workmanlike disposition to find merit in any work that serves the common good' (Veblen, 1923: 115). Thus, the instinct of emulation applies to both production and the admiration of work that serves the good of the collectivity as well as consumption and the admiration of those who demonstrate achievement and distinction in it. In the world that Veblen examined, the chief means of demonstrating achievement, and thereby demonstrating that one was worthy of emulation, was conspicuous consumption. Veblen is suggesting that emulation is the primary motive behind consumption patterns. For Veblen (1899/1934: 26) the incentive for ownership *and* consumption has been 'from the outset the invidious distinction attaching to wealth'.

Emulation implies that social relations matter in terms of consumer behavior – we do not consume objects for their intrinsic worth, but because these objects are socially meaningful. Consumer goods ultimately derive meaning from comparison to other commodities – an invidious distinction based on pecuniary worth. While Veblen specifically focuses on the consumption habits of the leisure class, he acknowledges that 'no class of society, not even the most abjectly poor, forgoes all customary conspicuous consumption' (1899/1934: 85). Although we all may participate in conspicuous consumption, according to Veblen, only the leisure class has the power to determine which consumer goods are worthy of display for all social strata. 'The leisure class stands at the head of the social structure in point of reputability; and its manner of life and its standards of worth therefore afford the norm of reputability for the community' (1899/1934: 84). As the motive of emulation drives the desire to consume, invidious distinctions are made between members within the leisure class itself. Similar distinctions are made between members of the leisure class and those in lower social strata. The motive of emulation plays a crucial role throughout the entire system of stratification as 'members of each stratum accept as their ideal of decency the scheme of life in vogue in the next higher stratum' (1899/1934: 84). The leisure class continually strives to set itself apart from, or above, those classes below it, while those in lower classes continually strive to emulate the consumer habits established by the leisure class and which have trickled down through the various classes in the social hierarchy. However, as soon as those in the lower strata begin to conspicuously consume goods that are similar to those being consumed by the leisure class, the latter deems new goods worthy of conspicuous consumption in order to distinguish itself from the vulgar consumption practices of the masses.

Social Class and Consumption

Veblen's theory of consumption is exclusively class-based as he describes how the top stratum, the leisure class, sets the standards of reputability – or the consumer code – for all other classes in society. The lower classes 'must conform to the accepted code' (1899/1934: 84) and remain passive, while 'it is for this class [the elite] to determine what scheme of life the community shall accept as decent and honorific' (1899/1934: 104).

Veblen's theory of consumption has been described as a 'trickle-down' model (Davis, 1992: 110). The leisure class is the point of origin for all reputable consumer goods. And, 'each class envies and emu-lates the class next above it in the social scale' (Veblen, 1899/1934: 103–4). In reference to the importance of class distinction (a theme explored in detail by Bourdieu in *Distinction*, 1984), Veblen claims, as we have seen, that when the lower strata adopt a certain consumer good, the leisure class loses interest in it. A consumer product is no longer a luxury nor a signifier of wealth if both the lower classes and the leisure class are consuming it. Thus the leisure class is forced to search out new consumer products or fashions to demarcate, and in a way reproduce, itself. A source of Bourdieu's concepts such as cultural capital and habitus can be found in Veblen's work, in such ideas as the 'cultivation of the aesthetic faculty' (1899/1934: 74) and the way the gentleman of the leisure class 'must know how to consume [goods] in a seemly manner' (1899/1934: 75). While Veblen is merely suggestive, Bourdieu develops these two ideas into a rich account of the way different classes develop a distinctive system of 'taste' and learn a specific classificatory schema and reproduce this schema through consumption practices.

Critiquing and Extending Veblen's Class-Based Approach

The key point to be derived from Bourdieu's work, at least in reference to Veblen's, is that it is not enough to say that the classes below the leisure class emulate its consumption patterns. While this may be true, at least to some degree, there is far more to the consumption patterns of classes ranking below the leisure class. Each class elaborates its own distinctive consumption pattern which can be thought of as reflect-ing a distinctive 'taste'. Veblen's theory fails to give classes below the leisure class the ability (one they clearly possess) to create their own patterns of consumption that are an idiosyncratic mix of emulation and independence.

The class-based model of consumption presented by Veblen holds a certain allure, especially in the case of American life at the beginning of the twentieth century when, in the view of at least some, a more rigid class hierarchy existed. However, a century later, a theory of consump-tion based on a rigid class system is very limiting (see Featherstone, 1991: 83; Lipovetsky, 1994). With the advent of mass society, the leisure class has lost its position of leadership – both politically and culturally. Mass society has a democratizing effect which leads to a weakening of class power and identity. Perhaps the most liberating element of mass society is that the exclusionary category of class becomes less of a determinant of behavior (Kornhauser, 1959: 14), resulting in an 'increase in opportunities for many to intervene in areas previously reserved for a few' (Kornhauser, 1959: 28). Veblen's theory does not allow for the consumption patterns of the lower strata to be emulated by those above them in the stratification system, especially the leisure class. Veblen's trickle-down model thus cannot explain the multiple locations from which interest in consumer goods, especially fashion, originates.

How would Veblen explain the fact that haute couture that caters to the leisure class has adopted fashions that come 'from below' like Dr Martens, clogs, cargo pants, Levi blue jeans, grunge, punk, and hip-hop styles, tattoos and Harley Davidson motorcycles? The movement of preferences for consumer goods at the millennium is more complex than a series of commodities cascading down a one-way chute from the leisure class to the social classes below. Today, consumer goods have other origins and other meanings than those associated simply with social class.

Furthermore, besides the conspicuous display of pecuniary strength – or class – other 'signifieds' can be read into the display of consumer goods. For example, today many people conspicuously consume 'lifestyles' that do not reflect wealth or class distinctions as much as distinctions based on gender, race, ethnicity, youth, or other specific sub-cultures. In other words, in consumption we no longer emulate the leisure class exclusively or even predominantly. We are increasingly likely to emulate the consumption patterns associated with a wide array of lifestyles. Think, for example, of the young executive who used to go to Grateful Dead concerts (or now, with the end of the 'Dead', Phish concerts). Once there, the executive is apt to discard his suit and tie, buy a pair of baggy pants and a tie-dyed t-shirt (perhaps announcing 'I love drugs') available at the outdoor market on the grounds of the concert (and perhaps even some drugs and drug-paraphernalia), and dance the night away. Likewise, there is the case of the 'white' businessman entertaining clients at an inexpensive Thai restaurant. In so doing, he is consuming ethnicity while displaying his cultural capital – familiarity with exotic ethnic food. One can even think of the trend toward casual days in corporate offices as an example of the upper classes emulating the mode of dress of the lower classes.

While Veblen did not directly address the concepts of 'lifestyle' or 'status', it is clear that this is what he had in mind when describing the leisure class. The defining characteristic of the leisure class is not just that its members possessed a vast amount of wealth but that they also lived a specific lifestyle – one in which physical labor (industry) was less and less a part. Clearly the leisure class can also be thought of as a status group in the Weberian sense of having a distinctive style of life. And in this Weberian view, perhaps it is not always a 'pecuniary comparison' that is being made between consumer goods, but a 'status comparison'. Thus, as Goffman (1951: 294) points out, one has a 'specialized means of displaying one's position'. Such sign-vehicles have been called status symbols. According to Goffman, status symbols carry both categorical as well as expressive significance. Status symbols serve to identify the social status of the person who displays them and as well as 'the style of life' and the 'cultural values' of the person. Although high class position and high status ranking often go hand in hand, this is not always the case – one can accumulate great amounts of wealth but have a low status (the successful drug dealer, for example). And as Bourdieu has shown, one can have a high status but possess relatively little wealth (for example, many intellectuals or opera singers). In other words, the possessor of economic capital does not always possess a great deal of cultural capital, and vice versa. Nevertheless, today we may be as likely, and perhaps even more likely, to emulate a high status group than one that ranks high in social class.

Changes Since Veblen's Day

There are now many different status groups whose lifestyle is 'worthy' of emulation. The advent of Hollywood dramatically increased the celebrity lifestyle[7] and the degree to which it has come to be held in high esteem – many envy and emulate the glamorous life of beautiful people. Professional athletes have also achieved celebrity status. Celebrity endorsements of consumer products attract suburban consumers who seem to believe that wearing Air Jordans is one step closer to the lifestyle of Michael Jordan. Speaking of suburbia, the suburban lifestyle itself has become a 'reputable' way of life emulated by many who seek an alternative to the city lifestyle. However, the city lifestyle is emulated by many who wish to be a part of where the action is. Youth subcultures have also created distinctive lifestyles that have been emulated not only by other youths, but co-opted by the mass market. Today, the 'hipster' lifestyle associated with the city is generally considered cool and marketed to youth as one worthy of emulation.

This brings us to another important societal change that has occurred since the time of Veblen: the birth of mass media, especially television (and now the Internet). While advertisers existed in Veblen's time, never before have they had access to such a wide array of outlets to promote goods and services. Rather than the leisure class determining which consumer goods are worthy of display, today a group of professionals exists – Bourdieu's 'cultural intermediaries' – who continually dream up the next 'worthy' consumer good. One could argue that the new cultural intermediaries fabricate entire lifestyles composed of consumer goods designed to be displayed and emulated. If one wants to 'look' like part of the hip-hop scene, one can purchase the baggy pants, etc. that display that lifestyle. Goffman (1951: 296) describes the type of person who makes such purchases as one 'who manipulates symbols in what appears to be a fraudulent way – displaying the signs yet possessing only a doubtful claim to what they signify'.

The influence of the mass media is pervasive and it has become a 'mediating factor' in the emulation process. Rather than observing and emulating people we have seen and met personally, we now emulate images displayed on television, billboards, advertisements, and music videos. It could be argued that we are far more likely today to study and to emulate images rather than people.

Veblen actually provides a rather primitive, though insightful, semiotic reading of consumer goods. Even in Veblen's (1899/1994: 86) time he observed that 'the means of communication and the mobility of the population now expose the individual to the observation of many persons who have no other means of judging his reputability than the display of goods (and perhaps breeding) which he is able to make while under their direct observation'. Veblen's message is more significant today as the means of communication have grown not only in scope, but in speed. The mobility of people may still be physical – moving frequently between one city, or one country, to another, but with the mass media and especially the Internet we need not leave our living rooms to observe what other people are consuming. Even if we live in the city, our direct gaze may be focused more on media images than 'real' people. Take, for example, people on a New York City subway reading or flipping through popular magazines. They may be studying the images in the magazine far more closely than they are observing the people in the subway car.

Overall, the point is that there is much more to conspicuous consumption today (and probably in Veblen's day, too), as well as to consumption more generally, than simply emulation of the leisure class. While invidious distinctions are still made between consumer goods and the people who purchase these goods, pecuniary worth is no longer the sole criterion on which these comparisons are made. Furthermore, the leisure class is no longer the sole arbiter of consumption styles. A variety of social groups with different tastes and lifestyles also provide leadership in consumption – to the extent that even the upper classes emulate the consumption styles of social classes below them. This phenomenon suggests that perhaps status, rather than class, is a more important variable when studying consumption practices. Consumers today, surrounded by advertisements and popular culture, study media images more closely than they do the consumption habits of the leisure class. These media images, which flow from a wide range of class, status and lifestyle groups, are surely a 'mediating factor' that influence consumer behavior. Other classes create their own styles, upper classes often emulate those below them, and a variety of groups with different lifestyles provide leadership in consumption. The issue may be more now one of status group than class, and people today study media images far more closely than they do the behavior of the leisure class and those media images flow from a wide range of class, status and lifestyle groups.

Other Criticisms

One of the great paradoxes in Veblen's theory is that, on the one hand, he argues that business people are inclined to reduce production in order to maintain profits. However, those very same people, when they act as consumers in the leisure class, behave in a way that leads to an increase in production. There is an interesting contradiction here that remains unexplored and unexplained by Veblen. This can be looked at from the point of view of the idea of 'unanticipated consequences'. As members of the leisure class and as seekers of invidious distinction, business leaders in their role as consumers go blithely along engaging in conspicuous consumption. Every new product they find to consume eventually trickles down the class system affecting the way virtually everyone consumes. All of this serves to fuel consumption and, ultimately, industry, which reacts by increasing productivity. However, increased production worries the business people as business people and they respond by reducing production in order to maintain profits and prices. What business people do not realize is that it is their actions as consumers that are ultimately responsible for increases in production. Thus, in a sense, business people are their own worst enemies, at least as producers.

Another major criticism of Veblen's theory is his blindness to the positive contributions of waste, especially in the realm of consumption. Veblen's view on waste was colored by his critical attitude toward waste in business and his negative view of business leaders and the leisure class of which they were an important part. He simply extended this critical attitude toward waste in production to waste in consumption. However, what he failed to see, and we can now see quite clearly, is that wasteful consumption is a crucial motor for industry. That is, if people only consumed what they needed, what was truly functional, industry today would grind to a halt and the economy would plunge into recession. Thus, the industry that Veblen admired so now *requires* conspicuous consumption in order to function optimally.

Of course, it is possible to argue that industry is being fueled by the wrong thing. Instead of being fueled by waste, it should, Veblen might argue, be fueled by the production of things that are useful to the community as a whole. Thus instead of baubles for the well-to-do and those who emulate them, what should be produced are things to improve the well-being of the less well off, to help rebuild and improve our infrastructure, and so on. However, the capitalistic system is far better at creating baubles and the need for them than it is at handling these other matters. It may well be that Veblen's critique of business was not an adequate critique of the underlying nature of the capitalistic system.

Conspicuous Consumption and the New Means of Consumption

The issue in this section is what do the new means of consumption, and the consumption that takes place in them, tell us about Veblen's theory of consumption? For one thing, the distinction that Veblen made between conspicuous consumption and conspicuous leisure is no longer viable. Given the importance of the new means of consumption oriented to leisure (casinos, cruises, theme parks, eatertainment, retailtainment), it is clear that much of modern consumption has as much to do with leisure as it does with goods. Furthermore, Veblen was making a distinction that is no longer viable. That is, the consumption of leisure is no longer easily separable from the consumption of goods; indeed both goods and leisure can be seen as commodities. Veblen was unable to see this because he was writing at the peak of the industrial revolution when services paled in significance in comparison to goods. It is certainly *not* the case that conspicuous consumption has replaced conspicuous leisure, or that the latter is only characteristic of some earlier age. In fact, with the increasing importance of amusements and fun, leisure may once again be in the process of gaining ascendancy over the consumption of goods. A more modern view would be to see *both* conspicuous leisure and conspicuous consumption as bases of commodity consumption. A cruise and a gambling junket are as much commodities as a Mercedes Benz and a mink coat.

A second point is that people do not simply consume commodities, they also consume the means of consumption. Another basis of invidious distinction is the places in which one consumes. Thus, the means of consumption are stratified and participating in those that have high status yields higher status for the individual. Shopping at Nordstom's (and, given the importance of signs in a postmodern world, leaving with that shopping bag with the Nordstrom's logo) yields higher status than shopping at J.C. Penney. In Las Vegas, staying at the Bellagio confers higher status than staying at the Holiday Inn. While Veblen saw property as trophies, it is now the shopping bags, T-shirts, and kitsch that carry the labels and logos of Nordstrom's and Bellagio, to say nothing of Hard Rock Cafe and Planet Hollywood, that are our new trophies.

This remarkable trend toward wearing all manner of clothing (and many other things) with labels prominently displayed cries out for comment in a chapter that deals with conspicuous consumption. Subtlety has clearly all but disappeared when it comes to displaying the signs associated with the goods we consume. Most of us are no longer confident that those around us can 'read' the clothes we wear. Thus, we leave nothing to doubt; we literally wear the labels on our sleeves. David Howes (1996: 1) describes this 'labeling trend': 'Brand names and trademark symbols such as Marlboro, Nike, and Rolex are now known around the world. These marks transcend language and make it possible to display one's status and one's desires by simply pointing to the appropriate symbol.' Incidentally, there is a paradox here. On the one hand, we no longer seem to trust one another as readers of signs. On the other, this distrust is increasing at a time when we have all become much more sophisticated and sensitive readers of those signs. Thus, wearing labels seems like overkill, but this is just fine as far as manufacturers are concerned since in the past they had to pay for this kind of advertising (for example, people walking the streets wearing 'sandwich boards'). In fact, this is but one of many examples of getting customers to do work for nothing (others are the salad bar at the fast-food restaurant and the ATM) that in the past workers had to be paid to do.

However, the most important point to be made on the basis of an analysis of the new means of consumption is that while there is certainly conspicuous consumption today, what defines much of consumption, at least as far as the new means of consumption are concerned, is a kind of *conspicuous inconspicuousness*. With the boom in chains of many of the new means of consumption, the vast majority of people regardless of class and lifestyle are consuming in the same settings and coming home with many of the same goods or experiencing much the same service. Thus, labels like Wal-Mart, Target, the Gap, Princess Cruise Line, Walt Disney, and McDonald's adorn the shopping bags and the commodities of many people. Most of us are shopping in essentially the same places and buying essentially the same things. While there is certainly some effort at creating invidious distinctions going on here ('we went on that Destiny cruise or to Disney World, you didn't'), there is also a demonstration of the fact that we are consuming like everyone else; we are inconspicuous in our consumption patterns. Rather than distinguishing ourselves through what we consume, we seem to want to be like everyone else. However, we continue to want to be conspicuous, but now about our inconspicuousness.

This may indicate a shift in the sensibilities of at least some of us on this issue. While in the past we may have wanted to distinguish ourselves from others, it may be that we are now more interested in demonstrating our commonality with the vast majority of other people. It may be that people do not want to stick out too much from the crowd. We may want to distinguish ourselves from our neighbor by buying a red Honda rather than a green one, but we may not want to buy a Rolls-Royce even if we could afford it. Perhaps consumers inconspicuously conform to similar brand names or styles, and make conspicuous distinctions in small details such as car color or model, or cuff lengths in clothing. Perhaps in this perceived high-crime era, most people prefer to be largely indistinguishable, at least in their public consumption and appearance, than easily distinguished from others.

However, this is probably too psychologistic an explanation. The fact is that people are sporting the same labels because, at least in part, of the domination of the means of consumption that have generally succeeded in driving smaller and local competitors out of business. All of those Wal-Marts, McDonald's, Bed, Bath and Beyonds and Princess Line cruise ships mean that most of us consume in the same places and they offer us more or less the same selection of goods and services. To a large extent, we are being forced into conspicuous inconspicuousness; the new means of consumption (for example, retail clothing chains like the Gap, Banana Republic, and Old Navy – all owned by the same corporation, Gap Inc.) and their commodities that are essentially the same from one time or place to another are increasingly our best, or in some cases our only, option.

What of the modern parallel of Veblen's leisure class? Aren't they still engaging in conspicuous consumption? The answer is clearly yes. They can still afford the one-of-a-kind vacation, the designer dress, or the custom-made shoes. And in consuming such things they are attempting to make an invidious distinction between themselves and those below them in the stratification system. However, it is interesting to note that even in the leisure class, we see an increasing amount of inconspicuous consumption and for many of the same reasons discussed above. Many are less interested in sticking out from the crowd because, among other reasons, they fear that they would be more likely to be labeled as *nouveau riche* or to become crime victims. More importantly, we are witnessing the expansion of chains of the elite means of consumption such as Valentino's, Gucci, Neiman-Marcus, and the like. Then, the mass chain stores are so readily accessible, convenient and attractive that even the elites shop in them. The result is that the elite, wherever they may be, are also increasingly likely to consume in the same settings and purchase many of the same things. Thus, elites find it more difficult to distinguish themselves from other members of the upper class. Further, while frequenting the elite means of consumption may set them apart from classes below them in the stratification system, it is increasingly difficult in the age of low-priced 'knock-offs' of high-priced goods to distinguish between those who carry Gucci bags and those who carry the copies. And, of course, 'original' and copy are made even more indistinguishable by the fact that they are both simulations. Gucci bags are simulations and the knock-offs are simulations of those simulations.

Veblen argued that no class, not even the poorest, forgoes all conspicuous consumption and this is even more true of conspicuously inconspicuous consumption. Even the poorest of the poor can afford a T-shirt with Caesar's Palace logo on the half-price rack at Wal-Mart or a hamburger in a bag sporting McDonald's golden arches. Even the street person may be able to afford these things or, failing that, is able to fish them (or their remnants) out of the local trash can. Many of the poor spend inordinate amounts on such inconspicuous consumption and, in the process, may ignore aspects of their lives (for example, the state of their underwear, the quality of their mattress) that are less visible to others. This tends to be supportive of Veblen's view that people will endure a quite shabby private life in order to have the public symbols they deem desirable.

The Treatment of 'Conspicuous Consumption' in the Mass Media

We have looked at various corrections to, and amendments of, Veblen's theory of consumption in general, and of conspicuous consumption in particular, in the preceding sections. We now turn to the way the term 'conspicuous consumption' has been appropriated by the mass media at the turn of the twenty-first century. The overarching question is: To what extent has Veblen's concept of conspicuous consumption become a popular term in describing the consumption habits of Americans a century after Veblen introduced his idea? It turns out that in this age of hyperconsumption, the term is widely used in the mass media.

We conducted a simple Internet search for the key words 'conspicuous consumption' which yielded 3,452 hits. In comparison, searches for the 'Protestant Ethic' and the 'fetishism of commodities/commodity fetishism' turned up 242 and 33 hits, respectively. This is interesting since it seems to suggest a preoccupation in the media with consumption. It demonstrates how far out of touch contemporary sociology is with the modern world. While in sociology in general, and sociology textbooks more particularly, production and terms associated with it (for example, alienation) get the lion's share of attention, the popular press is far more attuned to what is actually happening in society and is using terms like conspicuous consumption to help it understand that new reality ...

There are two key points to make in this last section. First, the concept of conspicuous consumption has become one of the most widely used ideas derived from sociology and related social sciences. This is true, in part, because it is one of the few concepts created by a discipline that has been so absorbed in productivist issues that it has all but missed the revolution in consumption. Second, its utility may also come from the fact that free of the need to be true to what Veblen meant by the concept, those in the popular media who appropriate it can use it any way they want. The result is the huge difference between those who deploy it to criticize consumption and those who use it to praise consumption or even in the hopes of increasing it. Such are the risks of producing relevant and catchy sociological concepts. While the discipline has generally failed miserably in this, and this has helped to make it so irrelevant to popular concerns, the fact remains that there is a downside to being successful at creating such ideas – they are likely to be wildly distorted in popular usage. We should be cautious about what we wish for. However, a bit of distortion is probably less of a problem than our current productivist irrelevance. But say this for Veblen, he may have been another of the classical productivists, but unlike others that did not blind him to the importance of consumption. And as his reward for being prescient and relevant, he gets to be used *and* misused by the popular media.

Notes

The material in this chapter is published here for the first time. It was co-authored by James Murphy and Wendy Weidenhoft, and was presented at meetings of the American Sociological Association, Chicago, 1999.

1   Veblen's work is also seen as a contribution to at least one other contemporary field, leisure studies (Rojek, 1995).

2   Another term favored by Veblen (1923), especially in his later writings, is *absentee ownership*.

3   Veblen also saw most labor unions, especially the American Federation of Labor, as engaged in such sabotage.

4   Riesman (1953/1995) argues that one of the ways to look at the basic conflict in Veblen's work is that between workmanship and wastemanship.

5   It is this that leads Veblen (1904: 241) to argue: 'Depression is primarily a malady of the affections of the business men.'

6   Implicitly, Veblen, like Marx, valorizes use value and is critical of what happens when exchange value becomes predominant. This is another factor that lies at the base of the critical orientation of both toward consumption.

7   In fact, C. Wright Mills (1956: 71) criticizes Veblen for not dealing with the importance of celebrities and argues that 'with the elaboration of the national means of mass communication, the professional celebrities of the entertainment world have come fully and continuously into the national view. As personalities of national glamour, they are at the focal point of all means of entertainment and publicity. Both the metropolitan 400 and the institutionalized elite must now *compete* with and borrow prestige from the professionals in the world of the celebrity.'

11

OBSCENE FROM ANY ANGLE: FAST FOOD, CREDIT CARDS, CASINOS AND CONSUMERS

Over the past decade I have been thinking and writing about processes – McDonaldization, consumerism – and entities – fast-food restaurants, credit cards, and the new means of consumption – that can be seen as 'obscene powers'. From a modern perspective, all can be viewed as part of increasing external (especially corporate) control over our lives, especially as consumers, and as posing threats to social justice, human rights, and democratic decision making. Of course, such a set of judg- ments implies that analysts are operating with an 'Archimedean point' that allows them to judge certain social phenomena 'obscene' in the sense that they are perceived as threats to foundational notions of what is social justice, what rights humans should possess, and what counts as democratic decision making. It is tempting to get into the difficulties, even impossibilities, of making such judgments in the age of the pre- eminence of postmodern perspectives, but that is already a road well traveled in the literature on postmodern social theory. Thus, instead of debating that issue at length at the beginning of this chapter, I simply will operate, at least at first, as a modernist and discuss the degree to which the phenomena of concern here are 'obscene powers' in the sense described above. I will leave postmodern social theory, or at least one perspective derived from it, to the second section. Although I will offer some thoughts on the reconciliation of the two views, there is as we will see an apparent contradiction here between modern obscenity trace- able to the invisibility of a wide range of problems and postmodern obscenity tied to hypervisibility.

When one casts aside postmodern doubts and equivocations, one is immediately confronted with the problem of being overwhelmed by the obscenities associated with these processes and entities. There are so many that it is difficult to decide which to discuss and in what order to discuss them. I will manage to select a few and to present them in some sort of order, but before I do I feel compelled to point out that these entities and processes are not without their redeeming qualities. The vast majority of the 'haves' within advanced societies eagerly embrace processes like McDonaldization and consumerism and are anxious to eat in fast-food restaurants, utilize credit cards to their upper limits, and to shop and spend their leisure time in such new means of consumption as shopping malls, mega-malls, theme parks and cruise ships. The great preponderance of 'have nots' within those societies would dearly love to change places with the haves and to be more involved in these processes, to spend more time in the new means of consumption and to have access to more credit cards with higher credit limits. Similar desires characterize many of those in less 'advanced' societies who up to now have had little access to and experience with these obscene powers. After all, even the seemingly ubiquitous McDonald's has 'only' managed, at last count, to make its way into 115 of the world's nations. In short, most of those connected with these processes and entities are quite content with them and those with little or no involvement crave to be more implicated in them.

Furthermore, these obscene powers have many redeeming qualities. To mention just a few – McDonaldization not only standardizes goods and services, but serves to elevate the quality of one or both in some parts of the world (Watson, 1997a); consumerism serves to increase demand and lower price thereby bringing a wide array of goods and services to an ever-increasing number of people; fast-food restaurants bring a kind of McDonaldized diversity to parts of the world that had heretofore been more monocultural as far as various kinds of foods are concerned; credit cards are a boon to those consumers who pay their credit card bills in full each month ('convenience users') and thereby get a month of 'free' credit; and the new means of consumption offer large numbers of people spectacular settings that they can consume, and in which they can consume a wide range of goods and services. There are good reasons why so many people are eager to eat in McDonald's, carry Visa cards in their wallets, and take a vacation at Disney World. In spite of the near universal acceptance of these entities and processes, and their many desirable aspects, I will focus in the first section of this chapter on what are, from a modern perspective, some of their most obscene characteristics.

A Modern View: Invisible Worlds, Invisible Obscenities

From a modern point of view which emphasizes the need to get at the truth hidden behind appearances, invisibility is central to the obscenity of the processes and entities of interest here. Many of their most 'obscene' qualities are barely visible and even invisible and thus it becomes necessary to reveal at least some of those obscenities. It is the very lack of visibility of the workings of these processes, to say nothing of the problems associated with them, that help to make them obscene. In fact, it is just those aspects of these processes and entities that are invisible that are likely to have the most negative impact on people. A discussion of this invisibility is not only important in itself, but it would also go a long way toward allowing us to ameliorate some of the greatest obscenities associated with them.

The spread of McDonald's and fast-food restaurants is obvious to all, but far less visible is the degree to which innumerable phenomena throughout the world have been McDonaldized (Ritzer, 1996) ... McDonald's restaurants are themselves by design very obvious, as is the proliferation of those outlets as well as the similar spread of other American chains of fast-food restaurants. Far less visible, and perhaps even invisible, is the degree to which other social structures and settings are adopting and adapting these principles; the degree to which they are becoming McDonaldized. For example, the media are becoming increasingly McDonaldized as reflected in the success of *USA TODAY* ('McPaper') in the newspaper business and CNN Headline News on television. Then there is the McDonaldization of the university and the rise of what has been labeled by several scholars 'McUniversity' (Parker and Jary, 1995). The medical profession has experienced McDonaldization as reflected in the rise of hospital chains and the development of local, drive-in, no-appointment-necessary McDoctors. Within medicine, birth and death have been McDonaldized as reflected in advanced technologies that allow us to choose the characteristics of our offspring ('designer babies') and to keep people alive almost indefinitely. While most of us are aware that the media, the university, medicine and many settings have changed, few see it as part of a wide-ranging process of McDonaldization. If we cannot connect these developments, how can we see that the problems associated with each are part of a broader process and a larger set of problems? Furthermore, the invisibility of the process makes it all but impossible to develop any sort of coordinated strategy for dealing with them.

Similarly invisible is the spread of McDonaldization to other cultures. Again, the incursion of McDonald's and other, largely American, chains into other societies is abundantly obvious, but what is not at all clear is the development of indigenous chains that emulate McDonald's and are based on the principles of McDonaldization. Examples abound, including Juicy Burger in Beirut, with J.B. the clown standing in for Ronald McDonald, and the chain Russkoye Bistro in Russia, which is consciously modeled after McDonald's and regards it like an older brother. The most famous restaurant in Beijing – Quanjude Roast Duck Restaurant – sent its management staff to McDonald's in 1993 and then introduced its own 'roast duck fast food' in early 1994. In a sense, it is the largely invisible incursion of the principles of McDonaldization into local institutions that is a far greater threat to indigenous cultures than the spread of McDonald's itself (and other American fast-food restaurants) to other nations. After all, McDonald's is, by design, highly visible and this is especially the case outside the United States.

This visibility is reflected in the fact that McDonald's often becomes the target of protests, such as those that occurred in recent years in Yugoslavia over NATO bombing and in France over US tariffs on French cheese. However, when local institutions McDonaldize, the process and its roots in the American chain become invisible to the indigenous population and ultimately to those who work in and even run those settings. It is far harder to see, let alone oppose, McDonaldization when it worms its way into local settings than when it takes the form of the importation of a McDonald's or Pizza Hut restaurant.

Yet, there is a sense that even McDonald's becomes a part of local culture and, as a result, its role in a larger international process becomes invisible to the local population. For example, there are so many McDonald's restaurants in Japan, they have by now been around so long, and they have adapted in so many ways to Japanese culture, that many Japanese, especially children, now see McDonald's as a Japanese chain. Thus, when a Japanese Boy Scout arrived in Chicago on a tour he was surprised to find a McDonald's there; he thought McDonald's existed only in Japan and was a Japanese institution (Watson, 1997a). Such an infiltration into local culture makes it very difficult to see that the process, as well as the problems associated with it, are international in scope. However, it is still the incursion of the principles of McDonaldization into local settings that poses the greatest threat to local communities, largely because in that instance the process becomes so much more invisible.

Given the various ways in which McDonaldization has grown invisible, what are some of the major obscenities, or what I call irrationalities of rationality, associated with that process? We can start with homogenization since if the process itself is invisible, then the degree to which it is homogenizing not only American culture, but also culture around the world, would also be invisible. McDonaldization involves a set of four basic principles and to the degree that those principles are applied more or less uniformly across areas of the United States or nations of the world, it is an homogenizing process. The appearance of McDonald's in every major nation in the world, and the application of those basic principles to indigenous restaurants and restaurant chains, makes for a great deal of uniformity in the ways in which people around the world eat as well as engage in other activities that have been similarly McDonaldized. While there are certainly many local adaptations, the basic principles are applied universally. To the degree that McDonaldization is invisible, the trend toward homogeneity is similarly imperceptible.

Another problem associated with McDonaldization is disenchantment. Premodern, nonrational settings tend to be more enchanted than their contemporary counterparts. A major factor in the progressive disenchantment of these settings, as Max Weber demonstrated long ago, is the process of rationalization, or what I have termed more contemporaneously McDonaldization, utilizing a different paradigm (the fast-food restaurant) than that used by Weber (the bureaucracy). While some McDonaldized settings make their lack of enchantment abundantly obvious – the basic structure of fast-food restaurants and 'warehouse' supermarkets and hardware stores come to mind – most seek to conceal the absence of enchantment behind a veil of simulated enchantment. Thus, while fast-food restaurants are bare, highly functional structures, they seek through various tie-ins to associate themselves with enchanted worlds. Particularly notable here is the relationship between McDonald's and Disney, especially the fact that McDonald's actively promotes, and thereby associates itself with, the 'magical world of Disney'. Such associations are designed to obscure the absence of enchantment in eating in a fast-food restaurant, especially from children who are so important to those restaurants both as consumers and as agents luring parents and other adults into these settings.

To take one more major irrationality, McDonaldized settings are highly dehumanized settings in which to eat (and in which to work in 'McJobs'). Yet, these settings strive to put on a human face in order to obscure the dehumanization that lies at their core. Thus, Wendy's has its founder, the avuncular Dave Thomas, serve as a major figure in most, if not all, of its TV ads. Kentucky Fried Chicken used to do the same thing with its founder, Colonel Sanders, but since he is long dead, it must be satisfied with a cartoon version of the 'Colonel'. While his face is somewhat obscured by greasepaint, the smiling and endlessly friendly Ronald McDonald plays this role for McDonald's. To take one other McDonaldized (or as Bryman, 1999b has argued 'Disneyized') setting, Disney World is a highly rationalized theme park which seeks to hide that fact behind the benign and friendly image of the long-dead Walt Disney himself, as well as the super-friendly (albeit scripted) actions of park employees, in and out of costume.

The list of obscenities associated with McDonaldization, but obscured by McDonaldized systems, could be extended greatly – environmental destruction hidden behind public relations campaigns and some reforms (often coerced by external forces), danger to people's health obscured by claims about the nutritional value of fast food and the token offering of more nutritional foods, lack of a hospitable environment hidden behind advertisements that seem to communicate a sense of community among those who dine in fast-food restaurants (in fact, fast-food restaurants are so inhospitable that a large proportion of diners use the drive-throughs and take their meals with them, perhaps eating them in their cars parked in the adjacent parking lot or while driving on to their next McDonaldized activity), and so on. Such hidden obscenities are very familiar to modernists who often take as their task the tearing away of veils in order to reveal the irrationalities that lie just below the surface.

It should come as little surprise to anyone that we have just completed a decade (the 1990s) in the United States (and other developed nations) of unprecedented economic growth fueled by, and fueling, rampant consumerism – hyperconsumerism. While this is hardly hidden from general view, many aspects of consumerism (some of which will be touched on below in discussions of specific aspects of our consumer society) are less visible, including, for example, the degree to which sectors we do not usually associate with consumerism have come to be affected (infected) by it. For example, while we do not usually think of college students (and their parents) as consumers of educational services, that is exactly what they are, and there is evidence that they are coming to think of themselves increasingly as such. Similarly, hospital patients and those who use a wide range of other medical services are similarly thinking of themselves as consumers of medical sites and services. Changes like these mean that consumerism is leaching its way out of its well-known commercial domains and coming to affect increasing aspects of society. Thus, consumerism involves far more than shopping at the mall or at an e-tailer; it involves obtaining goods and services at universities, hospitals, as well as museums, athletic stadia and churches and synagogues. Largely hidden from view is the fact that consumerism has come to affect an ever-increasing number of structures and institutions. The result is that being a student is frequently no longer about getting a good education but getting a 'good deal', going to the hospital may involve assessing the quality of the rooms and the food being served more than the skills of the medical staff, going to a ball game is often more about buying souvenirs and shopping in the various concession stands than it is about watching the game, and being involved in religion is sometimes more about participating in clubs, socials, trips, and spectacular, albeit peripheral, events than it is about the 'religious experience'.

Similar obscenities, as well as efforts to conceal them, are associated with the other entities and processes of concern in this chapter. Credit cards (Ritzer, 1995) are presented by the banks and credit card companies as the consumer's helper. Short of cash, as most consumers are, people are urged to charge their purchases. Consumers can have what they want now and the only cost to them will be a 'modest' interest charge each month until the balance is paid. The credit card is presented as merely a 'tool' that is firmly under the control of the consumer.

While such claims have a significant element of truth, what they obscure is that a large number of people, perhaps a third of all credit card users, who 'revolve' their accounts rather than pay them in full (as 'convenience' users do), end up being controlled by their credit cards, or more accurately by the credit card companies. Many find themselves in perpetual debt to the credit card companies and that 'modest' interest rate (often a usurious 18 per cent) turns into a crushing debt when it is multiplied month after month, and credit card after credit card (since many people have multiple credit cards). Large numbers of people have several cards, and often in college and increasingly before, because the credit card companies function, albeit silently, as 'pushers', seeking, because of the great profitability of the credit card business, to get credit cards into as many hands as possible. The credit card companies do not want this known; for obvious reasons they do not want to be put in the same category as drug dealers ...

Then there are the new (post-Second World War) means of consumption ... (Ritzer, 1999). One of the things that all of the new means of consumption have in common is the use of spectacle in order to attract customers and to hide the fact that their simulated forms of enchantment obscure the disenchanted, rationalized systems that lie at their core. The need to conceal this underlying reality is shared with all other McDonaldized systems.

However, what I would like to focus on here in discussing the new means of consumption is the hidden mechanisms that they employ in order to control people and to get them to consume more and to spend more money ...

There is a whole hidden world of such control in all the new means of consumption and this is made clear by Paco Underhill, a consultant to many of them, in his book, *Why We Buy: The Science of Shopping*. Take the following example, in which a vice president of a national chain of young women's clothing stores (one of the new means of consumption) seeks to control the presentation of T-shirts so that something that costs them $3 can be sold for $37:

> 'We buy them in Sri Lanka for $3 each,' she began. 'Then we bring them over here and sew in washing instructions, which are in French and English. Notice that we don't say the shirts are made in France. But you can infer that if you like. Then we merchandise the hell out of them – we fold them just right on a tasteful tabletop display, and on the wall we hang a huge, gorgeous photograph of a beautiful woman in an exotic locale wearing a shirt. We shoot it so it looks like a million bucks. Then we call it an Expedition T-Shirt, and sell it for $37. And we sell a lot of them, too.' (Underhill, 1999: 206–7)

Underhill (1999: 207) describes this as a 'depressing', but 'valuable' lesson. A number of steps are described here to deceive consumers and lead them to purchase a product at an unconscionable mark-up. Needless to say, retailers do not want their subterfuges known to consumers, and they certainly do not want consumers to know how much of a mark-up is involved in the pricing of goods like these T-shirts.

Interestingly, a parallel kind of deception is involved in Underhill's book. Underhill sees himself as doing a 'science of shopping' and he sells his research and advisory services to various organizations, especially retailers. He provides them with data and with recommendations about how to attract more consumers and how to get them to consume more. For example, he shows that people are limited in what they can buy if they only have use of their hands. Thus, he recommends the widespread deployment of baskets and speaks highly of the chain Old Navy where customers are offered a handsome bag on entry that allows them to load up on items. Not missing a trick, Old Navy cashiers even ask at the checkout whether consumers also want to purchase the bag! The tools that he offers to retailers to heighten consumption are hidden beneath a rhetoric that emphasizes that his researchers are only track-ing what customers do and recommending that retailers give them what they want. More extremely, Underhill (1999: 33) has the audacity to present his organization as 'providing a form of consumer advocacy'. Perhaps he regards getting people to pay $37 for a $3 item an example of consumer advocacy. The reality that Underhill is offering retailers methods to heighten consumerism and increase profits is made less visible, while a more humble (and deceptive) role of merely providing consumers with what they want and serving as an advocate for them is the most visible aspect of the book.

A Postmodern View: Visible Worlds, Visible Obscenities

A starkly different view on the obscenity of the processes and entities of concern here is derivable from Jean Baudrillard's (1983/1990) ideas on the scene and the obscene. Baudrillard argues that the contemporary world has grown obscene because things that were at one time invi-sible (and therefore a 'scene') have grown increasingly visible. What makes something a scene is some degree of mystery, of enchantment and that is only possible when at least some aspects are hidden from view. The problem with the contemporary world from this perspective is that the kinds of processes and structures of concern here have been made increasingly visible and thereby they have lost their ability to enchant us. Baudrillard's paradigm for this is pornography. His point is that concealing parts of the body is more likely to be enchanting and even sexually arousing than simply confronting the viewer with a naked body or specific body parts. The partially covered, or even fully clothed, body would be more of a scene, whereas the naked body, especially dis-played to satisfy prurient interests, is obscene.

In what ways are the entities and processes of interest here obscene in this sense of the term? Let's start with the fast-food restaurant. Most have an open 'kitchen' in which everything that goes on is visible to consumers waiting in line to place or receive their orders. Clearly, there is little mystery involved in what goes into the preparation of fast food. This stands in stark contrast to the traditional restaurant where food preparation is done out of the view of the consumer. Then, there is the fact that customers do much of the work (on an unpaid basis, by the way) – carrying their own food to the table, making their own salads, filling their own soda cups, bussing their own debris, and so on. There is clearly no mystery involved when customers perform such tasks on their own (except, perhaps, to the proprietors who might wonder why customers do it).

The spread of fast-food restaurants, and more generally of McDonaldization, often takes highly visible forms. Originally, McDonald's restaurants sported huge golden arches that loudly announced their arrival and presence as well as signs that crassly kept track of how many millions, then billions, of hamburgers they sold. Forced to mute structures and signs in recent years, the opening of a new McDonald's, especially in an area or country that heretofore lacked one, is often marked by a major publicity campaign. Then there is the enormous amount of money spent by McDonald's on advertising, especially on television. The advertisements and the arches (albeit in a muted form) seem to be everywhere one turns. Much the same could be said about other McDonaldizing systems. Visible structures, active publicity campaigns, and a ubiquitous presence on TV and other media define virtually all of them.

Credit cards also have a high profile, as reflected in the innumerable offers one receives in the mail, the signs on the door of virtually every retailer, and the highly visible advertisements and advertising campaigns. Also highly visible is the fact that when we are in a consumption setting, virtually everyone around us is paying by credit card. Thus, a consumer is now likely to feel self-conscious about paying with cash at a department store. Almost everyone uses a card and the employees often make it plain that they prefer payment by credit card.

Since spectacle defines the new means of consumption, and spectacles must be visible in order to be, well, spectacles, visibility defines the new means of consumption. Las Vegas in general, and its most important casino-hotels, are among the most visible aspects of our consumer society. There are the advertisements, of course, but there is also the free media coverage frequently given to the city and its casinos. The openings of recent casino-hotels like New York, New York, Bellagio, Venetian and Paris are big news. More importantly, visibility is the name of the game in Las Vegas. The hotels compete with one another to see which one can attain the greatest visibility. Lights, water displays, sea battles and the like are used in an effort to make one casino-hotel stand out from the other. More generally, the Las Vegas strip is one of the most visible places in the world – its lights can undoubtedly be seen from high in the stratosphere. Inside the casino-hotels, the most visible aspect is the casino. There is no effort to hide it; indeed it is usually right in one's face when one enters the hotel lobby. And most visible within the casino are its biggest and most reliable moneymakers – the slot machines. And, they are ringing, whistling, illuminating and displaying how much can be won on a particular machine. There is no subtlety here; no effort to seduce the gambler into playing the slots. Rather, gamblers are beaten over the head with and by them.

Similar points could be made about Disney World and cruise ships. Disney World has succeeded in making itself extraordinarily visible throughout much of the world. Indeed, it, like Las Vegas, has become a 'destination' for large numbers of the world's tourists. Few people are unaware of Disney World and what it has to offer. The advertisements, especially those featuring the winners of major sporting events announcing at the conclusion of a game or match 'We're going to Disney World', have served to embed Disney World in people's consciousness. The Disney cable network can be seen as one long advertisement for the various Disney enterprises, including Disney World. The big draw is the well-known and quite spectacular attractions at the park. People go to see those attractions. In fact, given the long lines at many attractions, they spend far more time looking at them than participating in them. Of course, there is much that is unseen, or 'behind the scenes' at Disney World, but people are led to gaze on what's visible. Similarly, what distinguishes the modern cruise ship is its enormous size and this is abundantly visible not only to passengers, but those who see the ships as they pass from port to port.

Thus, in various ways, a case can be made that what characterizes these entities and processes is their great visibility. Furthermore, it could be argued that that is about all there is to them; there is nothing, at least as far as the visitor/customer is concerned, below the surface. From the postmodern perspective, the superficial and most visible aspects exhaust what these entities and processes have to offer. There is nothing more to them than what meets the eye. As a result, from a Baudrillardian perspective, the absence of a scene, of hidden elements, means that these entities and processes lack the ability to seduce. Thus, they are disenchanted domains and it is that lack of any mystery that gets to the essence of their problematic character, at least to the postmodernist. There are no deeper problems, of the type discussed in the preceding section, to be uncovered by the debunking modernist sociologist.

Reconciling Modern and Postmodern Obscenities

Can both of these perspectives be true ('truth', of course, is an issue anathema to postmodernists)? Are the phenomena discussed throughout this chapter obscene both because they are highly invisible *and* highly visible? Or, are these alternative perspectives to be bought into depending on whether one adopts a modern or a postmodern perspective?

One way of reconciling these two perspectives is to argue, undoubtedly from a modernist perspective, that a high degree of visibility exists to distract the consumer from the hidden problems and prospects. Distracted or enthralled by the visible, the consumer is less likely to think about the invisible irrationalities that lie hidden below the surface. Thus, one obscenity allows the other to exist. Of course, it would seem that postmodernists would have none of this. There are no underlying, hidden realities to postmodernists; all we have are the superficial surface appearances. However, on this issue, as on so many others, we must be wary of discussing postmodern social theory in global terms. In fact, there *are* postmodernists who think in just this way and one example is Paul Virilio (1995: 65), who argues that 'new apperceptual techniques essentially tended *to cover what was invisible to the naked eye with the mask of the visible'*.

While I find postmodern social theory in general, and especially Baudrillardian theory, extremely useful, I do not find it particularly helpful in this case (Virilio is one exception). I would agree that hypervisibility is an issue, even a concern, in the contemporary world, but it just does not strike me as nearly as important as the kind of underlying problems of concern to the modernist. Of course, that may well be due to the fact that I approach these issues as a modernist schooled in postmodern ideas and not as a postmodern social theorist. Thus, to relate this to the work of Zygmunt Bauman (1992), I am doing a sociology of postmodernity rather than a postmodern sociology. While I have great respect for the latter as a source of new and refreshing ideas, I find it far more useful to disengage those ideas from their roots in postmodern social theory and to use them in modern analyses of issues of the day.

Of course, I am mindful, following Bauman and others, that there are grave dangers associated with modernism in general and modern social theory in particular. In fact, much of my recent work involves, as should be clear above, a critical analysis of the deeper problems associated with modern processes – McDonaldization, consumerism, and structures – fast-food restaurants, credit cards, and the new means of consumption. However, what I do seem to be guilty of, again following Bauman, is of being a legislator seeking to dictate the appropriate interpretation of these structures and processes and the problems associated with them. Fearful of that, allow me to reinterpret what I am saying here as an effort to serve as an interpreter offering a sociological interpretation of these phenomena to an audience with varying backgrounds, some of whom are unfamiliar with a sociological view. Thus, what I offer is not an 'answer', but rather one perspective among many possible perspectives on the objects and processes discussed here. I do not think this will assuage my postmodern critics, but it at least puts this analysis in its properly humble position and dissociates me from a long line of modernists who, often quite disastrously, thought they best understood a problem and had the optimum solution to that problem.

The Obscene Consumer

Much of the above has focused on the obscenities associated with sites of consumption (fast-food restaurants and other new means of consumption), those things that facilitate their use (especially credit cards), and processes associated with them (McDonaldization, consumerism). However, there is far more to consumption, including the consumer, the goods and services consumed, as well as the process of consumption. Unable to cover all of these issues here, I would like to close with a few thoughts on the consumer from the perspective of the obscene.

Zygmunt Bauman (1997) has correctly argued that along with the transition from the predominance of production to that of consumption, concern in postmodern society has shifted from the problematic producer to the problematic consumer. He labels the latter 'flawed consumers', or those who are 'unable to respond to the enticements of the consumer market because they lack the required resources'; the resources needed 'to be seduced by the infinite possibility and constant renewal promoted by the consumer market, of rejoicing in the chance of putting on and taking off identities, of spending one's life in the never ending chase after ever more intense sensations and even more exhilarating experience' (Bauman, 1997: 14).

In the terms of this present chapter, Bauman is arguing that flawed consumers are obscene from the perspective of postmodern society because they do not have the resources to participate adequately in the consumer society. In other words, they do not consume enough. However, I do not think that Bauman has taken this argument far enough. It is not only that flawed consumers do not consume enough, but when they do consume – and in a consumer society virtually everyone consumes – they consume the 'wrong' things, things that pose serious threats to those who are deeply involved in, or profit from, consumption. I would argue that we need to further specify the 'flaws' of the 'flawed consumer' and it would be more accurate to identify the problematic type as the *dangerous consumer*.

Part of the reason that this group is dangerous is that, following Bauman, they simply do not consume enough. The danger here is that escalating consumerism requires that nearly everyone consume at ever – increasing levels. The absence of a high and escalating level of consumption poses a threat to those who profit from and have a vested interest in a robust economy driven by consumerism. However, the threats posed by the 'dangerous consumer' go beyond merely not consuming enough; the dangerous consumer consumes the wrong things. For example, because they lack adequate resources, such people consume a variety of public and welfare services that are a drain on the economy. Because they lack the resources, but share the goals of a consumer society, they are more likely to engage in criminal activities and thereby to 'consume' the services of the police, the courts, and the prisons and thereby further drain the economy of resources. Further, when they consume in a more conventional sense, they are more likely to consume the 'wrong' things, things that are apt to be perceived as 'wrong' by the winners in our 'winner take all' consumer society. For example, they are more likely to consume the 'wrong' drugs. Rather than champagne or even cocaine, they are likely to consume heroin, crack and the like. The latter are more likely to be seen as dangerous drugs leading to more threatening behaviors. Minimally, they are the drugs that are more likely to be criminalized and absorb the interest of the criminal justice system. Dangerous consumers are more likely to consume guns, or at least those guns that are likely to be used in crimes against property and the relatively well-to-do people who own that property. Thus, dangerous consumers are so designated because *both* what they do, and what they do not, consume poses a threat to consumer society. Bauman's 'flawed consumers', those unable to participate adequately in consumption, are too limited and too passive to pose a real threat to consumer society. Dangerous consumers, both by their relative inactivity and by their activity, pose a much more active and serious threat to consumer society. Of course, Bauman recognizes this in discussing the fact that the flawed consumers are those who tend to be ghettoized and criminalized.

It is important to recognize that even those who are threats to consumer society are themselves consumers. No one is able to escape the imperatives of the consumer society, even those who are seen as threatening it. The fact that they are consumers, and aspire to be bigger and better consumers of conventional goods and services, indicates that ultimately 'dangerous' consumers pose no real threat to consumer society. They are already playing the game and if they were to obtain more resources through illegal means, they would proceed to be more active, more mainstream consumers. This complements Bauman's argument that because consumption is inherently individualizing, it is therefore far less likely to produce a revolutionary class than production which is a collective enterprise and thereby apt to produce collective opposition in the form of a revolutionary social class.

Thus, just as there are obscene sites of consumption, and processes implicated in those sites, there are also obscene consumers – those who threaten the raucous consumer party going on all around us at the dawn of the new millennium. Of course, they are obscene from the modern optic of what Bauman calls (and practices) the (modern) sociology of postmodernism. From the perspective of Baudrillardian postmodern sociology we would need to identify another type of obscene consumer – almost certainly one whose practice of consumption and display of consumer goods is hypervisible. Interesting, the obscene consumer from this perspective sounds strikingly like Veblen's modernist conspicuous consumer (see Chapter 10). But, however we identify the obscene consumer, it is clear that the notion of the obscene applies as well to the consumer as it does to the other concerns in this chapter.

Nevertheless, it is difficult to see the consumer in the same light as the processes and entities of concern earlier in this chapter. That is, the latter are far greater obscenities, especially from a modern point of view, than the 'obscene' consumer. To point the finger at the consumer is in modern terms to 'blame the victim' for obscenities that are far more traceable to processes like McDonaldization and consumerism and entities like fast-food restaurants, credit cards and the new means of consumption. It is in these arenas that the real obscenities lie and it is there that both modernists and postmodernists should focus their attention.

Note

This chapter is based on a paper presented at the conference on 'Obscene Powers: Corruption, Coercion and Violence', John Hansard Gallery, University of Southampton, Southampton, England, 11–12 December 1999 and was published previously in *Third Text*, SI (Summer), 2000, pp. 17–28.

REFERENCES

Abercrombie, Nicholas, Hill, Stephen and Turner, Bryan S. (1994) *Dictionary of Sociology*, new edition. London: Penguin.

Abu-Lughod, Janet (1997) 'Going Beyond the Global Babble', in A.D. King (ed.), *Culture, Globalization and the World-System*. Minneapolis: University of Minnesota Press.

Achenbach, Joel (1990) 'The Age of Unreality', *Washington Post*, 22 November: C1, C14.

Alfino, Mark, Caputo, John S. and Wynyard, Robin (1998) *McDonaldization Revisited: Critical Essays on Consumer Culture*. Westport, CT: Greenwood.

American Banker (1991) 'EFT Experts Look Ahead with Costs on Their Minds', 20 May: 22A.

Appadurai, Arjun (1990) 'Disjuncture and Difference in the Global Cultural Economy', in Mike Featherstone (ed.), *Global Culture: Nationalism, Globalization and Modernity*. London: Sage. pp. 295–310.

Appadurai, Arjun (1996) *Modernity at Large: Cultural Dimensions of Globalization*. Minneapolis: University of Minnesota Press.

Baker, Wayne E. and Jimerson, Jason B. (1992) 'The Sociology of Money', *American Behavioral Scientist*, July/August: 678–93.

Bakhtin, M.M. (1968) *Rabelais and His World*. Cambridge, MA: MIT Press.

Ball, Edward (1987) 'The Great Sideshow of the Situationist International', *Yale French Studies*, 73: 21–37.

Baran, Paul and Sweezy, Paul (1966) *Monopoly Capital: An Essay on the American Economic and Social Order*. New York: Monthly Review Press.

Barber, Benjamin (1995) *Jihad vs. McWorld*. New York: Times Books.

Barboza, David (1999) 'Pluralism under Golden Arches', *New York Times*, 12 February.

Baudrillard, Jean (1970/1998) *The Consumer Society*. London: Sage.

Baudrillard, Jean (1973/1975) *The Mirror of Production*. St Louis: Telos Press.

Baudrillard, Jean (1976/1993) *Symbolic Exchange and Death*. London: Sage.

Baudrillard, Jean (1983) *Simulations*. New York: Semiotext(e).

Baudrillard, Jean (1983/1990) *Fatal Strategies*. NY: Semiotext(e).

Bauman, Zygmunt (1992) *Intimations of Postmodernity*. London: Routledge.

Bauman, Zygmunt (1993) *Postmodern Ethics*. Oxford: Blackwell.

Bauman, Zygmunt (1997) *Postmodernity and Its Discontents*. New York: New York University Press.

Beilharz, Peter (1999) 'McFascism? Reading Ritzer, Bauman and the Holocaust', in Barry Smart (ed.), *Resisting McDonaldization*. London: Sage. pp. 222–33.

Bell, Bill, Jr (1998) 'Environmental Groups Seeking Moratorium on New or Expanded "Animal Factories"', *St Louis Post-Dispatch*, 4 December: C8.

Benjamin, Walter (1986) 'Paris, Capital of the Nineteenth Century', in *Reflections: Essays, Aphorisms, Autobiographical Writings*. New York: Schocken. pp. 146–62.

Berman, Russell, Pan, David and Piccone, Paul (1990–91) 'The Society of the Spectacle 20 years Later: A Discussion', *Telos*, 86: 81–101.

Best, Steven, and Kellner, Douglas (1997) *The Postmodern Turn*. New York: Guilford.

Best, Steven, and Kellner, Douglas (Forthcoming). 'Debord and the Postmodern Turn: New Stages of the Spectacle',

Binkley, Christina (1997) 'Starless Nights in the "New" Las Vegas', *Wall Street Journal*, 9 May: B1.

Binkley, Christina (1998) 'Gambling on Culture: Casinos Invest in Fine Art', *Wall Street Journal*, 15 April: B10.

Bloomberg Business News (1996) 'McDonald's Sells Discovery Zone Shares', *Houston Chronicle*, 27 December: 10.

Boas, Max and Chain, Steve (1976) *Big Mac: The Unauthorized Story of McDonald's*. New York: NAL.

Boorstin, Daniel (1961) *The Image: A Guide to Pseudo-Events in America*. New York: Harper Colophon.

Bourdieu, Pierre (1984) *Distinction: A Social Critique of the Judgment of Taste*. Cambridge, MA: Harvard University Press.

Bourdieu, Pierre and Wacquant, Loic (1992) 'The Purpose of Reflexive Sociology (The Chicago Workshop)', in P. Bourdieu and L.J.D. Wacquant (eds), *An Invitation to Reflexive Sociology*. Chicago: University of Chicago Press. pp. 61–215.

Bowman, John (1995) 'Playing Around: Local Leaps and Bounds to Close in Wake of Discovery Zone Buying Chain', *Business First-Louisville*, 9 January, section 1: 4.

Brachet-Marquez, Viviane (1997) 'Mexican Sociology: Contradictory Influences', *Contemporary Sociology*, 26: 292–6.

Bracken, Len (1997) *Guy Debord – Revolutionary*. Venice, CA: Feral House.

Braverman, Harry (1974) *Labor and Monopoly Capital: The Degradation of Work in the Twentieth Century*. New York: Monthly Review Press.

Bryant, Adam (1992) 'It Pays to Stick to Basics in Credit Cards', *New York Times*, 31 October: 35.

Bryant, Christopher G.A. and David Jary (2000) 'Anthony Giddens', in George Ritzer (ed.), *The Blackwell Companion to Major Social Theorists*. Malden, MA: Blackwell, pp. 670–95.

Brym, Robert and Saint-Pierre, Celine (1997) 'Canadian Sociology', *Contemporary Sociology*, 26: 543–6.

Bryman, Alan (1995) *Disney and His Worlds*. London: Routledge.

Bryman, Alan (1999a) 'Theme Parks and McDonaldization', in Barry Smart (ed.), *Resisting McDonaldization*. London: Sage. pp. 101–15.

Bryman, Alan (1999b) 'The Disneyization of Society', *Sociological Review*, 47: 25–47.

Buck-Morss, Susan (1989) *The Dialectics of Seeing: Walter Benjamin and the Arcades Project*. Cambridge, MA: MIT Press.

Bulkeley, William M. (1996) 'Hold the Ketchup! Chic Restaurants Aim to Sell Haute Cuisine through Chains', *Wall Street Journal*, 1 April: B1, B8.

Campbell, Colin (1989) *The Romantic Ethic and the Spirit of Modern Consumerism*. Oxford: Blackwell.

Canedy, Dana (1999) 'Web Grocers Betting on Time-Starved Consumers', *International Herald Tribune*, 11–12 September: 9, 13.

Carlson, Peter (1990) 'Who Put the Sunshine in the Sunshine Scent?', *Washington Post Magazine*, 16 December: 21.

Chain Store Executive (1992) 'Evaluating the Payments: More Is Better', September: 28.

Chaney, David (1993) *Fictions of Collective Life*. London: Routledge.

Chase-Dunn, Christopher, Kawano, Yukio and Brewer, Benjamin D. (2000) 'Trade Globalization since 1795: Waves of Integration in the World-System', *American Sociological Review*, 65 (1) (February): 77–95.

Chicago Tribune (1992) 'French "Cast Members" Get Used to the Rules in a Magic Kingdom of Jobs', 31 January: 2.

Chinoy, Ira and Babington, Charles (1998a) 'Low-Income Players Feed Lottery Cash Cow', *Washington Post*, 3 May: A1, A22.

Chinoy, Ira and Babington, Charles (1998b) 'Lotteries Lure Players with Slick Marketing', *Washington Post*, 4 May: A1, A10.

Clammer, John (1997) *Contemporary Urban Japan: A Sociology of Consumption*. Oxford: Blackwell.

Clark, T.J. and Nicholson-Smith, Donald (1997) 'Why Art Can't Kill the Situationist International', *October*, 79: 15–31.

Clarke, Simon (1990) 'The Crisis of Fordism or the Crisis of Social Democracy?', *Telos*, 83: 71–98.

Clawson, Dan (1997) 'Market Censorship – Books Under Attack', *Contemporary Sociology*, 26: vii–viii.

Cohen, Richard (1990) 'Take a Message – Please!', *Washington Post Magazine*, 5 August: 5.

Cohen, Roger (1993) 'Euro Disney in Danger of Shutdown', *Washington Post*, 23 December: D3.

Cohen, Roger (1999) 'Fearful Over the Future, Europe Seizes on Food', *New York Times – Week in Review*, 29 August: 1, 3.

Coleman, Brian and King, Thomas R. (1994) 'Euro Disney Rescue Package Wins Approval', *Wall Street Journal*, 15 March: A3, A6.

Coleman, James William (1992) 'Crime and Money: Motivation and Opportunity in a Monetarized Economy', *American Behavioral Scientist*, July/August: 827–36.

Connors, Philip (1999) 'Not All McDonald's Are Carbon Copies, A "Collector" Attests', *Wall Street Journal*, 16 August: A1, A6.

Consumer Reports (1992) 'Hello, Central, Get Me 0055516960349583693941685905048876598765976', August: 7.

Corrigan, Peter (1997) *The Sociology of Consumption*. London: Sage.

Crary, Jonathan (1984) 'Eclipse of the Spectacle', in Brian Wallis (ed.), *Art After Modernism: Rethinking Representation*. Boston, MA: David R. Godine. pp. 283–94.

Crenshaw, Albert B. (1991) 'Keeping Tabs on Card Holders', *Washington Post*, 20 January: H4.

Crossette, Barbara (1998) 'Worldwide, Most are Consuming More, and Rich Much More', *New York Times*, 13 September, section 1: 3.

Davis, Fred (1992) *Fashion, Culture, and Identity*. Chicago: University of Chicago Press.

Debord, Guy (1967/1994) *The Society of the Spectacle*. New York: Zone Books.

Debray, Regis (1995) 'Remarks on the Spectacle', *New Left Review*, 214: 134–41.

Delillo, Don (1985) *White Noise*. New York: Viking.

Derrida, Jacques (1967/1974) *Of Grammatology*. Baltimore, MD: Johns Hopkins University Press.

Detweiler, Gerri (1993) *The Ultimate Credit Handbook*. New York: Plume.

Dezalay, Yves (1990) 'The *Big Bang* and the Law: The Internationalization and Restructuration of the Legal Field', in Mike Featherstone (ed.), *Global Culture: Nationalism, Globalization and Modernity*. London: Sage. pp. 279–94.

Dinmore, Guy (1999) 'Milosevic Playing Well at Home', *Chicago Tribune*, 31 March.

Dorfman, Joseph (1934/1966) *Thorstein Veblen and his America*. New York: Augustus M. Kelley.

Duhamel, Georges (1931) *America the Menace: Scenes from the Life of the Future*. Boston, MA: Houghton Mifflin.

Duignan, Peter and Gann, Lewis (1992) *The Rebirth of the West: The Americanization of the Democratic World*. London: Blackwell.

Edwards, Richard (1979) *Contested Terrain: The Transformation of the Workplace in the Twentieth Century*. New York: Basic Books.

Esquivel, Laura (1992) *Like Water for Chocolate*. New York: Doubleday.

Faiola, Anthony (1996) 'Satisfying DC's Appetite: Dining Out Is In, and So are Big National Restaurant Chains', *Washington Post – Washington Business*, 16 December: 12–13.

Featherstone, Mike (ed.) (1990) *Global Culture: Nationalism, Globalization and Modernity*. London: Sage.

Featherstone, Mike (1991) *Consumer Culture and Postmodernism*. London: Sage.

Featherstone, Mike and Lash, Scott (1995) 'Globalization, Modernity and the Spatialization of Social Theory: An Introduction', in M. Featherstone, S. Lash and R. Robertson (eds), *Global Modernities*. London: Sage.

Ferry, Luc and Renaut, Alain (1985) *French Philosophy of the Sixties*. Amherst, MA: University of Massachusetts.

Ficklen, Mary (1998) 'Love These Days Can be So Viagravating', *Dallas Morning News*, 8 June: 12C.

Fine, Gary Alan (1999) 'Art Centres: Southern Folk Art and the Splintering of a Hegemonic Market', in Barry Smart (ed.), *Resisting McDonaldization*. London: Sage. pp. 148–62.

Fine, Gary Alan and Manning, Phil (2000) 'Erving Goffman', in George Ritzer (ed.), *Blackwell Companion to Major Social Theorists*. Malden, MA: Blackwell. pp. 457–85.

Ford, Henry (1922) *My Life and My Work*. Garden City, NY: Doubleday Page & Co.

Fowlie, Wallace (1950) *Age of Surrealism*. Bloomington, IN: Indiana University Press.

Frank, Robert (2000) 'Big Boy's Adventures in Thailand', *Wall Street Journal*, 12 April: B1.

Friedland, Jonathan (1997) 'Can Yanks Export Good Times to Latins?', *Wall Street Journal*, 6 March: A11.

Friedland, Roger and Boden, Deirdre (eds) (1994) *NowHere: Space, Time and Modernity*. Berkeley, CA: University of California Press.

Friedman, Jonathan (1994) *Cultural Identity and the Global Process*. London: Sage.

Friedman, Jonathan (1995) 'Global System, Globalization and the Parameters of Modernity', in M. Featherstone, S. Lash and R. Robertson (eds), *Global Modernities*. London: Sage.

Friedman, Thomas (1999) *The Lexus and Olive Tree: Understanding Globalization*. New York: Farrar, Straus, Giroux.

Fuchs, Stephan and Ward, Steven (1994) 'What is Deconstruction, and Where and When Does It Take Place? Making Facts in Science, Building Cases in Law', *American Sociological Review*, 59: 481–500.

Gabriel, Yiannis and Lang, Tim (1995) *The Unmanageable Consumer: Contemporary Consumption and Its Fragmentation*. London: Sage.

Galanoy, Terry (1980) *Charge It: Inside the Credit Card Conspiracy*. New York: Putnam.

Galtung, Johan (1997) 'On the Social Costs of Modernization: Social Disintegration, Atomie/Anomie and Social Development', in Cynthia Hewitt de Alcántara (ed.), *Social Futures, Global Vision*. Oxford: Blackwell.

Gane, Mike (1991) *Baudrillard's Bestiary: Baudrillard and Culture*. London: Routledge.

Gans, Herbert (1977a) 'Best Sellers by Sociologists: An Exploratory Study', *Contemporary Sociology*, 26: 131–5.

Gans, Herbert (1977b) 'Reply', *Contemporary Sociology*, 26: 789–91.

Garcia Canclini, Nestor (1995) *Hybrid Cultures: Strategies for Entering and Leaving Modernity*. Minneapolis: University of Minnesota Press.

Garfield, Bob (1991) 'How I Spent (and Spent and Spent) My Disney Vacation', *Washington Post/Outlook*, 7 July: B5.

Garson, Barbara (1977) All the Livelong Day. Harmondsworth: Penguin.

Gerth, Hans and Mills, C. Wright (1953) Character and Social Structure. New York: Harcourt Brace and World. pp. 3–74.

Gerth, Hans and Mills, C. Wright (1958) 'Introduction', in Hans Gerth and C. Wright Mills (eds), From Max Weber. New York: Oxford University Press.

Giddens, Anthony (1989) 'A Reply to My Critics', in D. Held and J.B. Thompson (eds), Social Theory of Modern Societies: Anthony Giddens and His Critics. Cambridge: Cambridge University Press. pp. 249–301.

Giddens, Anthony (1990) The Consequences of Modernity. Stanford, CA: Stanford University Press.

Gisler, Peggy and Eberts, Marge (1995) 'Reader Disagrees with Advice for Mom Too Tired to Read', Star Tribune (Minneapolis), 3 July: 3E.

Goffman, Erving (1951) 'Symbols of Class Status', British Journal of Sociology, 2: 294–304.

Goldman, Steven L., Nagel, Roger N. and Preiss, Kenneth (1994) 'Why Seiko has 3,000 Watch Styles', New York Times, 9 October: 9.

Gombin, Richard (1972) 'French Leftism', Journal of Contemporary History, 7: 27–50.

Goodman, Ellen (1991) 'Fast-Forwarding Through Fall', Washington Post, 5 October: A19.

Gray, Christopher (1974) The Incomplete Work of the Situationist International. Liverpool: Free Fall.

Gumbel, Peter and Turner, Richard (1994) 'Fans Like Euro Disney but Its Parent's Goofs Weigh the Park Down', Wall Street Journal, 10 March: A1, A12.

Hage, Jerald and Powers, Charles H. (1992) Post-Industrial Lives: Roles and Relationships in the 21st Century. Newbury Park, CA: Sage.

Hall, Stuart (1997) 'The Local and the Global: Globalization and Ethnicity', in A.D. King (ed.), Culture, Globalization and the World-System: Contemporary Conditions for the Representation of Identity. Minneapolis: University of Minnesota Press.

Hannerz, Ulf (1990) 'Cosmopolitans and Locals in World Culture', in M. Featherstone (ed.), Global Culture: Nationalism, Globalization and Modernity. London: Sage.

Hannigan, John (1998) Fantasy City: Pleasure and Profit in the Postmodern Metropolis. London: Routledge.

Hansell, Saul (1994) 'Into Banking's Future, Electronically', New York Times, 31 March: D1, D13.

Harvey, David (1989) The Condition of Postmodernity: An Enquiry into the Origins of Cultural Change. Oxford and Cambridge, MA: Blackwell.

Hernandez, Donald J. and Charney, Evan (eds) (1998) From Generation to Generation: The Health and Well-Being of Children in Immigrant Families. Washington, DC: National Academy Press.

Hobsbawm, Eric (1997) 'The Future of the State', in Cynthia Hewitt de Alcántara, (ed.), Social Futures, Global Visions. Oxford: Blackwell.

Hockstader, Lee (1995) 'Attack on Big Mac', Washington Post, 8 August: A13.

von Hoffman, Nicholas (1978) 'The Fast-Disappearing Family Meal', Washington Post, 23 November: C4.

Honan, William H. (1995) 'Professors Battling Television Technology', New York Times, 4 April: D24.

Horovitz, Bruce (1998) 'The Price of Family Fun: Disney Raises Theme Park Admission Prices', USA Today, 13 April: B8.

Howes, David (1996) 'Introduction', in David Howes (ed.), Cross-Cultural Consumption: Global Markers, Local Realities. London: Routledge. pp. 1–16.

Hundley, Kris (1998) 'The Inpatient Physician', St Petersburg Times, 26 July: 1Hff.

Huxtable, Ada Louise (1997a) The Unreal America: Architecture and Illusion. New York: New Press.

Huxtable, Ada Louise (1997b) 'Living with Fake and Liking It', *New York Times*, 30 March, section 2: 1, 40.

Illouz, Eva (1997) *Consuming the Romantic Utopia*. Berkeley, CA: University of California Press.

Independent (London) (1997) 'E coli Outbreak Forces Closure of Meat Plant', 22 August: 12.

Ingwerson, Marshall (1997) 'That Golden Touch to the Arches in Russia', *Ohio Slavic and East European Newsletter 25*, Spring 1997. (Originally published in the *Christian Science Monitor*, 1997.)

Jary, David and Jary, Julia (1995) *Collins Dictionary of Sociology*. Glasgow: HarperCollins.

Kay, Julia (1997) 'High-Tech Playground to Lure Families to Burger Restaurant', *Times-Picayune*, 27 January: E14.

Keohane, Robert O. and Nye, Joseph S. (1989) *Power and Interdependence*. Boston: Little Brown.

Kleege, Stephen (1994) 'Privacy a Concern with Marketing Based on Card Data', *American Banker*, 14 March: 15.

Knorr-Cetina, Karin (1997) 'Sociality with Objects: Social Relations in Postsocial Knowledge Societies', *Theory, Culture and Society*, 14 (4): 1–30.

Knorr-Cetina, Karin (2001) 'Postsocial Theory', in George Ritzer and Barry Smart (eds), *Handbook of Social Theory*. London: Sage.

Kornhauser, William (1959) *Politics of Mass Society*. New York: The Free Press.

Kowinski, William Severini (1985) *The Malling of America: An Inside Look at the Great Consumer Paradise*. New York: Morrow.

Kraft, Scott (1994) 'Agog at Euro Disneyland', *Los Angeles Times*, 18 January: H1.

Kuhn, Thomas (1962/1970) *The Structure of Scientific Revolutions*, rev. edn. Chicago: University of Chicago Press.

Kuisel, Richard (1993) *Seducing the French: The Dilemma of Americanization*. Berkeley, CA: University of California Press.

Lash, Scott and Urry, John (1994) *Economies of Signs and Space*. London: Sage.

Leach, William (1993) *Land of Desire: Merchants, Power, and the Rise of a New American Culture*. New York: Pantheon Books.

Lechner, Frank J. and Boli, John (eds) (2000) *The Globalization Reader*. Malden, MA: Blackwell.

Lefebvre, Henri (1971) *Everyday Life in the Modern World*. New York: Harper and Row.

Leidner, Robin (1993) *Fast Food, Fast Talk: Service Work and the Routinization of Everyday Life*. Berkeley, CA: University of California Press.

Levine, Donald (ed.) (1971) *Georg Simmel*. Chicago: University of Chicago Press.

Levine, Stephen (1991) 'McDonald's Makes a Play to Diversify', *Washington Post*, 30 August: G1, G4.

Lipovetsky, Gilles (1994) *The Empire of Fashion: Dressing Modern Democracy*. Princeton, NJ: Princeton University Press.

Lipton, Eric (1995) 'Visit to Groomer's Takes Deadly Turn', *Washington Post*, 31 March: B1.

Los Angeles Times (1993) 'Road to Cashlessness Paved With Plastic', 20 December: C1.

Lukacs, Georg (1971) *History and Class Consciousness*. Cambridge, MA: MIT Press.

Luke, Tim (1990) 'Postcommunism in the USSR: The McGulag Archipelago', *Telos*, 84: 33–42.

Luxenberg, Stan (1985) *Roadside Empires: How the Chains Franchised America*. New York: Viking.

Maayan, Myriam (1989) 'From Aesthetic to Political Vanguard: The Situationist International, 1957–1968', *Arts Magazine*, 65: 49–53.

MacGregor, Alison (1998) 'Fountain of Sexual Youth Carries Risks for Couples; Sex Can Ruin Some Relationships, Therapists Warn', *Ottawa Citizen*, 27 May: A8.

Mandell, Lewis (1990) *The Credit Card Industry: A History*. Boston, MA: Twayne.

Maragliano, Giorgio (1989) 'The Invisible Insurrection', *Flash Art*, 147: 87–90.

Marx, Karl (1867/1967) *Capital: A Critique of Political Economy*, vol.1. New York: International Publishers.

Marx, Karl (1884/1981) *Capital*, vol. 2. New York: Vintage Books.

Mattox, William R., Jr (1997) 'The Decline of Dinnertime', *Ottawa Citizen*, 30 April: A14.

MacCreary, Edward A. (1964) *The Americanization of Europe: The Impact of Americans and American Business on the Uncommon Market*. Garden City, NY: Doubleday.

McDonough, Thomas (1997) 'Rereading Debord, Rereading the Situationists', *October* 79: 3–14.

McHugh, Josh (1996) 'A Shoe that Really Fits', *Forbes*, 3 June: 126–7.

Meyer, John W., Boli, John, Thomas, George M. and Ramirez, Francisco (1997) 'World Society and the Nation-State', *American Journal of Sociology*, 103 (1) July: 144–81.

Miles, Stephen (1998) *Consumerism as a Way of Life*. London: Sage.

Miller, Michael B. (1981) *The Bon Marché: Bourgeois Culture and the Department Store, 1869–1920*. Princeton, NJ: Princeton University Press.

Mills, C. Wright (1956) *The Power Elite*. New York: Oxford University Press.

Mills, C. Wright (1959) *The Sociological Imagination*. New York: Oxford University Press.

Mitroff, Ian and Bennis, Warren (1989) *The Unreality Industry: The Deliberate Manufacturing of Falsehood and What It Is Doing to Our Lives*. New York: Birch Lane Press.

Munch, Richard and Smelser, Neil (1987) 'Relating the Micro and Macro', in Jeffrey C. Alexander et al. (eds), *The Micro–Macro Link*. Berkeley, CA: University of California Press. pp. 356–87.

Myerson, Allen R. (1996) 'America's Quiet Rebellion Against McDonaldization', *New York Times*, 28 July: E5.

Nasaw, David (1993) *Going Out: The Rise and Fall of Public Amusements*. New York: Basic Books.

Nocera, Joseph (1994) *A Piece of the Action: How the Middle Class Joined the Money Class*. New York: Simon and Schuster.

O'Brien, Tim (1998) 'Farming: Poison Pens', *Guardian* (London), 29 April: 4.

Ohnuki-Tierney, Emiko (1997) 'McDonald's in Japan: Changing Manners and Etiquette', in James Watson (ed.), *Golden Arches East: McDonald's in East Asia*. Stanford, CA: Stanford University Press.

Oldenburg, Ray (1989) *The Great Good Place*. New York: Paragon House.

O'Neill, John (1999) 'Have You Had Your Theory Today?', in Barry Smart (ed.), *Resisting McDonaldiization*. London: Sage. pp. 41–56.

Oransky, Ivan and Gottlieb, Scott (1998) 'Fertility Doctors Hold Couples Captive', *USA TODAY*, 30 September: 15A.

Parker, Martin and Jary, David (1995) 'The McUniversity: Organization, Management and Academic Subjectivity', *Organization*, 2: 1–20.

Penman, Danny (1997) 'Judgment Day for McDonald's', *Independent* (London), 19 June: 20ff.

Perl, Peter (1992) 'Fast Is Beautiful', *Washington Post Magazine*, 24 May: 26.

Pieterse, Jan N. (1995) 'Globalization as Hybridization', in M. Featherstone, S. Lash and R. Robertson (eds), *Global Modernities*. London: Sage.

Pine, Joseph (1993) *Mass Customization: The Frontier in Business Competition*. Cambridge, MA: Harvard Business School Press.

Piore, Michael and Sabel, Charles (1984) *The Second Industrial Divide: Possibilities for Prosperity*. New York: Basic Books.

Piskora, Beth and Kutler, Jeffrey (1993) 'ATM, Debit Cards and Home Banking: Finally, Many Bank Customers Seem To Be Ready for the Future', *American Banker*, 27 September: 1A.

Plant, Sadie (1992) *The Most Radical Gesture*. New York: Routledge.

Poster, Mark (1975) *Existential Marxism in Postwar France*. Princeton, NJ: Princeton University Press.

Postman, Neil (1985) *Amusing Ourselves to Death: Public Discourse in the Age of Show Business*. New York: Viking.

Quint, Michael (1990) 'D'Agostino to Accept Debit Cards for Purchases', *New York Times*, 19 May: 43.

Reiter, Ester (1991) *Making Fast Food*. Montreal and Kingston: McGill–Queen's University Press.

Richman, Phyllis (1996) 'The Golden Years Arches: McDonald's Mature Burgers Don't Cut the Mustard', *Washington Post*, 10 May: D1.

Richman, Phyllis (1998) 'Savoring Lunch in the Slow Lane', *Washington Post*, 22 November: M1.

Riding, Alan (1992) 'Only the French Elite Scorn Mickey's Debut', *New York Times*, 13 April: A1.

Rieff, David (1994) 'The Culture That Conquered the World', *Washington Post*, 2 January: C1–C4.

Riesman, David (1953/1995) *Thorstein Veblen*. New Brunswick, NJ: Transaction Publishers.

Ringle, Ken (1998) 'Daniel Yergin: Turning a Prophet', *Washington Post*, 9 April: B1–B2.

Ritzer, George (1981) *Toward an Integrated Sociological Paradigm: The Search for an Exemplar and an Image of the Subject Matter*. Boston, MA: Allyn and Bacon.

Ritzer, George (1991a) 'The 1980s: Micro-Macro (and Agency-Structure) Integration in Sociological Theory', in *Metatheorizing in Sociology*. Lexington, MA: Lexington Books. pp. 207–34.

Ritzer, George (1991b) 'The Recent History and the Emerging Reality of American Sociological Theory: A Metatheoretical Interpretation', *Sociological Forum*, 6: 269–87.

Ritzer, George (1995) *Expressing America: A Critique of the Global Credit Card Society*. Thousand Oaks, CA: Pine Forge Press.

Ritzer, George (1996) *The McDonaldization of Society*, rev. edn. Thousand Oaks, CA: Pine Forge Press.

Ritzer, George (1997) *Postmodern Social Theory*. New York: McGraw–Hill.

Ritzer, George (1998) *The McDonaldization Thesis*. London: Sage.

Ritzer, George (1999) *Enchanting a Disenchanted World: Revolutionizing the Means of Consumption*. Thousand Oaks, CA: Pine Forge Press.

Ritzer, George (2000) *The McDonaldization of Society: New Century Edition*. Thousand Oaks, CA: Sage.

Ritzer, George (2001) *Explorations in Social Theory*. London: Sage.

Ritzer, George and Gindoff, Pamela (1992) 'Methodological Relationism: Lessons for and from Social Psychology', *Social Psychology Quarterly*, 55: 128–40.

Ritzer, George and Liska, Allan (1998) '"McDisneyization" and "Post-Tourism": Complementary Perspectives on Contemporary Tourism', in Chris Rojek and John Urry (eds), *Touring Cultures: Transformations in Travel and Theory*. London: Routledge.

Ritzer, George, Goodman, Douglas and Wiedenhoft, Wendy (2001) 'Theories of Consumption', in George Ritzer and Barry Smart (eds), *Handbook of Social Theory*. London: Sage.

Ritzer, George and Walczak, David (1986) *Working: Conflict and Change*, 3rd edn. Englewood Cliffs, NJ: Prentice Hall.

Robertson, Roland (1992) *Globalization: Social Theory and Global Culture*. London: Sage.

Robertson, Roland (1995) 'Globalization: Time-Space and Homogeneity–Heterogeneity', in M. Featherstone, S. Lash and R. Robertson (eds), *Global Modernities*. London: Sage.

Robertson, Roland (2001) 'Globalization Theory 2000+: Major Problematics', in George Ritzer and Barry Smart (eds), *Handbook of Social Theory*. London: Sage.

Robins, Marjorie (1992) 'Awfully American for Grown-ups', *Los Angeles Times*, 3 May: L1.

Rojek, Chris (1995) 'Veblen, Leisure and Human Need', *Leisure Studies*, 14: 73–86.

Rosenau, Pauline Marie (1992) *Post-Modernism and the Social Science: Insights, Inroads, and Intrusions*. Princeton, NJ: Princeton University Press.

Ross, Kristin (1997) 'Lefebvre on the Situationists: An Interview', *October*, 79: 69–83.

Rothenberg, Sheila and Rothenberg, Robert S. (1993) 'The Pleasures of Paris', *USA TODAY* (Magazine), March: 38ff.

Rule, James, McAdam, Douglas, Stearns, Linda and Uglow, David (1980) *The Politics of Privacy*. New York: Elsevier.

Ryan, Michael (1988) 'Fast Food vs. Supermarkets', *Parade*, 13 November: 6.

Schnedler, Jack (1994) 'Mastering Mall of America: Full-Throttle Day of Shop-Hopping Tames Minnesota's Mighty Monster', *Chicago Sun-Times/Travel*, 6 February: 1ff.

Schneider, Mark A. (1993) *Culture and Enchantment*. Chicago: University of Chicago Press.

Schor, Juliet B. (1998) *The Overspent American: Upscaling, Downshifting, and the New Consumer*. New York: Basic Books.

Schrage, Michael (1990) 'Personalized Publishing: Confusing Information with Intimacy', *Washington Post*, 23 November: B13.

Schrage, Michael (1992) 'The Pursuit of Efficiency Can Be an Illusion', *Washington Post*, 20 March: F3.

Schrambling, Regina (1991) 'The Curse of Culinary Convenience', *New York Times*, 10 September: A19.

Schumpeter, Joseph (1950) *Capitalism, Socialism, and Democracy*, 3rd edn. New York: Harper and Brothers.

Schutz, Alfred. 1932/1967. *The Phenomenology of the Social World*. Evanston: Northwestern University Press.

Servan-Schreiber, J.-J. (1968) *The American Challenge*. New York: Atheneum.

Shelton, Allen (Unpublished Essay) 'Writing McDonald's, Eating the Past: McDonald's As a Postmodern Space'.

Shimbun, Yomiuri (1995) 'Golden Arches Better-Known in Japan', *The Daily Yomiuri*, 26 January: 17.

Shipway, Mark (1987) 'Situationism', in M. Rubel and J. Crump (eds), *Non-Market Socialism in the Nineteenth and Twentieth Centuries*. Houndsmills: Macmillan. pp. 151–72.

Shiver, Jube, Jr (1988) 'Scoring System for Loan Seekers Stirs Debate', *Los Angeles Times*, 30 October: IV5.

Simmel, Georg (1904/1971) 'Fashion', in Donald Levine (ed.), *Georg Simmel*. Chicago: University of Chicago Press. pp. 294–323.

Simmel, Georg (1907/1978) *The Philosophy of Money*. London: Routledge and Kegan Paul.

Simmel, Georg (1991) 'Money in Modern Culture', *Theory, Culture and Society*, 8: 29.

Slater, Don (1997) *Consumer Culture and Modernity*. Cambridge: Polity Press.

Sloane, Leonard (1992) 'Buying by Catalogue Is Easy: Timely Delivery May Not Be', *New York Times*, 25 April: 50.

Slow (1998) July–September, Issue 10, www.slowfood.com/publications/slow10/Ritzer.html

Smart, Barry (ed.) (1999) *Resisting McDonaldization*. London: Sage.

Smith, Adam (1789/1994) *The Wealth of Nations*. New York: Modern Library.

Smith, Anthony D. (1990) 'Towards a Global Culture?', in M. Featherstone (ed.), *Global Culture*. London: Sage.

Smith, Peter (1991) 'On the Passage of a Few People: Situationist Nostalgia', *Oxford Art Journal*, 14 (1): 118–25.

Smolowe, Jill (1990) '"Read This!!!!"', *Time*, 26 November: 62ff.

Sociale Wetenschappen (1996) 39: 1–81.

Spector, Jack (1997) *Surrealist Art and Writing*. New York: Cambridge University Press.

Spencer, Maryellen (1983) 'Can Mama Mac Get Them to Eat Spinach?', in Marshall Fishwick (ed.), *Ronald Revisited: The World of Ronald McDonald*. Bowling Green, OH: Bowling Green University Press. pp. 85–93.

Sprague, Joey (1998) '(Re)Making Sociology: Breaking the Bonds of our Discipline', *Contemporary Sociology*, 27: 24–8.

Stallybrass, P. and White, A. (1986) *The Politics and Poetics of Transgression*. London: Methuen.

Stanley, T.L. (1998) 'Strategy: Refurbished DZ to Be Tie-in Friendly', *Brandweek*, 26 January.

Stearns, Patty Lanoue (1998) 'Double-Sized Fast Foods Means Double the Trouble', *Pittsburgh Post-Gazette*, 10 October: B6.

Sterngold, James (1994) 'Tokyo's Magic Kingdom Outshines Its Role Model', *New York Times*, 7 March: D1, D7.

Stewart, John (1991) 'The Credit-Reporting Mess', *Credit Card Management*, July: 55ff.

Sullivan, Barbara (1995) 'McDonald's Sees India as Golden Opportunity', *Chicago Tribune-Business*, 5 April.

Swardson, Anne (1999) 'A Roquefort David Strikes a Coke Goliath', *International Herald Tribune*, 23 August: 5.

Swisher, Kara (1991) 'A Mall for America?', *Washington Post/Business*, 30 June: H1, H4.

Sztompka, Piotr (2000) 'Robert K Merton', in George Ritzer (ed.), *The Blackwell Companion to Major Social Theorists*. Malder, MA: Blackwell. pp. 435–56.

Terkel, Studs (1974) *Working*. New York: Pantheon. p. 159.

Tester, Keith (1999) 'The Moral Malaise of McDonaldization: The Values of Vegetarianism', in Barry Smart (ed.), *Resisting McDonaldization*. London: Sage. pp. 207–21.

Thompson, William N., Kenty Pinney, J. and Schibrowsky, John A. (1996) 'The Family that Gambles Together: Business and Social Concerns', *Journal of Travel Research*, 34: 70–4.

Time (1985) 'Fast Food Speeds Up the Pace', 26 August: 60.

Time (1999) 27 December.

Tiryakian, Edward A. (1992) 'Pathways to Metatheory: Rethinking the Presuppositions of Macrosociology', in George Ritzer (ed.), *Metatheorizing*. Newbury Park, CA: Sage. pp. 69–87.

Tobias, Andrew (1994) 'Beware the Plastic Loan Shark', *Time*, 10 January: 20.

Turner, Bryan (1986) 'Simmel, Rationalisation and the Sociology of Money', *Sociological Review*, 34: 93–114.

Turner, Bryan (1999) 'McCitizens: Risk, Coolness and Irony in Contemporary Politics', in Barry Smart (ed.), *Resisting McDonaldization*. London: Sage. pp. 83–100.

Underhill, Paco (1999) *Why We Buy: The Science of Shopping*. New York: Simon and Schuster.

Updegrave, Walter L. (1987) 'How Lenders Size You Up', *Money*, April: 145ff.

USA TODAY (1999) 'Internet 100', 9 August: 3b.

Vaneigem, Raoul (1967/1984) *The Revolution of Everyday Life*. London: Rebel Press/Left Bank.

Varney, Kenneth R. (1994) 'Automated Credit Scoring Screens Loan Applicants', *Washington Post*, 15 January: E1, E13.

Veblen, Thorstein (1899/1934) *The Theory of the Leisure Class: An Economic Study of Institutions*. New York: Modern Library.

Veblen, Thorstein (1899/1994) *The Theory of The Leisure Class: An Economic Study of Institutions*. New York: Penguin.

Veblen, Thorstein (1904) *The Theory of the Business Enterprise*. New York: Charles Scribner's Sons.

Veblen, Thorstein (1919/1964) *The Vested Interests and the Common Man*. New York: Augustus M. Kelley.

Veblen, Thorstein (1921) *The Engineers and the Price System*. New York: Viking Press.

Veblen, Thorstein (1922/1964) *The Instinct of Workmanship and the State of the Industrial Arts*. New York: Augustus M. Kelley.

Veblen, Thorstein (1923) *Absentee Ownership and Business Enterprise in Recent Times: The Case of America*. New York: Viking Press.

Vidal, John (1997) *McLibel: Burger Culture on Trial*. New York: The New Press.

Virilio, Paul (1995) *The Art of the Motor*. Minneapolis: University of Minnesota Press.

Visser, Margaret (1989) 'A Meditation on the Microwave', *Psychology Today*, December: 38ff.

Waldman, Amy (1995) 'Lonely Hearts, Classy Dreams, Empty Wallets: Home Shopping Networks', *Washington Monthly*, 27: 10ff.

Wall Street Journal (1989) 'The Microwave Cooks Up a New Way of Life', 19 September: B1.

Wallerstein, Immanuel (1974) *The Modern World-System: Capitalist Agriculture and the Origins of the European World-Economy in the 16th Century*. New York: Academic Press.

Warwick, David R. (1993) *Reducing Crime by Eliminating Cash*. San Francisco: National Council on Crime and Delinquency.

Washington Times (1989) 'Call Boy Probe Chronology', 20 October: A10.

Waters, Malcolm (1996) *Globalization*. London: Routledge.

Watson, James (ed.) (1997a) *Golden Arches East: McDonald's in East Asia*. Stanford, CA: Stanford University Press.

Watson, James (1997b) 'Transnationalism, Localization, and Fast Foods in Asia', in James Watson (ed.), *Golden Arches East: McDonald's in East Asia*. Stanford, CA: Stanford University Press.

Watson, James (1997c) 'McDonald's in Hong Kong: Consumerism, Dietary Change, and the Rise of a Children's Culture', in James Watson (ed.), *Golden Arches East: McDonald's in East Asia*. Stanford, CA: Stanford University Press.

Weber, Max (1921/1968) *Economy and Society*, 3 vols. Totowa, NJ: Bedminster Press.

Weber, Max (1927/1981) *General Economic History*. New Brunswick, NJ: Transaction Books.

Weber, Max (1958) 'Science as a Vocation', in Hans Gerth and C. Wright Mills (eds), *From Max Weber*. New York: Oxford University Press. pp. 129–56.

Wieviorka, Michel (1997) 'Intellectuals, Nor Professionals: Sociology in France', *Contemporary Sociology*, 26: 288–92.

Wiggershaus, Rolf (1994) *The Frankfurt School: Its History, Theories, and Political Significance*. Cambridge, MA: MIT Press.

Williams, Francis (1962) *The American Invasion*. New York: Crown.

Williams, Rosalind H. (1982) *Dream Worlds: Mass Consumption in Late Nineteenth-Century France*. Berkeley, CA: University of California Press.

Wilson, E.O. (1998) 'Back from Chaos', *Atlantic Monthly*, 281 (3): 41–62.

Witchel, Alex (1994) 'By Way of Canarsie, One Large Hot Cup of Business Strategy', *New York Times*, 14 December: C1, C8.

Wollen, Peter (1993) *Raiding the Icebox*. Bloomington, IA: Indiana University.

Woodard, Colin (1998) 'Fish Farms Get Fried for Fouling', *Christian Science Monitor*, 9 September: 1ff.

Wu, David Y.H. (1997) 'McDonald's in Taipei: Hamburgers, Betel Nuts, and National Identity', in James Watson (ed.), *Golden Arches East: McDonald's in East Asia*. Stanford, CA: Stanford University Press.

Wu, Olivia (1998) 'Raising Questions; Environmentalists Voice Concerns Over Booming Aquaculture Industry', *Chicago Tribune*, 9 September: 7Aff.

Yan, Yunxiang (1997) 'McDonald's in Beijing: The Localization of Americana', in James Watson (ed.), *Golden Arches East: McDonald's in East Asia*. Stanford, CA: Stanford University Press.

Zelizer, Viviana A. (1994) *The Social Meaning of Money*. New York: Basic Books.

Zukin, Sharon (1991) *Landscapes of Power: From Detroit to Disney World*. Berkeley, CA: University of California Press.

INDEX